T0305091

The Great Recession and the Contradictions of Contemporary Capitalism

NEW DIRECTIONS IN MODERN ECONOMICS

Series Editor: Malcolm C. Sawyer, *Professor of Economics, University of Leeds, UK*

New Directions in Modern Economics presents a challenge to orthodox economic thinking. It focuses on new ideas emanating from radical traditions including post-Keynesian, Kaleckian, neo-Ricardian and Marxian. The books in the series do not adhere rigidly to any single school of thought but attempt to present a positive alternative to the conventional wisdom.

For a full list of Edward Elgar published titles, including the titles in this series, visit our website at www.e-elgar.com.

The Great Recession and the Contradictions of Contemporary Capitalism

Edited by

Riccardo Bellofiore

Professor of Political Economy, University of Bergamo, Italy

Giovanna Vertova

Assistant Professor of Political Economy, University of Bergamo, Italy

NEW DIRECTIONS IN MODERN ECONOMICS

Edward Elgar

Cheltenham, UK • Northampton, MA, USA

Published by
Edward Elgar Publishing Limited
The Lypiatts
15 Lansdown Road
Cheltenham
Glos GL50 2JA
UK

Edward Elgar Publishing, Inc.
William Pratt House
9 Dewey Court
Northampton
Massachusetts 01060
USA

A catalogue record for this book
is available from the British Library

Library of Congress Control Number: 2014941539

This book is available electronically in the ElgarOnline.com
Economics Subject Collection, E-ISBN 978 0 85793 853 4

ISBN 978 0 85793 852 7

Typeset by Servis Filmsetting Ltd, Stockport, Cheshire
Printed and bound in Great Britain by T.J. International Ltd, Padstow

Contents

Contributors

Riccardo Bellofiore is Professor at the University of Bergamo. He is currently teaching advanced macroeconomics, history of economic thought, monetary economics and international monetary economics. His current research interests are contemporary global and European economy, endogenous monetary approaches, Marxian value and crisis theories.

François Chesnais is Emeritus Professor at the University of Paris-Nord. His current research interests are financialization in its interconnections with globalization and issues related to sovereign debt. He is an active member of the NGO Attac and editor of the journal *Carré rouge*.

Meghnad Desai is Emeritus Professor of Economics at the London School of Economics (LSE) and the author of over twenty-five books including *Testing Monetarism* (1981) and *Marxian Economics* (1979). There is a two-volume collection of his selected essays, *Macroeconomics and Monetary Theory* (Volume I) and *Poverty, Famine and Economic Development* (Volume II) (both 1995), published by Edward Elgar.

Gérard Duménil is Economist and former Research Director at the Centre National de la Recherche Scientifique. His current interests are the analysis of neoliberal capitalism, its crisis, macroeconomics, and basic issues in Marxism. His latest books, with Dominique Lévy, are *The Crisis of Neoliberalism* (2011), published by Harvard University Press, and *La grande bifurcation. En finir avec le néolibéralisme* (2014), published by La Découverte.

Dominique Lévy is Economist and former Research Director at the Centre National de la Recherche Scientifique. He tightly collaborates with Gérard Duménil, sharing the same interests, and together they have worked on many publications (see Gérard Duménil).

Christian Marazzi is Professor at the Swiss Italian University of Applied Sciences. He is author of several books on post-Fordism and financial capitalism. He is currently working on the transformations of monetary policy.

Jo Michell is Lecturer in Economics at the University of the West of England, Bristol. He is currently teaching macroeconomics and banking and finance. His current research interests are macroeconomic modelling, business cycles, income distribution and the Chinese economy.

Alain Parguez is Emeritus Professor of Economics of the University of Franche-Comte, Besancon (France), and was associated with the Economics Department at the University of Ottawa. He has worked extensively on developing the Theory of the Monetary Circuit. He has written widely on monetary policy, crisis theory and economic policy, including many articles on the impact of austerity measures. He was the editor of *Monnaie et Production* from 1984 to 1996. He is currently writing a book on the General Theory of the Monetary Circuit and its economic policy implications.

Sergio Rossi is Full Professor of Economics at the University of Fribourg, Switzerland, where he has held the Chair of Macroeconomics and Monetary Economics since 2005. His research interests are in macro-economic analysis, particularly as regards national and international monetary and financial issues. He has authored and edited many books, contributed several chapters to books and is widely published in academic journals.

Jan Toporowski is Professor of Economics and Finance at the School of Oriental and African Studies (SOAS), University of London. He teaches macroeconomics and monetary and financial economics. His research interests are in banking and finance, Kalecki, and the history of economic thought.

Vittorio Valli is Emeritus Professor at the University of Turin, where he teaches comparative economic development. He was the first president of AISSEC (Italian Association of Comparative Economic Systems) and of EACES (European Association of Comparative Economic Studies). He is co-editor of EJCE (*European Journal of Comparative Economics*). He has published several books and articles on the Italian, US, German and Japanese economies and on issues of economic policy, labour economics, growth theory and comparative economic development.

Alessandro Vercelli is Professor at the University of Siena, where he teaches economics of sustainable development, and Professorial Research Associate at SOAS (University of London). He has been a member of the Presidential Council of the Società Italiana degli Economisti (SIE) and vice-president of the International Economic Association (IEA). His current research interests focus on sustainable development, financializa-tion, theory and history of economic fluctuations, history of analysis, and economic methodology.

Giovanna Vertova is Assistant Professor at the University of Bergamo. She is currently teaching political economy and international political economy. Her current research interests are the economics of globalization, national systems of innovation, and gender and feminist economics.

Introduction

Riccardo Bellofiore and Giovanna Vertova

According to *The Telegraph*[1], 'During a briefing by academics at the
London School of Economics on the turmoil on the international markets
the Queen asked: "Why did nobody notice it?"' That the mainstream(s)
failed, and that capitalism was put into question, was an opinion widely
shared for a few years after the 2007 subprime crisis, and the more so
after Lehman Brothers collapsed in September 2008. So much so that
The Financial Times, and even *The Economist*, had articles and series on
the crisis in economics and the future of capitalism. We say mainstreams,
using the plural, because the failure was equally distributed between
freshwater and saltwater macroeconomics, as Paul Krugman calls them –
between Chicago monetarism and new classical macro, and Harvard new
Keynesian macro, as we knew them.

The country where we live and teach, Italy, is an exception to this, since
even to politely ask these questions raises the suspicion of some nostalgia
for real socialism or of lobbying for unproductive State employees (as happened to one of us who edited a special supplement on the crisis). In the
meantime, Willem Buiter of *The Financial Times*[2] wrote in his blog about
'the unfortunate uselessness of most "state of the art" academic monetary
economics', where he argued that 'the typical graduate macroeconomics
and monetary economics training received at Anglo-American universities
during the past 30 years or so, may have set back by decades serious inves-
tigations of aggregate economic behaviour and economic policy-relevant
understanding. It was a privately and socially costly waste of time and
other resources'. In late 2008, Joseph Stiglitz compared the fall of Wall
Street to the fall of the Berlin Wall, and a few years later, Paul Krugman,
with Brad DeLong, changed the characterization of the crisis from a Great
Recession to a Lesser Depression.

The chapters included here provide a varied series of 'takes' on the
current capitalism in crisis, which have been presented since 2008 to
the students of our university in Bergamo and have their roots in a

[1] 5 November 2008.
[2] 3 March 2009.

1

heterogeneous, but qualified, set of traditions and authors that have resisted the test of time much better than Neoclassical or standard Keynesian economics in their various combinations: from Keynes to his antagonist Hayek, from Marx to Kalecki, from Minsky to Schumpeter, to the circuit theory of money.

This book opens with a general perspective on the recent dynamics of capitalism leading to the current crisis, written by Riccardo Bellofiore. This author deconstructs the notion of Neoliberalism and refers to those authors, like Minsky or Magdoff–Sweezy, who already since the 1970s foresaw the exhaustion of Keynesianism and stressed the increasing role of private debt. Money manager capitalism was in fact not the return of laissez-faire but a 'real subsumption of labour to finance', because the last phase of financialization was able to include households and workers subordinately under finance. A politically active kind of management of capitalism through monetary policy was integral to this model, which may be also labelled private Keynesianism, or an asset-bubble-driven Keynesianism. Traumatized workers went hand-in-hand with manic-depressive savers and indebted consumers. The Great Recession started from an implosion of this model in the US, and it was exported to Europe because of the Neo-mercantilist posture of that capitalism. The chapter explores in more detail how the crisis affected Europe.

In the following chapter, Gérard Duménil and Dominique Lévy summarize their own interpretation of the crisis of Neoliberalism and critically discuss other interpretations of Marxian inspiration. They contrast views of the Great Recession as just a financial crisis with the opposed perspective seeing the crisis as the outcome of a classical falling rate of profits dynamics, or of underconsumption. Criticizing the former views, the two authors enquire (theoretically and empirically) into the different quantitative measures of the rate of profits for the US economy. Criticizing the latter views, they analogously enter into a discussion of the US share of wages. The restoration of the rate of profit and overconsumption are placed on the background of the specific class structure and financial hegemony typical of Neoliberalism.

In his chapter, Meghnad Desai outlines the three approaches to understanding the causal explanation and the policy cures proposed by Marx, Keynes and Hayek. He insists that the current difficulties are not of a Keynesian nature, which typically arises from a collapse of effective demand due to over-saving. The Great Recession was, rather, caused by governments' and households' excessive spending because of too easy credit facilitated by global imbalances: and it is here that the legacy of Hayek's work during the 1930s becomes relevant. The failure of Keynesian policies implemented as a response to the crisis – deficit fiscal spending and quantitative easing – is explained through households' deleveraging and governments' difficulties in bond markets.

A different perspective is put forward by François Chesnais. Massive over-accumulation of industrial capacity and the persistent existence of a huge mass of financial claims on present and future production, together with the pile-up of derivatives yielding high speculative nominal profits, marked the initial phases of the global economic and financial crisis since August 2007. During the same crisis, financial institutions shaped Western countries' government policies in an unprecedented way, to save and prolong the life of the debt-led growth regime set up in the 1990s. The chapter was written at a time when the Eurozone banking and sovereign debt crisis was in full sway: the situation has only worsened in the recent years.

Christian Marazzi presents an interpretation of the crisis based on André Orléan's 'conventionalist' analysis on financial rationality. The economics of convention enables one to see true uncertainty as fundamental in the formation of financial bubbles. Financial markets are 'cognitive machines' whose role is to produce a reference opinion, perceived by all operators as an expression of 'what the market thinks'. Money is the absolute convention, the principle of sovereignty and, at the same time, a vehicle of potential violence which may erupt in various forms: as hyperinflation, deflation or crisis. Marazzi's analysis rereads the dynamics of this financial capitalism using the concept of 'collective convention', as well as looks at the mimetic behaviour of the market agents operating. In the last thirty years, the typical distinction between the financial sphere and the real economy sphere collapsed, giving rise to Minsky's money manager capitalism.

Jan Toporowski's chapter examines the social and economic impact of debt in a society in which a property-owning middle class accounts for the bulk of household saving. He rejects the Ricardian view of saving and income distribution, based on notions of usury and a class structure with only workers and capitalists. Changes in asset values are closely linked with income and wealth inequality. Inflation of asset values allows a property-owning middle class to generate cash flow from asset markets, making property owners independent of State systems of welfare for which that class pays taxes. The result is a growing middle class hostility towards social welfare paid for by the State. With saving determined by middle class debt behaviour, a 'post-modern' business cycle emerges, in which the working class pays the debts of the middle classes.

Jo Michell's chapter investigates the speculative choices taken by firms and households when making investment decisions and operating in financial markets. A simple stock-flow system is used to demonstrate the implications of different assumptions about investment, profits and methods of financing. The Minskian notion of 'financial fragility' is considered within such a system, and an alternative interpretation of the relationship between the prices of real and financial assets is presented. This serves to demonstrate some of the potential difficulties in modelling such market processes within fully specified mathematical stock-flow systems.

With Sergio Rossi's chapter we enter into the international payment system discussion. He argues that the global financial crisis that broke out in 2007 is the result of a structural disorder that has been increasingly harming the world economy since so-called post-Bretton Woods, a regime which puts the US dollar at centre stage in international transactions. International payments have become provisional, as settlements for any foreign transactions are carried out using so-called key currencies, which are, in fact, simply promises of payment. Rossi shows that the international economy is actually a barter trade system, since money is denatured when international transactions are paid using national currencies as if they were 'reserve assets' beyond the issuing country's borders. In light of Keynes's proposal to set up an international clearing union, Rossi suggests the introduction of a real-time gross-settlement system between countries, to be run by an international settlement institution issuing supranational currency every time a final payment has to be carried out between any two monetary spaces. Establishing a new international monetary order will help to rebalance trade between countries.

In his contribution to the book, Alain Parguez, arguing from the point of view of the General Theory of the Monetary Circuit, explains the fundamental rules of a good and stable management of public finance. Austerity policies produce bad deficits, instead of good deficits. The latter are the planned result of a long-term policy aimed at creating a useful and productive stock of capital, either tangible (as material and social infrastructure) or intangible (as employment in health, education, advanced research, etc.). The dismantling of the State, by privatizing its public finance, is responsible for bad deficits. These happen when private agents expect more cuts and more poverty, thus refraining from investing and consuming. Parguez concludes that the European public debt crisis was built-in in the Euro-System, a system which violates the rules.

The chapter by Vittorio Valli is dedicated to two crises of the Italian economy: the gradual relative economic decline since 1973 and the severe consequences of the 2007–08 financial turmoil originating in the US. The relative economic decline was mainly due to the energy crises, the vanishing of Gerschenkron's advantages of relative economic backwardness and of the Fordist model of growth, and the processes of population ageing, de-industrialization and relative technological decline. These tendencies induced weakness in the current account balance, which led, until 1996, to periodic devaluations of the Italian lira. When Italy entered the Eurozone in 1999, the remedy of devaluation was no longer available, and so in the 2000s Italy experienced a structural deficit in the balance of its current account and a growing external debt. Since the 1980s there has been a rapid increase in economic inequalities and in the evasion of taxes and social contributions, along with a sharp rise in public deficit and in public debt. The high public debt/GDP ratio increased Italy's vulnerability to financial distress. Restrictive policies have further worsened real GDP and the debt/GDP ratio.

In the first part of her chapter, Giovanna Vertova proposes a theoretical framework for the analysis of the current crisis with a gender perspective. The only way to do this is to analyse together the production and the social reproduction systems (a kind of 'extended' macroeconomic system). By looking at unpaid domestic labour, and not only at paid labour for the market, it is possible to see the invisible costs of labour carried out by women. So, the gender configurations of both systems are investigated before, during and in the aftermath of the crisis. Looking at the 'extended' macroeconomic system also enables one to assess the gender impact of the previous fiscal anti-crisis packages and the more recent European austerity plans. The second part of the chapter deals with the Italian case, which could be quite interesting because Italian gender inequality is still very strong, despite the fact that Italy is alleged to be a developed country. In Italy the gender division of labour is still very neat: most Italian men work in the productive system and most Italian women have difficulties in participating in the labour market, due to the burden of unpaid domestic and care labour. The results of the empirical investigation lead to the conclusion that the crisis has a strong gender impact – in both the productive and social reproductive system – and, moreover, that gender inequality may also be strengthened by austerity policy and the European sovereign debt crisis. The long and difficult process towards more gender equality is, therefore, at risk here.

In the closing chapter, Alessandro Vercelli explores the dynamic roots of two recent catastrophic events: the financial meltdown, triggered by the subprime mortgage crisis, and the partial nuclear meltdown of the three reactors of the Fukushima1 plant. The criticality of the chain-reaction dynamics is what makes both nuclear reactors and financial systems fragile and accident-prone. In Vercelli's point of view, a systematic examination of the dynamic analogies between the nuclear and financial chain reactions has a heuristic potential that has been unduly neglected. In particular, the common features of their dynamic behaviour impose similar constraints on their controllability and calls for a more precautionary policy in their design and regulation.

1. The Great Recession and the contradictions of contemporary capitalism

Riccardo Bellofiore

1. INTRODUCTION

Capitalism is once again in a Great Crisis. To understand it, I am convinced we need to refer to and innovate Marxian critical political economy and Financial Keynesianism. That is why in this chapter, before I discuss the dynamics of capitalist economies, I shall briefly refer to these theories. I urge for their renewal in light of the new realities, and especially taking into account the rise and fall of money manager capitalism.

The Neoliberal Great Moderation was a paradoxical kind of financial and 'privatized Keynesianism'. The heart of the Anglo-Saxon model was the attempt to overcome the stagnationist tendencies emerging from 'traumatized workers' resulting from the transformation of 'manic savers' into 'indebted consumers'. This 'autonomous' consumption, fuelled by finance and bank debt, was the driving force of a dynamic but unsustainable 'new' capitalism, manipulated by an innovative kind of monetary policy. The Neo-mercantilist export-led approach that dominated the European macroeconomic landscape since WWII, particularly since the 1960s and 1970s, was very different, but it profited from the US-based consumer-debt driven boom. The Maastricht Treaty was mainly a French project, which Germany resisted, and it was designed under the Iron Curtain. The real puzzle is to understand not only how the Euro actually came into being from such fragile foundations, but also why for many years it seemed such a happy experiment. The Eurozone's sovereign debt crisis was imported, but the Eurozone's institutional composition, coupled with Germany's self-defeating obsession with fiscal austerity, ultimately drove the area into a double-dip recession. A way out of the crisis requires not only monetary reforms and expansionary coordinated fiscal measures, but also a whole change of economic model, based upon a new 'engine' of demand and growth. A monetary financing of 'good' deficits is needed for the realization of a radicalized 'socialization of the investment': a class-based and Keynesian New Deal.

Are Marxian theory and Financial Keynesianism (I am referring here especially to the theory of the monetary circuit and to Minsky), in their original formulation, useful to understanding the current crisis? I suggest that we have to reformulate them outside the dominant interpretations, and to apply them creatively to the phase of capitalism we are living in. The most widespread readings of Marx's theory of the crises are the 'tendential fall in the rate of profits' and an under-consumptionist view about 'realization crises'. Those who believe the falling rate of profits story (related to the rise in capital composition) see the problem in the inadequacy of the surplus value produced. Those who are persuaded by the under-consumption narrative think that worsening income distribution led to a realization crisis. From this perspective, the problem was that there was too much potential surplus value. I find more interesting a position that starts from two of the heretics of Keynesianism and Marxism, Minsky and Sweezy, who stressed the role of private debt. We have to integrate finance, effective demand and capital accumulation. Financialization was a 'real subsumption of labour to finance', coupled with 'centralization without concentration', which produced a recovery in the rate of profits since the 1980s (against the falling rate of profit view) and turned Monetarism into a paradoxical privatized Keynesianism (against under-consumptionism). This configuration, 'money manager capitalism', mutated in fundamental ways the monetary circuit and the roots of financial instability, but it was nevertheless unsustainable. Its collapse opens the way to a 'socialization of investment' and requires policies based on permanent 'good' public deficits.

2.   MARX'S THEORY OF THE CRISIS

The theory of crises is a most controversial area in Marxist political economy[1]. A first line of thought is the fall in the profit rate. Mechanization of production, for Marx, is not just a reaction to distributive struggles; it is also an autonomous push by capital to control living labour. If mechanization is a powerful lever to regulate both the exchange value and the use value of labour power, it nevertheless creates a difficulty, because it may end up removing workers from production. When the 'technical' composition of capital (an index of the 'material' ratio of means of production to

---

[1] The argument here is based on Bellofiore (2011). The reader is referred to that article for bibliographical references.

workers) goes up, this is a factor contributing to the expulsion of workers; but living labour is the exclusive source of value and surplus value. If this is reflected in a rise in the 'value' composition of capital, the rate of profit tends to fall.

For Marx, a rise in the rate of surplus value could not permanently counteract the negative sway on the rate of profit of a higher (value) composition of capital. The strongest case is the reference to an absolute limit to the (surplus) labour that may be pumped out from a given population. If variable capital tends to zero, surplus value exhausts the new value which is the monetary expression of the total social working day. The composition of capital is now the reciprocal of the maximum rate of profit, which in turn acts as the ceiling for the actual rate of profit. In other words, Marx is suggesting that the numerator of the maximum rate of profit meets a natural constraint in the living labour extracted from workers, while the continuous increase of its denominator pushes it down. At the ruling prices, individual capitalists are forced to introduce more capital-intensive techniques, lowering unit costs and gaining temporary extra-profits, even though the long-run effects of their behaviour force a 'devaluation' of commodities and thereby depress the average rate of profit.

This argument seems not to consider that the progress in the productive power of labour through technical change devalues all commodities, including the elements of constant capital. It cannot be excluded a priori that the devaluation of constant capital might be strong enough to raise the maximum rate of profit, removing the limit Marx thought was bounding the actual rate of profit. A parallel criticism is that – since the actual rate of profit is a function, not only negatively to the composition of capital, but also positively to the rate of exploitation – the upsurge in the rate of surplus value could outweigh the increase in the composition of capital. It must, however, be considered that Marx's law is stated with reference to the rise in the 'organic', and not in the 'value' composition of capital. The latter fully reflects the revolution in the prices of constant and variable capital produced by mechanization, whereas the former measures inputs at the prices before the introduction of the new techniques. 'Organic' composition of capital thus automatically reflects the 'technical' composition.

Once the rate of surplus value goes up to repress the tendency of the rate of profit to fall, it is more and more likely that the system stumbles upon a second type of crisis: a realization crisis. The stress here is not so much on the 'overproduction of capital' (i.e., not enough surplus value is extracted to adequately valorize capital), but on 'overproduction of commodities' (i.e., a positive excess of supply over demand). Some Marxists

(Hilferding, Lenin, Tugan-Baranovsky) stress 'disproportionalities', that is, sectoral imbalances between supply and demand, due to the unplanned, chaotic nature of market economies: the unevenness of capitalist development may eventually degenerate into a 'general glut' of commodities. In principle, however, this difficulty should be overcome thanks to price-and-quantity adjustments, and it should disappear in a more organized form of capitalism. The other variety is sometimes labelled as 'under-consumptionism'. It is maintained that the decrease in the wage share, and hence in the portion of income which is consumed, converts into a decrease in effective demand. A more sophisticated, non-under-consumptionist version is the one by Rosa Luxemburg as interpreted by Joan Robinson: net investments are unable to make up for decreasing consumption, since long-term profitability of new machine goods depends on future outlets, and the latter are less and less predictable. The difficulty has to do with the incentive, or motive, to invest. As in Keynes and the authentic Keynesian tradition, the problem is not located in lacking consumption, but in the insufficiency of investments.

Some insist that crises of realization are of increasing severity and lead to a final breakdown. For Luxemburg this happens when the 'external' factor mitigating them – net exports to non-capitalist areas – are exhausted, and capitalism is entirely globalized. Other writers in the same tradition, such as Kalecki, objected that the insufficiency of effective demand may be resolved by what are dubbed (net) 'domestic' exports, such as governments' budget deficits financed by the injection of new money. A similar role may be played by the unproductive consumption coming from 'third persons' drawing their incomes from deductions from total surplus value. To be compatible with a smooth accumulation of capital, these 'solutions' call for the continuation of the pressure on living labour. In this event, the profit squeeze may eventually come directly from workers' struggles within the capitalist labour process. Overproduction of commodities can be extended in time by credit and finance, which stimulate both investment and consumption. But sooner or later the insufficiency of effective demand makes its effects felt.

I do not think that these two lines in Marxian crisis theory are able to interpret this crisis. The tendential fall in profit rate goes against the almost complete recovery in the rate of profits since 1980. Moreover, rather than under-consumption, we witnessed in the centre of Neoliberalism a situation of over-consumption. A promising rereading of Marx's theory of crisis looks at the 'tendential fall in the rate of profit' as a meta-theory of crises, incorporating the different kind of crises which can be derived from Marx's oeuvre, and extending into an historical narrative of the evolution of capitalism. From this point of view, the tendency towards a fall in the rate of profit due to a rising value composition of capital was confirmed during the late 19th century Great Depression (1873–96), also known as the Long Depression. The increasing rate of exploitation, needed to overcome the tendency for the rate of profit to fall, was implemented by Fordism and Taylorism, which jointly strengthened the tendency for the relative wage to fall. The rise in the rate of surplus value, however, created the conditions for a realization crisis, the Great Crash of the 1930s. The so-called Golden Age of capitalism was predicated on a higher pressure on productive workers to obtain enough living labour and gain higher and higher surplus labour. This opened the way to a social crisis of accumulation, located inside the immediate valorization process: a key factor of the Great Stagflation of the 1970s.

From this point of view, the Great Moderation, leading to the current Great Recession, must be interpreted as capital's reaction to a crisis originating from a rupture in the same capital–labour social relation of production. The 'real subsumption of labour to finance' within 'money manager capitalism' – that is, the subordinated integration of households into the stock exchange market, and their going deeper and deeper into bank indebtedness – is one side of this reaction. The 'deconstruction' of labour within a new phase of capitalist accumulation characterized by new styles of corporate governance leading to a 'centralization without concentration' – and then to the weakening of workers in the labour market and in the labour process – is the other.

3.   FINANCIAL KEYNESIANISM

Marx's discourse was framed in a relatively underdeveloped form of monetary institutional setting of capitalism. It needs to be integrated into a Post-Keynesian analysis of finance. I shall concentrate on the French–Italian circuit theory of money and on Minsky's financial instability hypothesis. Both may be labelled as Financial Keynesianism (see Bellofiore 2013a and the references therein).

In the 1930 *Treatise on Money*, Keynes stresses 'initial finance'. Banking sector loans allow the business sector to pay the wage bill to buy workers' labour power and start capitalist production, both for consumption and investment goods. Privileged access to (endogenous) money as purchasing power let entrepreneurs fix the composition of output, irrespective of consumers' sovereignty. In the 1936 *General Theory*, Keynes assumed given (but not exogenous) money supply and rather focused on the 'final finance' firms have to recover on the stock markets. The demand for money balances as a store of wealth may skyrocket, and liquidity preference may lead to involuntary unemployment equilibrium, whatever the degree of price and wage flexibility. In his later articles on finance, Keynes proposed a first integration of the two views on money, as a flow and as a stock.

'Monetary circuitism' returns to the first theme, initial finance. Capitalism is pictured as a sequence of concatenated phases, opened by the creation of purchasing power by banks. Money is neither a commodity nor bilateral credit, but a credit instrument in a triangular transaction, allowing the payer to finally settle the payment with the payee by means of promises to pay from a third agent (nowadays, a bank). The differential access to money as finance gives way to asymmetries of power and shapes the real structure of the economy. The simplest circuit model considers a closed economy without the State: the basic agents are the commercial banking sector (the Central Bank is initially excluded, and added in a second step), firms and households (workers). Banks create credit-money, allowing firms to cover their current costs of production (i.e., the wage bill). Since loans create deposits, the banking system does not face any constraint: a view connected with Post-Keynesian 'horizontalism'. Production then follows, implementing entrepreneurs' choices about the level and allocation of employment. Finally, workers choose how to divide money income between consumption and savings. Monetary demand for consumption against the real output firms sell to workers settles the price of consumption goods and, hence, the real wage (a similar result follows from oligopolistic firms charging a mark-up on their direct costs). Savings may be spent on the financial markets, buying securities issued by firms (on which a long-term interest rate is paid), or be kept as money balances (liquidity preference). If all savings go on the financial market, firms get back from households the whole finance they received and may then return the principal to the banks. Financial markets are where firms recover the 'initial' finance, which is not spent on consumption. If savers add bank deposits to liquid balances, firms remain indebted to banks: the permanence of a money stock signals an equivalent credit of households with the banking sector. If the State or a foreign sector is included, there can be inflows of money to firms that, in a sense, are 'free' from the payment of interests to banks.

Minsky extends Keynes by integrating an investment theory of the business cycle into a financial theory of investment. Capitalism is production of money by means of money. Economic units are 'money in–money out' devices, estimating money receipts from their assets, deducting financial commitments of holding positions, and assessing their liquidity. Like banks, they finance the ownership and control of longer-term, illiquid and risky assets with short-term liabilities. Availability and terms of financial agreements govern investment; investment brings about gross profits; gross profits feed back into the financial structure. Positions in capital assets require long-term finance, and this latter is a combination of internal and external funds. They may be financed by intermediaries other than banks, or directly by savers, through instruments whose liquidity is subject to their convertibility into bank money. As commercial banks, financial intermediaries are profit-seeking agents, which constantly try to extend credits, financing new positions. A given amount of reserves may support more bank loans and demand deposits; and a given amount of bank loans and demand deposits may support a higher volume of finance. During periods of prosperity, economic units lower their margins of safety; their liability structures embody a higher degree of risk, while the money (and finance) supply becomes infinitely elastic. In a complex financial system, investment may also be financed through portfolio adjustment, reducing balance sheets' liquidity and causing a rise in the price of capital assets. The late Minsky rejected the idea that a Central Bank is able to control reserves.

In a period of tranquil growth, the economy is financially robust, most agents are in a hedge-financing position and liability structures spontaneously shift to fragility. The validation of outstanding debts and risky projects foster euphoric growth, developing into boom, and then a bubble. A rising debt–equity ratio is associated with higher short-term financing of fixed capital and long-term financial assets. The share of speculative or ultra-speculative positions goes up, and the demand for finance becomes almost inflexible. The crisis breaks out when 'something happens' and the supply of finance is constrained by more prudent bank attitudes or tougher restrictive actions from the Central Bank, with a sudden, severe and unexpected increase in the cost of financing. The missing validation of cash payment commitments on outstanding debts leads to the revaluation of borrowers' and lenders' risks, and to the reassessment of liability structures; while rising rates of interest endanger the liquidity and solvency of banks and financial intermediaries. Liquidity preference jumps up, demand deposits contract, financial instruments may not be 'accepted' by the banking system. The struggle to 'make position by selling positions' turns out to be ruinous because of the immediate fall in asset prices. Investments completely stop and gross profits plummet. Even hedge-financing units become speculative or Ponzi. Debt-deflation and financial turbulence strike the real economy, curbing income growth and bringing about mass unemployment.

With a small government and without a lender of last resort, the lower turning point is reached only after monetary contraction and bankruptcies restore 'robust' finance. Big Government and Big Bank may instead sustain gross profits (which are positively related to government budget deficits) and support the liability structure (thanks to the higher cash inflows helping to meet cash commitments, and to the refinancing and reserves helping to prevent banks' and financial intermediaries' bankruptcies). According to Minsky, 'Keynesian' economic policies are, however, unable to abolish the fundamental processes leading to instability. A better solution would be a 'socialization' of investments (through public productive expenditure), of employment (the State as employer of last resort or, better, as direct provider of employment), of banking and finance (the support to small and medium-sized banks, and policies in favour of equity finance), and other structural reforms.

One too easy way to apply circuitism to the current crisis is to see in household indebtedness the means by which under-consumption was overcome after the Volcker shock and in the Neoliberal era. To look at the Great Recession as a 'Minsky moment', where the financial instability hypothesis was confirmed in its original formulation, is also too straightforward. The changes in capitalism in the last few decades – but also internal theoretical difficulties – urge a reappraisal of both Minskian and circuitist traditions. On the one hand, Kalecki and Steindl showed (converging with circuitism) that when profits increase or, equivalently, household saving decreases, investment comes to finance itself. There is thus no compelling reason why an increase in leverage should necessarily materialize. On the other hand, Minsky's approach mostly focused on investment goods demand and its financing. In the last decades, credit creation has been fuelled not so much by the non-financial business sector's indebtedness but rather by household indebtedness. Consumption became autonomous, driven by a paper wealth appreciation accompanied and even stimulated by a new monetary policy. Households' consumption has been financed through collateralized debt, set in motion by capital asset inflation. In turn, capital asset inflation itself has hedged for a while firms' financial positions. On the policy side, Central Banks acted as 'lenders of first resort' to support rentiers' behaviour and 'irrational euphoria' on asset markets. Neoliberalism is not what it looked like, and what its ideologist proclaimed: in fact, early Monetarism mutated into an asset-bubble-driven 'privatized Keynesianism'.

This paradoxical new form of Keynesianism is, in a sense, a third, new understanding of the label Financial Keynesianism, which can be fully understood only through a critical reappraisal of the circuitist and Minskian traditions. As Seccareccia has argued, the monetary circuit changed dramatically. The connection between firms and banks has been largely amputated, and the centre stage has been taken by the link between banks and financial intermediaries: 'the practical disappearance of household saving and the ever growing household indebtedness has fueled the expansion of speculative derivatives because of the demand arising from the growing savings of the non-financial corporate sector' (Seccareccia 2010, p. 6). Minsky was right in stressing that 'banks are not passive managers of household savings but are, instead, in the business of making profit by actively seeking creditworthy borrowers, in this case in the household sector' (*idem*).

4.   MONEY MANAGER CAPITALISM, PRIVATIZED KEYNESIANISM AND THE GLOBAL CRISIS

To understand the current crisis we have to look deeper into this new money manager capitalism. Already in the 1980s, Minsky himself noted that globalization promoted securitization, which spurred the banking model from 'originate to hold' to 'originate to distribute'. Banks maximize fees and commissions by issuing and managing assets in off-balance-sheet affiliate structures. In this context, bankers had no interest in credit evaluation and delegated it to rating agencies. With governments trying to reduce their deficits everywhere, the household sector became a net borrower, and the non-financial business sector a net lender. Though household saving behaviour was helping to counter stagnation, banks lost their best customers. Financial innovations won the day: they reduced risk individually, but increased it globally (an example being 'subprime' lending).

In terms of social class relations, these dynamics had devastating consequences. Workers were 'traumatized' in the labour markets and within the labour process, so that the Phillips curve was flattened and wage-induced inflation was not a problem (price inflation rather came from 'commodities', raw materials, oil, etc.). Pension and institutional funds fostered that 'capital asset inflation' which, at least for a while, was hedging *ex post* corporations' balance sheets: instability was hidden, the appearance was of a seemingly stabilized economy, but the unsustainability of the process was becoming ever greater. Savers entered into a 'manic' phase, deceived by assets' appreciation, and the propensity to save out of income fell. Effective demand was internally boosted by 'indebted' consumers, providing outlets, also externally, to Asian and European Neo-mercantilism.

This renewed phase is often labelled 'financialization', but it should be better understood as a real subsumption of labour to finance. The reason is that workers' and lower income households' reliance on the stock exchange and banks, and more generally from the fictitious capital bubbles, had quite non-fictitious effects not only on demand, but also on firms' corporate governance and on real production. The traumatization of workers in the exploitation arena and the worsening distribution for wage-earners were sterilized in its effects on effective demand, but the subordinated incorporation of households within capital's financial dimension retroacted on working conditions, with a lengthening of the social working day and the intensification of labour, and a rise in labour supply. This 'subordination' of labour to finance was 'real' not only because it affected production and valorization within the labour processes; it also transformed the relationship between banks and firms, and endogenously boosted effective demand. The resulting full employment was not characterized by 'decent' wages and stable jobs. It was, instead, a full underemployment, with unemployment penetrating into the employed labour force through the spreading of part-time and casual/informal occupations.

Wage deflation, capital asset inflation and the increasingly leveraged position of households and financial companies were complementary elements of a perverse mechanism where real growth was doped by toxic finance. It was a dynamic configuration of capitalism capable of manufacturing consent and yielding hegemony. The middle classes, too, were sedated by escalating property values and found an illusory security from uncertainty (Toporowski 2010). However, households' indebtedness in no way corresponded to a state of economic and social welfare. The US 'overspending' consumer matched the US 'overworking' job-earner. Growing debt had its ultimate *raison d'être* in the insufficiency of income to support consumption of non-manufacturing goods and services. This caused an escalation in expenditures generating rents for the financial sector. Being based on a burgeoning private debt, the process was unsustainable and collapsed a first time with the dotcom crisis. The risk was there that savers turned from the 'manic' to the 'depressive' phase, with households reducing consumption to reduce their debt exposure. The risk was avoided with a return to military Keynesianism (after September 11th) and then to a revised form of the asset-bubble-driven privatized Keynesianism. This second bubble phase ended rather quickly. The new monetary policy was unable to make ends meet in inflation, considering oil and raw material prices. Although capital asset prices were not considered a problem – and wage inflation was not on the agenda – commodities price inflation worried the Federal Reserve and other Central Banks; and, from 2004, the Fed began to increase interest rates such that by 2005 US house prices softened. The proliferation of subprime mortgages, with the enticement of poor households to enter the financial swamp, was an attempt to keep the real-estate bubble inflating by any means. The hope that the increase in borrowing costs could be offset by a further rise in asset values, thereby expanding the value of the collateral used in loan applications, faded away. The widespread view that opaque securitization packages would efficiently distribute risk and that the emerging countries' savings would cover the deficits of the US, Britain, Australia and Spain, were revealed to be a double deception. This time the 'depressive' phase was irresistible, and the economy fell into the biggest crisis since the Great Crash.

5.   EUROPEAN NEO-MERCANTILISM

It was precisely the indebted consumer that had served as the engine of growth in US-centred money manager capitalism that provided the final consumers for the exports of the Neo-mercantilist economies of Japan, Germany and other parts of Europe, and, more recently, China[2]. When the subprime crisis broke out in July 2007, toxic finance spread throughout the world. The collapse of inter-bank relations augmented the negative impact of financial imbalances. European finance was the first to crumble; and with a lag, the large exporting countries were severely hit by the plummeting demand of indebted US consumers. The consequent sharp reduction in China's growth impacted hugely on Europe's main manufacturing nations, with Germany and Italy at the forefront, dissolving any illusion of a 'de-linking'.

The Neo-mercantilist model dates back to the late 1940s and the persistent German surpluses, originally recycled through the European Payments Union (1950–58), which served to reduce intra-European deficits. During the 1960s, the trade balance gave rhythm to economic policies, with 'stop and go' being used to gain net exports in Germany, Italy and France. Net exports for the whole European area were an impossible goal because when deficit countries compress income to adjust, this retroacts on the exports and employment of surplus countries. With no clearing mechanism, deficit countries have to bear the burden of adjustment by going into recession, with negative repercussions on the exports and related employment of the surplus countries. To maintain a net surplus, Germany had then, as now, to reduce economic activity, with a corresponding increase in unemployment. An alternative for deficit countries is to let their currency devalue. However, this alternative is not an option under a fixed exchange rate system, such as Bretton Woods (1944–71), the European Monetary System (EMS 1979–92), or todays' European Monetary Union (EMU). Nevertheless, it surfaced as an option after Bretton Woods collapsed in 1971.

The main danger to Germany and France came from Italy. During the 1970s, by pegging the Lira to the US Dollar (which was falling relatively to

---

[2] This part of the chapter takes up again and develops the argument in Bellofiore (2013b).

the Deutsche Mark and the Yen), Italy more than compensated for inflationary excesses through competitive devaluations. At the time, Italy's export fundamentals were the strongest both in Europe and in the bilateral trade with Germany. This served as a motivation for the EMS, with its exchange rate mechanism (ERM), which emerged during the 1980s as a German concern that was also strongly favoured by the Netherlands and Belgium. The Netherlands were organically connected with Germany, whilst Belgium had strong links with France. These countries, together with Switzerland, Austria and Scandinavia (especially Finland and Sweden), are Germany's 'satellites': their economies earn intra-European trade surpluses, while maintaining trade deficits with Germany (the only exception being the Netherlands, whose positive account is due to the fact that it provides the German economy with financial and services support). Their position is similar to Berlin's: net exports through productivity growth, stable prices and limited fiscal budgets, plus net foreign balances to finance welfare expenditures without burdening the State deficit.

The key role of the financial sector encouraged France to take an anti-inflationary stance and to join Germany and the 'satellites', with the aim (less and less achieved) of gaining net exports by drastically reducing imports. In the meantime, despite the wider band assigned to the Lira in the first half of the 1980s, its devaluations did not compensate for inflation, causing Italy's net exports to decline. This tendency was reinforced during the second half of the 1980s (especially after 1987), when the EMS mutated into a fixed exchange rate system without any change in parities. The added paradox was that the Bank of Italy fixed interest rates high enough to encourage huge capital imports, making the Lira a 'strong' currency in the ERM, Italy's deteriorating trade balance notwithstanding. That policy was instrumental in forcing a capitalist restructuring and wage squeeze. But it also actively contributed to a further deterioration of the public debt because of the widening share of interest payments within budget deficits; and the government debt has been at the mercy of capital markets ever since.

The EMS/ERM caused a division of Europe into two parts, from the point of view of the current account balance. On the positive side of the ledger there were Germany and the 'satellites'; on the negative side Italy, whose trade surplus could rise steeply any time the Lira was devalued – the more so if, as happened in 1992, wage contracts were decoupled from inflation. Portugal and Spain, with Greece, were deeper into negative territory. France represented a case of its own; mistakenly considering itself to be on a par with Germany, it slid further and further into an economic reality which puts her on the negative side. This situation encouraged the French *élite* to try to share the benefits of German financial stability and command over money through a 'single currency'. During the EMS regime – and until reunification with East Germany in 1990 – the Federal Republic of Germany realized huge net exports as a proportion of GDP, reached again (and surpassed) only in 2007–08. The EMS made Europe as a whole the primary market supporting Germany's positive net exports and profits for its big business. Its external position with other trade partners was much more variable, based on exchange rates and product specialization. However, the price to be paid was a slow rate of growth. In the meantime, France did not profit from Italy's declining trade surpluses; and it became more and more a service and financial-based economy.

The EMS came to an end in 1992–93 because German reunification was only partially financed through taxes; it was also financed by fiscal deficits and capital imports. The Bundesbank was very much opposed to what became known as Kohl's 'Reaganomics on the Rhine' – namely, the incurring of large budget deficits financed by foreign debt instead of tax increases. It was for this internal conflict with Kohl, even more than the ever-present desire to discipline Italy and other EMS members, that Germany's Central Bank drastically raised the short-term rate of interest in 1991–92. A consequence was the sharp appreciation of the Deutsche Mark, especially in relation to the Lira; and from 1992 to 2000, Germany's current account was negative (although there was still a positive balance in its merchandize account). The primary reason for Germany's deteriorating current account balance was the net export performance for Germany as a whole: while West Germany realized an enormous surplus, this was far outweighed by East Germany's colossal deficit. It may seem that the Bundesbank's high interest rate policy – which, in the name of fighting inflation, countered the increase in domestic demand and wages resulting from public expenditures associated with reunification – eventually failed to achieve the aim of defending the Neo-mercantilist stance of German capital. At the same time, it may seem that the ability to finance the international expansion of German capital was vanishing. However, this was not in fact the case. The 1990s were not a lost decade. Rather, they were the beginning of a period of restructuring, inflicted on the German labour market and processes, involving a strong push towards the trans-nationalization of many German industrial conglomerates. During this period, German firms shifted from an automation strategy, characteristic of the 1970s and 1980s, to a strategy of off-shoring upstream activities, mainly to Eastern Europe, but also to Northern Italy and other areas in the old EU-15. Together with the introduction of the 'single currency' locking-in the participants of the EMU at fixed exchange rates, these economic policies and industrial behaviours were the pillars of the resurrection of Germany's export-led capitalism during the 2000s.

6. THE SINGLE CURRENCY AND THE CRISIS IN EUROPE

The European 'single currency' was born with an original sin. From the beginning, it embodied the tendency for permanent recessionary drift, differences in relative competitiveness among member nations, a wage squeeze, mounting social inequality, the dismantling of trade unions, and continuous industrial restructuring. It is understandable that, within the structurally heterogeneous European area, where there are radical variations in both the productive power of labour and (material and immaterial) infrastructures, the push for a nominal convergence cannot but give way to a progressive deepening of real divergences. The in-built and on-going tendency towards self-dissolution of the EMU can be counteracted only through a dual strategy of common fiscal (and transfer) policy governing resource redistribution between regions within the Eurozone and industrial policies aimed at overcoming the backwardness of certain of its constituent regions. By contrast, the European Union budget (in relation to GDP) is ludicrously low, fiscal competition among States is the rule and industrial policy is officially oriented towards deregulation (though actual practices diverge).

How was such a fragile construction able to take off at the end of the 1990s? And how could that have happened after the EMS was dissolved during the early 1990s and the Maastricht Treaty entered a coma? Some legends must be dispelled. The first is that the Maastricht Treaty was a consequence of the collapse of actually 'existing socialism'. The second is that there was continuity between the Treaty and the Euro. In reality, the Treaty was the offspring of the second term of the Delors Commission (1988–92), with the project being integrally defined in a Europe (and Germany) that had been split in two by the Iron Curtain. It is also important to note that the Eurozone was a French project, not a German one. During the late 1980s, US capitalism was considered an inferior model to Japanese and to some European capitalisms. In this context, France wanted to share control over monetary policy with Germany, which, at the time, was a manufacturing giant but a political dwarf. Whilst the UK could have filled the role of the Eurozone's financial centre, it never truly wanted to enter the game. The dismantling of the Berlin Wall and the subsequent disbanding of 'socialism' in Eastern Europe and the USSR were the events that marked the failure of the strategy; this was due to the economic fallouts already mentioned, and the fact that the political underpinnings were vanishing. Germany itself started looking towards the East; but it was unable to expand its influence as a consequence of Eastern Germany reconstruction and the turmoil in ex-Yugoslavia and Russia, where the role and interests of the US have not to be forgotten.

The answer to the question about how the *Euro* project was reborn from its own ashes like a phoenix, comes from the twin considerations that, during the 1990s, Germany was in a relatively weak position, and that the *made in the USA* 'new' capitalism was thriving. The reduction in interest rates during that decade helped the entire European area to meet the Maastricht criteria on public finance, whereas Germany had difficulties in fulfilling them completely. Germany overcame the reunification shock, while pushing forward a radical restructuring of the labour market and process. With the 'satellites', it benefited from faster capitalist development in the periphery. The real-estate bubble was spreading throughout Europe, as a consequence of which Ireland and Spain had significant GDP growth: this is why their public budgets were so 'virtuous' before 2007–08. In a world of lower and lower interest rates, the government deficits of Greece and Portugal, as well as the management of the Italian government debt, made room for on-going financial investments for German and French banks.

The multi-speed dynamics of Europe is well known by now, and can be grasped through a Luxemburg–Kalecki vision. Net exports were the driving force in the 'core' (Germany and the 'satellites'), with the resulting profits invested abroad. The insertion of Europe in the 'new' capitalism's financial world meant that these investments found their way into 'toxic' finance. Further, with the 'single currency', the Treasury-bonds of the European 'periphery' played for European banks and finance (especially, French and German) a role similar to subprime loans in the US. Germany, like the rest of Northern Europe, had an historical need to export to Southern Europe, where it realized the largest part of its profits. Thus, trade deficits in France, Italy, Spain, Portugal and Greece were crucial to Germany's competitiveness. They also held down the nominal valuation of Germany's currency, the Euro (compared with what it would have been under the Deutsche *Mark* or with an *Euro* restricted to the net exporters). Moreover, the 'single currency' deepens – not just because of wage repression, but also due to the increase in the productivity of labour – a competitive deflation, and thus a real devaluation benefiting the 'core' area, whose net exports rose exponentially. This structural strength is due to Germany's specialization in technology sectors, advanced machinery and high-quality manufacturing, and not just wage deflation.

After the dotcom crisis, Germany again saw its net export model of growth flourish (thanks also to the wage repression policy related to the so-called Hartz reforms), without the risk of competitive devaluations within the area; and Italy was able to put its external accounts into better shape, especially in certain of its manufacturing sectors, becoming the second largest exporter in Europe. Capitalist growth was vibrant and strong not in the country as a whole but in particular areas: less and less the much mythologized old industrial 'districts', rather the so-called fourth capitalism of small and medium-sized enterprises which were strong in innovation and marketing, and became globally competitive thanks to exports and foreign direct investments. After the dotcom crisis, these 'pocket-multinationals' have been particularly swift in moving into high value-added production. However, this new incarnation of the *made in Italy* model was inherently fragile. Firstly, it lacked systematic investment in R&D; secondly, it completely hinged upon a foreign-centred model of accumulation; and thirdly, it had no structural/inter-sectoral coherence. It could survive only at the price of continuous restructuring and becoming increasingly dependent on the worsening conditions of labour – just to be able to defer the competition coming from China and East Asia.

This being the case, the Eurozone crisis was not endogenous, but came from outside. The early chains of transmission were the already depressed state of expectations in Europe; the mortgage and financial crisis in the UK and the bursting of the housing bubble in Spain; the Eastern Europe financial troubles; and the fall in imports from the rest of Europe in all of these regions. Later came the collapse of exports to China and the fall of German and Italian manufacturing exports. In 2008–09 Europe avoided a complete breakdown because of three factors conflicting with the 'anti-Keynesian' rhetoric of European governments: the working of automatic stabilizers, targeted pro-industry programmes and State policies openly shielding workers from unemployment (e.g., Germany financed a temporary reduction in working hours). After having cut the rate of interest, which exceeded 4 per cent in the summer of 2008, the ECB did not follow its Monetarist prescriptions to the letter, instead rewriting its own material constitution, refinancing budget deficits in secondary markets and providing huge amounts of liquidity. The problem was that these manoeuvres were reactive, in the wake of the crisis, rather than providing the firepower or showing the determination needed to put an end to speculation: too late and (at that point) too little. It is curious that if, at the beginning of the crisis, Greece's debt had been wiped out, the costs for Europe would have been serious (because of balance sheet interconnections) but acceptable. As the domino effect spread the crisis to Ireland and then Portugal, even a cancellation of their debt would have been dangerous but still tolerable. During the summer of 2011, after having hit Ireland and Portugal, the crisis hit Spain and then Italy; at this point, the quantitative change in the dimension of the countries involved caused a qualitative leap in the scale of the crisis.

The crisis in Europe is not due to Greece, nor is it the result of government indebtedness of a particular country (both in absolute terms and in relation to GDP). As Toporowski (2011) argued, what matters is the willingness (or not) of the ECB to refinance government deficits. Even with a hypothetical *Euro* limited to Germany and its 'satellites', the sovereign debt crisis could burst. Belgium, for example, has a debt to GDP ratio close to 100 per cent. Excluding default, a first way out could be inflation, a second growth, a third a mix of the two. Both inflation and growth increase the denominator in the deficit (or debt) to nominal GDP ratio. Another misunderstanding is that trade imbalances within the Eurozone ought to be a problem for the EMU. As Lavoie (2013, p. 22) recently wrote:

> there is no limit to the debit position that a national central bank can incur on the books of the ECB, that is, its liabilities with respect to the rest of the Eurosystem are not limited. [. . .] Furthermore, national central banks in debit are charged the main official rate, which is also the rate gained by those with claims on the Eurosystem. Thus these imbalances can go on forever . . . [I]f there is some lack of confidence in the system, we should observe an increase in the size of the balance sheets of the central banks of the countries under suspicion, as well as an increase in the size of the balance sheet of the ECB. [. . .] A current account deficit of Spain or Italy with respect to the rest of the eurozone is no more meaningful than the current account deficit of the Mezzogiorno relative to Northern Italy.

7. THE SOCIALIZATION OF INVESTMENTS, AND THE GOOD DEFICITS

This is not the occasion to review the day-to-day policy recommendations accompanying the evolution of the European crisis. The proposals to solve it are multiple: from the banking union to the fiscal union, from the Eurobond to an upsurge in public investments – each appearing unable to work alone. The unblocking of the European real 'imbalances' involves an intervention that concerns not only a reflation on the demand side and/or a recoupling of wages to productivity. A strong intervention on the supply side and in the productive structure, along with financial stabilization, is also called for. Being a fiscal union in the short term is a utopia. The *Eurobond* solution, as a common guarantee for all the public debts of the Eurozone countries, and a coordinated fiscal expansion, going at a higher speed in the 'core', are part of an alternative platform. Eurobonds have to be regarded as the foundation for a coordinated expansion of expenditure and investments on a European scale. It amounts, in fact, to a proposal for a renewed and innovative *New Deal* for Europe with the potential to directly affect the structural basis of growth by improving the quality of output and increasing the productivity of labour. Given the nature of the world-wide crisis, originating from the collapse of the asset-bubble-driven 'privatized Keynesianism' centred on indebted consumption – and given the apparent impossibility to start a new phase of development on investment or net exports – a new policy based on an expansion of public expenditure looks to be the only way out. An increase in wages and a reduction of inequality would multiply the expansionary momentum.

Insight into a genuine way out of the current crisis may be found in the structural Keynesianism of those who are explicitly critical of capitalism and of the 'really existing' Keynesianism implemented after WWII. There is no such thing as economic development not based on debt. Recent decades have confirmed that *ex post* government deficits are the condition for the net creation of income in the private sector. However, as Parguez (Chapter 9 in this volume) insists, we should not forget that there are 'bad' and 'good' deficits. 'Bad' deficits are the non-planned result of the tendency to stagnation, of shock therapies, of deflationary policies, of the unsustainability of toxic finance, and so on. By contrast, 'good' deficits are planned *ex ante* ones. Their aim is to build up, and improve, a stock of productive resources. They are means for the production of wealth: a long-run investment in tangible goods (infrastructure, green conversion, alternative forms of transport, etc.) and intangible ones (health, education, research, etc.). A gender balanced and nature-friendly approach becomes inherent and crucial to this policy. Welfare itself has to be transformed from supplying nominal subsidies to direct intervention 'in kind', as part of a wider horizon of 'planning'. A deficit spending programme of this type immediately raises the government debt to GDP ratio – but the subsequent growth in the denominator will make this jump only temporary. Such an intervention may have positive effects seen from a capitalist point of view, those which fascinate Post-Keynesian economists. It would support the real economy from the demand side, it would stabilize the financial sector by providing 'sound' financial assets, and it would increase the productivity in the system. This kind of intervention can – and must – be part of a minimum programme of a class-oriented left. It is clear, however, that this yields not a stable model of a new capitalism, but rather an 'imbalance': an uneven terrain where the issue of overcoming capitalism in the end has to be dealt with.

Minsky's perspective of a 'socialization of investment', coupled with a 'socialization of employment' and a 'socialization of banking' is also to be reclaimed[3]. Minsky claims that the 'bastard' Keynesianism of the so-called

---

[3] The main reference here is to the last two chapters of Minsky (1975).

Golden Age had its origin in Keynes ambiguities. He would object to a return to 'Keynesianism', which has never been adequate. It was a form of capitalism where taxation and transfers governed consumption, monetary policy ruled investments, government spending brought about either waste or military expenditure, and where rent-positions and finance were nurtured. He called this a strategy of 'high profits–high investment', leading to an artificial consumption and putting at risk the biological and social environment. We have to come back to square one, he insisted: to 1933. We have to rethink a Keynesian *New Deal* that deals with the fundamental questions: 'for whom is the game played?' and 'what kind of product do we want?' Minsky favoured a society in which the real structure of consumption is determined by government investments, the driving force building a different supply side. Minsky explicitly supported a 'socialization of the towering heights', a 'communal' consumption, capital controls, the regulation of finance, banks as public utilities, and so on. Minsky, like Parguez, asks the State to create employment 'directly'. This might be inflected as a *Piano del lavoro* ('Employment Plan') in the tradition of Paolo Sylos Labini and Ernesto Rossi. The Great Recession – the final crisis of Neoliberalism as we knew it – and the European disaster, as the deadlock of Neo-mercantilism, are precisely putting the issues of 'how', 'what' and 'how much' to produce on the agenda.

REFERENCES

Bellofiore, R. (2011), 'Crisis theory and the Great Recession: a personal journey, from Marx to Minsky', *Research in Political Economy* (issue on: Revitalizing Marxist Theory for Today's Capitalism), **27**, 81–120.

Bellofiore, R. (2013a), 'Two or three things I know about her', *Cambridge Journal of Economics* (special issue: Perspective for the Eurozone), **37** (3), 497–512.

Bellofiore, R. (2013b), 'Endogenous money, financial Keynesianism and beyond', *Review of Keynesian Economics* (special issue: On Endogenous Money and Monetary Policy), **1** (2), 153–70.

Lavoie, M. (2013), 'The monetary and fiscal nexus of neo-chartalism: a friendly critique', *Journal of Economic Issues*, **47** (1), 1–31.

Minsky, H.P. (1975), *John Maynard Keynes*, New York: Columbia University Press.

Seccareccia, M. (2010), *Financialization and the Transformation of Commercial Banking*, Mimeo.

Toporowski, J. (2010), 'The wisdom of property and the politics of the middle class', *Monthly Review*, **62** (4), 10–15.

Toporowski, J. (2011), 'Not a very Greek tragedy', *Monthly Report Wiener Institut für Internationale Wirtschaftsvergleiche*, **5**, 5–7.

2. The crisis of the early 21st Century: Marxian perspectives

Gérard Duménil and Dominique Lévy

1. INTRODUCTION

That capitalism underwent a new structural crisis about three decades after the crisis of the 1970s, under circumstances evocative of the Great Depression, raised numerous interrogations. The purpose of the present chapter is to summarize our own interpretation, and discuss a set of other analyses of Marxian inspiration. Marxist scholars share a common critical analysis of capitalism in general and, more specifically, of neoliberalism, the latter phase of capitalism. But there should be no surprise in the discovery that the interpretation of the crisis remains controversial. The example of the Great Depression is telling in this respect: eighty years after the event, no consensus has yet been found concerning its actual roots, and the same sets of alternative explanations are often retaken in the discussion of the current crisis.

2. THE CRISIS OF NEOLIBERALISM

In the mid-1990s, we defined neoliberalism as a class phenomenon. More specifically, we described neoliberalism as a new 'social order' in which capitalist classes restored their powers and incomes, considerably diminished during the class compromise of the first post-World War II decades (the social-democratic or Keynesian decades). The control of financial institutions – now working to the benefit of capitalist classes – was a prominent component of the new social order. We denote as 'Finance' the upper fractions of capitalist classes and their financial institutions. Thus, the new neoliberal social order can be denoted as a *financial hegemony* (the second one since the late 19th Century). The transition, under capitalist leadership, to this new power configuration would, however, have been impossible if it had not been conducted in alliance with managerial classes, notably their upper and financial segments (within 'managers' we include both private and government components, and we denote capitalists and managers, considered jointly, as 'upper classes').

2.1. Our Interpretation of the Crisis

The overall interpretation we gave of the current crisis, as a 'crisis of neoliberalism,' that is, a 'crisis of financial hegemony,' is summarized in Figure 2.1. At the root of the entire process is 'neoliberalism under U.S. hegemony.' From this derive two strands of explanatory factors. In the upper part of the figure are mechanisms typical of neoliberal capitalism in every country: (1) the unquenchable quest for high income; (2) financialization; and (3) globalization. Capitalist classes always seek maximum income, but after the imposition of neoliberalism in the early 1980s, major transformations of social relations were realized in comparison to the previous decades, aiming at this maximization. A new discipline was imposed on workers and all segments of management (but, concerning management, this discipline was gradually transformed into the alliance mentioned above); new policies were defined to the benefit of upper classes; free trade placed all workers of the world in a situation of competition; capitals were now free to move around the globe seeking maximum profitability. To financialization and globalization, one can add deregulation that conditioned both processes.

The crisis could have come later to the world as a result of this neoliberal strategy pushed to the extreme, but it came from the United States during the first decade of the 21st Century. On the one hand, the U.S. economy was the most advanced among the large capitalist countries in

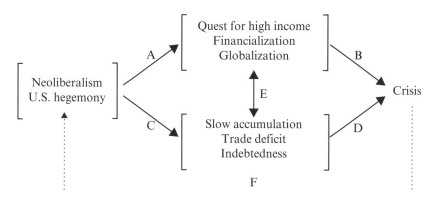

Source: Duménil and Lévy (2011a, p. 34).

Figure 2.1   Crisis of financial hegemony

the conduct of the above transformations. On the other hand, as depicted in the lower frame of the figure, a set of other 'specifically U.S.' features converged with these mechanisms. They can be described as 'the trajectory of disequilibria of the U.S. economy,' with both its national and international aspects. The main components of this trajectory are: (1) the declining rate of capital accumulation; (2) the rising share of consumption (including housing) in GDP; (3) the rising indebtedness of households; (4) the widening deficit of foreign trade; (5) the increasing financing of the U.S. economy by the rest of the world ('external debt' for short). The two later trends would have been impossible to maintain during thirty years in the absence of the international hegemony of the country, of which the position of the dollar as world currency is a consequence and means. These trends resulted in the construction of an increasingly fragile financial structure, where tremendous real and fictitious profits were made and also tremendous 'wages' were paid to financial managers.

These two sets of factors, both real and financial, are not autonomous. This is expressed in the vertical arrow E that denotes reciprocal relationships. For example, the increasing indebtedness of households (lower part of the figure) would have been impossible independently of the new trends typical of financialization and financial deregulation (upper part). Another facet of the same reciprocal relationships in arrow E is the crucial role played by globalization. The development of free trade in a world of unequal development and costs caused the rising U.S. deficit of foreign trade; a large fraction of the impact of credit policies tending to stimulate demand on U.S. territory ended up in increased imports and, correspondingly, growing trade deficits (given the comparative cost of labor in the United States and the eroding technical leadership of the country). The growth of the debt of households prior to the crisis was only made possible by the tolerance toward laxer lending practices and the corresponding wealth of daring financial innovations, which, finally, manifested themselves in the mortgage wave. More fundamentally, as contended in Box 2.1, the rise of the debt of households was the necessary counterpart of the growing deficit of foreign trade.

2.2.   Not a Mere Financial Crisis but a Strong Financial Component

From its first steps, the current crisis has often been described as a 'financial crisis' or, even more specifically, as the 'subprime crisis.' When analysts comment on the plunge of output in the United States and the rest of the world at the end of 2008, reference is made to a financial event, the fall of Lehman Brothers, certainly not the cause of everything.

It is unquestionable that the expansion of monetary and financial

BOX 2.1   THE DEFICIT OF FOREIGN TRADE AND THE DEBT OF HOUSEHOLDS

A deficit of foreign trade necessarily creates a corresponding lack of demand for domestic producers. Part of the income (equal to the value of output) resulting from production is used to finance purchases to producers not located on the U.S. territory. If imports are larger than exports, part of this purchasing power does not return to producers. This deficient demand must be compensated by new flows of lending (which are also partly used to purchase imported goods). If this compensation is not ensured, the rate at which the productive capacity on national territory is used declines, inducing enterprises to diminish their investment, with a negative effect on growth rates. A deficit of the government budget would have performed the task (the stimulation of demand) as well, but this device was not in line with neoliberal trends prior to the crisis. Thus, the rise of households' expenses, supported by their borrowing, was the outcome of macro policies rendered necessary by the trajectory of disequilibria of the U.S. economy in a globalized economy, not by the stagnation of the purchasing powers of wage-earners. For this reason, we believe the disequilibria inherent in the U.S. macro trajectory were a crucial factor of the crisis. As is well known, it is the collapse of the mortgage pyramid that destabilized the overall fragile financial structure and, finally, the real economy. But the pyramid was already there, the expression of unsustainable trends typical of neoliberalism in general, and the U.S. macroeconomy in particular.

mechanisms was a central aspect of the trends leading to the crisis[1]. Financialization has been a basic feature of capitalism from its origins, with a dramatic acceleration within neoliberalism. But one should not overlook the *explosion* after 2000, a crucial factor of the crisis. Of the various possible illustrations, we will only consider two examples. The first variable in Figure 2.2 is the issuance of Mortgage Backed Securities (MBSs) in the United States by private-label issuers (as opposed to

---

[1] In the Left school, one can mention the analysis by Peter Gowan, in which the emphasis is on financial innovations, 'a cluster of mutually reinforcing innovations which we have called the New Wall Street System' (Gowan 2009, p. 17). See also the work of the Research on Money and Finance study group (Lapavistas 2010).

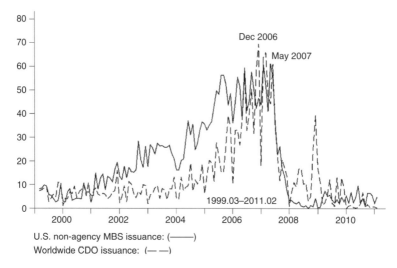

Source: Duménil and Lévy (2011a, p. 193).

Figure 2.2   Issuances of U.S. private-label MBSs and total CDOs worldwide (billions of dollars, monthly)

government sponsored enterprises such as Fannie Mae). The second variable is the issuance of Collateralized Debt Obligations (CDOs) worldwide, one type of 'vehicles,' among the riskiest, in which MBSs are pooled. The two variables point to the same tremendous expansion after 2000, from about 2 to 60 billions of dollars monthly.

It is, however, not appropriate to refer to the crisis as a 'merely financial' crisis or a 'financialization crisis.' First, the crisis is the 'crisis of neoliberalism,' fundamentally a class phenomenon. Besides financialization, all the aspects of globalization are involved, and the crisis was determined by the disequilibria of the U.S. economy, notably the slow capital accumulation and the deficit of foreign trade, not only financial phenomena. A difficulty here is that many mechanisms in capitalism combine real and financial aspects.

2.3.   The Crisis as a Stepwise Process

As of the end of 2011, four years after the first symptoms of the crisis were observed, the crisis entered into a second stage. Within the United States and Europe, the trough of the 2008 recession was reached in the second quarter of 2009. Thanks to active macro policies – the massive lending to the financial sector on the part of central banks and the huge deficits of governments (at least tolerated) – an upward movement of output was initiated. In the second quarter of 2011, the levels reached by GDPs prior to the crisis had almost been recovered. Industrial production remained, however, significantly inferior to pre-crisis levels.

The second phase of the crisis can be described as the crisis of sovereign debts, the debts of governments. The continuation of deficits led to the dramatic rise of government debts, and it is hard to identify new trends that could bring this growth to an end without destabilizing the macroeconomy. The explanation of this new situation lies in the 'structural nature' of the crisis and the extreme limitation of reforms. Keynesian demand policies only provide reprieves during contractions of output. During these periods, the macroeconomies are supposed to recover their capability to grow autonomously. None of the basic transformations required to draw the economy back to an autonomous growth trajectory has, however, been undertaken, neither in Europe nor in the United States. Large deficits remain necessary to support the macroeconomy. The Federal Reserve engaged in the bold practices of 'quantitative easing,' financing directly deficits; the European Central Bank follows a similar path, but only shyly, with the well-known consequences within the eurozone.

As of the end of 2011, the new policy trends are directed to the reduction of deficits. But cutting deficits will, most likely, cause a new plunge of output. One can, therefore, surmise that the crisis will enter a new, more spectacular, phase when the contraction is established as such.

3.   PROFITABILITY, DEMAND, AND LOANS

In the interpretation of the current crisis a large debate arose around the trend of the profit rate prior to the crisis. Did the profit rate diminish during the decade preceding the crisis and 'cause' the crisis? A crucial issue is the determination of the relevant measure of the profit rate to be used. However, not only profit rates are involved in the on-going debate, but also the share of profits (or of wages), supposed to impact demand patterns.

3.1.   Profit Rates, Taxes, and the Use of Profits

One difficulty in the discussion of the trends of the profit rate is that, even focusing on one country and one sector, a broad set of measures of the profit rate are considered. We focus here on the U.S. nonfinancial corporate sector (similar results are obtained when the entire U.S. corporate sector is considered).

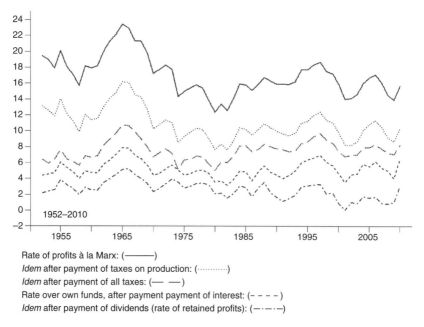

Rate of profits à la Marx: (———)
Idem after payment of taxes on production: (············)
Idem after payment of all taxes: (— —)
Rate over own funds, after payment payment of interest: (- - - -)
Idem after payment of dividends (rate of retained profits): (—·—·—)

Source: Duménil and Lévy (2011a, p. 58).

Figure 2.3   *Five alternative measures of profit rates: the U.S. nonfinancial corporate sector (percentage, yearly)*

The first variable in Figure 2.3 is a profit rate 'à la Marx.' Profits are total income minus the compensation of labor. Thus, profits are the sum of all taxes, interest and dividends paid, and the profits retained by enterprises. Capital is the net stock of fixed capital at replacement cost[2]. In this measure, the profit rate prior to 1965 oscillates around 19.2 percent and, after 1980, around 15.8 percent. In sharp contrast, the average value over the entire period of the rate of accumulation of fixed capital, that is, the ratio of net investment to the same measure of capital, was 2.9 percent. The distance between the two variables is striking and must be explained.

---

[2] Series at historical costs underestimate the value of the capital stock. They do not mirror the profit rate that can be expected of the continuation of investment in a given line, since new investments must be made at prices prevailing in the given year, not prices of the past. If enterprises made decisions concerning the distribution of dividends on the basis of a measure of profits ignoring that depreciations are estimated at historical cost, they would shortly feel the brunt, in the short run, of a liquidity squeeze and, in the long run, of the requirement to collect capital to compensate excess dividend distribution. Finally, if enterprises were the victims of this misreading of profitability trends, inflation would be the absolute weapon in capitalism against the tendency of the profit rate to fall.

In the second variable in Figure 2.3, production taxes have been subtracted from profits[3]. In the third variable, all taxes have been subtracted (profits still include net interest paid). In the fourth measure, interest is taken out of profits ('net interest,' that is, interest paid minus interest received); correspondingly, enterprises' own funds[4] (or shareholders' equity) must be substituted for the stock of fixed capital in the denominator. The last measure is the rate of retained profits, derived from the above, but after dividends have been paid out (dividends received minus dividends paid).

An important result follows. Clearly, using an *after-tax* estimate of profits (still including interest), the average profit rate after 2000 was larger than the average during the 1950s and 1960s. A complete restoration, or more, is observed. We consider the use of profit rates in which only production taxes are subtracted as misleading. As shown in Figure 2.4, the share of profit taxes in the total value added of the nonfinancial corporate sector was considerably diminished during the second half of the

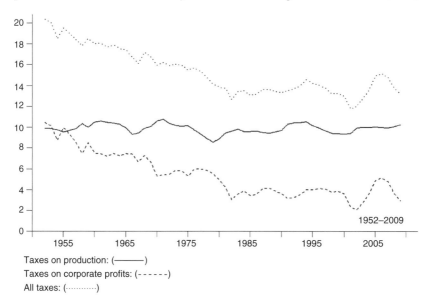

Taxes on production: (———)
Taxes on corporate profits: (- - - - - -)
All taxes: (············)

Source: National Income and Product Accounts (BEA).

Figure 2.4   *The shares of production and profit taxes in total value added: U.S. nonfinancial corporations (percentage, yearly)*

---

[3] In this measure, profits are denoted as 'net operating surplus' in national accounting frameworks.

[4] Total assets minus debt.

1970s, contrary to production taxes. This alleviation acted as a significant countertendency to the declining profit rate.

3.2.   How did Profitability Matter?

A crucial issue in the investigation of the potential role played by the profit rate in the current crisis is the determination of the mechanisms by which profitability impacts the economy. A common answer points to the effect of the profit rate on capital accumulation. Larger profit rates may allow for faster rates of growth of fixed capital for two sets of reasons. Firstly, large profit rates 'motivate' capitalists and/or enterprises in their propensity to invest. This first mechanism, *inducement*, plays a central role in Marx's analysis of competition and the formation of prices of production. Capitalists invest more in industries where profit rates are larger. Symmetrically, low profit rates discourage investment. Secondly, large profits contribute to the *financing* of investment and ensure the continuation of the activity of the enterprise as sufficient cash flows are generated. Concerning total investment (instead of its allocation among distinct uses), we believe this second channel is crucial.

More generally, a rather broad perspective is required in the discussion of investment. Three categories of mechanisms must be approached jointly: (1) investment in fixed capital with the purpose of increasing the productive capacity of nonfinancial corporations; (2) investment in the financial sector or, more generally, financial investment; and (3) the distribution of dividends to shareholders. The ways in which decisions are made in these three respects are typical of prevailing social orders such as the social compromise of the first decades after World War II or neoliberalism (we abstract here from, sometimes, important differences among countries). In the postwar compromise, a central feature of upper management (or 'corporate governance') was the arbitration in favor of productive investment; a large fraction of profits was conserved by nonfinancial corporations for the purpose of investment; in many countries, enterprises resorted to borrowing, loans being made available to borrowers under favorable conditions by a financial system in the service of accumulation; a limited fraction of profits was distributed as dividends. Under neoliberalism, the target of upper management is the maximizing of stock-market performances; consequently, dividends are lavishly distributed, and corporations buy back their own shares to the same end of increasing stock-market performances; investments (on the territory of the country, that is, domestic investment, or foreign direct investments) are self-financed; the pressure placed on management to maximize stock-market performances and the inducement created by globalization to export capital are such

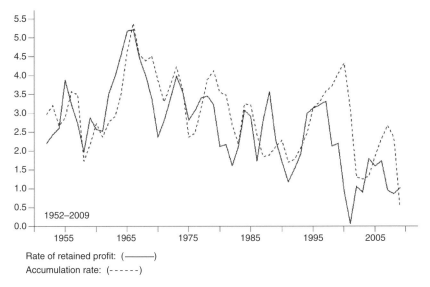

Rate of retained profit: (———)
Accumulation rate: (- - - - - -)

Sources: National Income and Product Accounts (BEA) and Fixed Assets Accounts (BEA).

Figure 2.5   *The rate of retained profits and the rate of accumulation: U.S. nonfinancial corporations (percentage, yearly)*

that domestic investment tends to be treated as a residual. Under such circumstances, it is the rate of retained profits which directly impacts accumulation.

In the United States, both the levels and fluctuations of the rate of retained profits (as in Figure 2.3) tightly match the profile of the rate of accumulation (the growth rate of the stock fixed capital, net of depreciation). This is shown in Figure 2.5, where the rate of retained profits is directly compared to the rate of accumulation. The tight correlation between the two variables mirrors the self-financing of investment by corporations. Nonfinancial corporations resort to a limited extent to borrowing and the issuance of new shares to finance their investment. This observation is in line with the above analysis of the determinants of investment.

3.3.   Changing Patterns of Income Distribution and Demand

There is a long tradition, deeply rooted within Marxian economics, of imputing crises in capitalism to the deficient purchasing power of

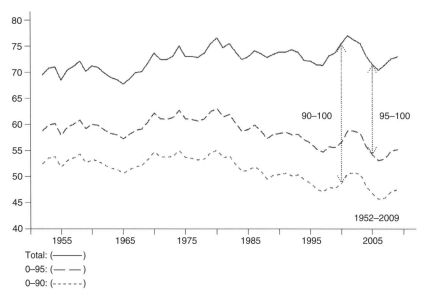

Source: Duménil and Lévy (2011a, p.49).

*Figure 2.6   Shares of wages in total income: U.S. nonfinancial corporate
             sector (percentage, yearly)*

wage-earners, as manifest in the low levels of the share of wages in total
income or a stagnant real wage. Reference is made to a quotation from
Volume III of *Capital*, out of its context, while it is generally not known
that Marx straightforwardly refuted this thesis in Volume II (Marx
1885/1978, p.486). We will not address here such theoretical issues, only
empirical observations. A preliminary step in this investigation is to check
whether the share of wages in total income actually diminished in the
United States during the neoliberal decades and, in particular, after 2000.
The variable is shown in Figure 2.6 for the nonfinancial corporate sector.
No significant trend downward is apparent.

  This observation contrasts with the well-known fact that the real wages
of the vast majority of wage-earners were stagnating (the average real
earnings of 'production workers' – about 80 percent of wage-earners –
increased much slower than the average). The solution of the apparent
contradiction lies in the observation that upper wages increased much
faster (wages include all supplements, bonuses, realized stock-options,
and the like). This is shown in the second variable in which the wages of
the 5 percent of wage-earners with upper wages has been taken out of the

mass of wages. The share of the remaining 95 percent displays a downward trend after 1980. In the third variable, the same sort of calculation is repeated but the upper 10 percent is subtracted, instead of 5 percent. The band between the two variables is constant. This observation shows that the concentration of income in favor of high wages was confined within the upper 5 percent, while the share of the 90–95 fractile was preserved and the share of the 0–90 diminished. These distributional trends echo important social transformations.

We interpret these changing patterns as the effect of 'managerial' trends, in particular the fate of managers within neoliberalism. Neoliberalism altered the trends of wage distribution to the benefit of very high wages. The households receiving such high wages are also those concentrating the great mass of capital income (interest and dividends, including capital gains).

Did the shifting income patterns diminish the overall propensity to spend of households? (In spending, we include consumption in the strict sense and residential investment.) Equivalently, do upper income fractiles spend proportionally less than lower strata? A positive answer could be expected: the beneficiaries of upper incomes are supposed to save more. It was so prior to neoliberalism, but gradually less and less throughout the neoliberal decades. Between World War II and 1980, the average rate of saving of households in the United States used to gravitate around 9 percent. During the neoliberal decades, it declined to almost zero. Thus, under the likely assumption that savings were concentrated within upper income strata, this observation points to the fact that the income brackets that were traditionally savers spent more and more. At least to 2000, this is confirmed by a study of the Federal Reserve (Maki and Palumbo 2001), where it is shown that the decline of saving occurred within the 80–100 income fractile[5].

Since data concerning the wages of income fractiles are not available within national accounting frameworks, the series, (– –) and (---), draw from the Internal Revenue Service statistics, and are obviously an approximation.

The overall conclusion is obvious. The concentration of income distribution in neoliberalism to the benefit of high income did not cause sagging demand patterns. To the contrary, the period witnessed a spending spree. Lower income strata certainly suffered from 'under-consumption' – not that they were not spending their income, but that their consumption did not measure up to decent standards – but there was no macroeconomic lack

---

[5] These spending trends are partially the outcomes of a 'wealth effect' – the consequence of the rise of stock-market indices and of the price of housing. The effect of gains on housing was larger than on the stock market (Sierminska and Takhtamanova 2007).

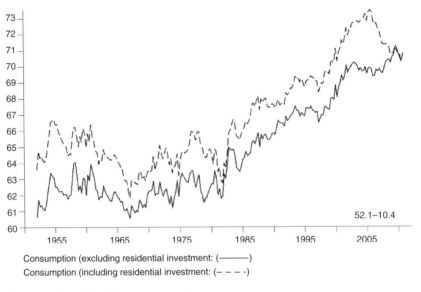

Consumption (excluding residential investment: (————))
Consumption (including residential investment: (– – – -)

Source: Duménil and Lévy (2011a, p. 147)

Figure 2.7   Demand: U.S. households (percent of GDP, quarterly)

of demand due to their low demand. This trend was much more than compensated by the spending of upper income fractiles. This wave of spending is clearly illustrated in Figure 2.7, where two measures of the spending of U.S. households are shown, one limited to consumption in the strict sense, and one including residential investment. Independently of the variable, spending gained almost 10 percentage points of GDP between 1980 and 2006. The current crisis was rather a crisis of 'over-consumption,' given the fraction of demand imported from foreign countries.

The observation of the dramatic spending of U.S. households during the neoliberal decades does not imply that the demand directed toward enterprises located on U.S. territory was sufficient to support *the activity of domestic enterprises* at adequate levels. These are two distinct issues to be carefully distinguished. Free trade is another major aspect of neoliberalism. A growing fraction of total demand was satisfied by imports from foreign countries. This was true of countries with low labor costs, such as China or Mexico, but also European countries such as Germany, or Japan. As is well known, the deficit of U.S. foreign trade went on growing throughout neoliberal decades to about 5 percent before the current crisis. The continuation of these deficits was only made possible by the towering position of the U.S. economy and the dollar in the world.

To sum up, considering production on U.S. territory, there was a deficit of domestic demand, but not because demand was low as a result of a bias in income distribution, but because of neoliberal globalization under U.S. hegemony. This chronic deficit of demand on U.S. territory was at the root of the requirement to boost the macroeconomy.

4. MARXIST ECONOMISTS INTERPRETING THE CRISIS

The present section discusses various aspects of the analyses of the current crisis by a number of Marxist economists (that we distinguish from interpretations derived from Fernand Braudel's historical analysis). Four categories of issues are considered: (1) the share of wages; (2) the lending boom to households; (3) the profit rate; and (4) financialization.

4.1.   A Decreasing Share of Wages?

Although the straightforward calculation in Figure 2.6 clearly shows the opposite, the view that the share of labor diminished during neoliberal decades is recurrently put forward in the literature devoted to the crisis. The mistake arises from the fact that the share of wages is not directly considered. An inference is made based on the comparison between labor productivity and the hourly real compensation of labor, as in Figure 2.8[6]. The growing gap between the two lines is interpreted as a declining share of wages.

This inference is wrong. As is well known, the share of wages can be expressed as the ratio of the hourly real wage to labor productivity, multiplied by the ratio of the consumer price index to the deflator of output:

$$Share\ of\ wages = \frac{Hourly\ real\ wage}{Labor\ productivity} \times Relative\ prices$$

What is omitted is that prices matter in the determination of the share of wages, and that the ratio of the consumer price index to the price of value added changed considerably, as shown by the third variable in Figure 2.8. The three variables reveal the following: (1) the hourly real wage was multiplied by 2 between 1960 and 2009; (2) relative prices, by 1.5; and (3)

---

[6] For example, Kotz (2009), Shaikh (2011) ('the slowdown of real wages relative to productivity'), and Valle (2008).

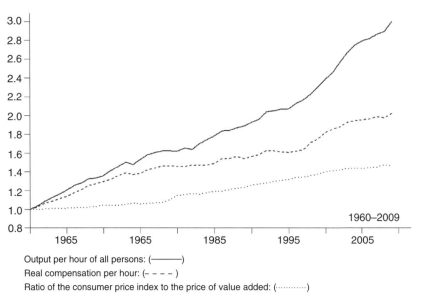

Output per hour of all persons: (———)
Real compensation per hour: (– – – –)
Ratio of the consumer price index to the price of value added: (···········)

Sources: National Income and Product Accounts (BEA) and Bureau of Labor Statistics.

Figure 2.8   Labor productivity, compensations of labor, and ratio of prices U.S., business sector (indices, 1960=1, yearly)

labor productivity, by 3. Thus, the share of wages remained about constant ($2 \times 1.5/3 = 1$), as shown in Figure 2.6. The business sector is the sum of the corporate and non-corporate sectors (mostly sole proprietors and partnerships).

4.2.   The Lending and Housing Booms

Capitalism is intrinsically prone to cumulative processes such as housing (or stock-market) booms and bubbles. The wave of residential investment caused the excessive rise of the prices of housing (the 'bubble' proper), which, in turn, fed the growing wave of borrowing as houses were used as collaterals[7]. This bubble unquestionably played a crucial role in *triggering* the crisis, although it cannot be considered the *cause* of the crisis.

A common, though problematic, interpretation of the roots of the

---

[7] Kotz (2009) provides interesting estimates of the 'gross equity extracted' due to the rise of home prices, which illustrate this process.

housing boom prolongs the above misled assessment of the trends of the share of wages. A link is established between the frustration of wage-earners after years of stagnating or declining purchasing powers and the rise of borrowing. This widely held explanation points specifically to the fractions of borrowers belonging to the lower income strata, as in sub-prime mortgages. We are told that deficient purchasing powers enhanced the inducement to get into debt. For example, in Moseley (2009): '[W]orkers were strapped with stagnant wages and were all too eager to borrow money to buy a house or a new car, and sometimes even basic necessities.' Or Shaikh (2011, p.45): 'The normal side effect to a wage deceleration would have been a stagnation of real consumer spending. But with interest rates falling and credit being made ever easier, consumer and other spending continued to rise, buoyed on a rising tide of debt.'

There is certainly a degree of truth in the two observations, the decline of the purchasing power of the great mass of wage-earners and the dramatic rise of the debt of households in the United States. But this is not sufficient to infer a causal relationship. Firstly, there is a uncontroversial reason. The financial sector, stimulated by large flows of income (capital income and high wages including all forms of supplements) derived from the lending boom, pushed these mechanisms to the extreme (with active lobbying in favor of financial deregulation). Various sources of incomes (fees and interest) were garnered, deriving from the lending itself, the securitization of the loans (as in Mortgage Backed Securities), and the insurance against defaults (as in Credit Default Swaps). Secondly, there is also, probably, a broad agreement that the mortgage wave during the last decade preceding the crisis stimulated the macroeconomy and, even, was encouraged to this end. The recovery from the recession of 2001 was only made possible by the tremendous increase in mortgages, which financed residential investment and consumption. But the role of central monetary authorities is overlooked, despite its crucial character. It is the function of central monetary authorities to control the levels of indebtedness. There was, instead, a growing 'tolerance' toward the new dangerous practices that made the boom possible; these practices were even welcomed by the Federal Reserve. Involved here is the discussion of the trajectory of disequilibria of the U.S. macroeconomy as in Box 2.1. At the root of the policy of the Federal Reserve was the growing deficit of foreign trade in the United States, the outcome of globalization and the resulting increasing deficient demand levels to producers still located on U.S. territory. The lack of demand was compensated by the expenses of households financed by borrowing. This was a macroeconomic requirement.

4.3. The Recovery of the Profit Rate

A broad number of Marxist economists acknowledge the substantial recovery of the profit rate (measured as the ratio of the excess of income on the labor cost and fixed capital net of depreciation) during the neo-liberal decades and do not see in the current crisis a 'profitability crisis' (contrary to the advocates of the Braudelian perspective below). Examples are Husson (2012)[8], Moseley (2009), Shaikh (2011), and Mohun (2013). In Moseley's formulation (2009): 'It has taken a long time, but the rate of profit is now approaching the peaks achieved in the 1960s.' The specific aspect in Shaikh's and Husson's analyses is the explanation of the recovery of the profit rate by a rise of the profit share. But the fact itself is clearly set out by Shaikh (2011, p. 45),

> At the same time, in countries such as the US and the UK there was an unprec-edented rise in the exploitation of labour, manifested in the slowdown of real wages relative to productivity. As always, the direct benefit was a great boost to the rate of profit

and by Husson (2012, p. 99),

> Inasmuch as productivity gains do not recover their level of the Fordist period, the main way of restoring the profit rate is a decline of the share of wages – that is, an increase in the rate of exploitation – and, therefore, an increase in the share of profits in value added. And this is exactly what happens from the mid-1980s onward.

There is a broad agreement that the purchasing power of the large mass of wage-earners was under pressure. But it is not correct to infer from this observation that the share of wages in total income diminished.

Once recognizing the new trend upward of profit rates, no mention is made of a long phase of 'over-accumulation,' quite the contrary. For example, Husson (2009) comments that: 'During the decades preceding the crisis, there was no tendency toward over-accumulation.' Reference is generally made to the low levels of investment. Significant exceptions are, however, Shaikh (2011), who points to: 'the great boom after the 1980s'[9],

---

[8] In Husson's measure the profit rate returned to its peak in the mid-1960s.
[9] A specific feature of Shaikh's (2011, p. 45) analysis is the emphasis placed on the declining interest rate: '[A] new boom began in the 1980s in all major capitalist countries, spurred by a sharp drop in interest rates which greatly raised the net rate of return on capital, i.e. raised the net difference between the profit rate and the interest rate [. . .], the rate of profit-of-enterprise. This is the central driver of accumulation.' We do not think that this measure of the profit rate is the most appropriate to account for the rate of accumulation (Duménil and Lévy 2011b).

or the analysis of 'overinvestment' by Kotz (2009)[10]. Special attention must, finally, be paid to Mohun's (2013) analysis. Mohun converges with us concerning the emphasis on what the Bureau of Labor Statistics calls 'supervisory wages,' and what we call the 'wages of managerial classes.' He boldly aggregates upper wages with profits. A new form of 'profit rate' follows. Mohun (2013, Figure 10.5) shows an upward trend of this profit rate, but with a fluctuation downward during the last decade prior to the crisis. We do not believe the current crisis can be interpreted in this manner, but the discussion of Mohun's framework lies beyond the limits of the present study.

4.4. Financialization

It is, sometimes, contended by Marxist economists that the absence of recovery of investment fueled financial activity. It is, notably so, in Husson's analysis: 'It is not the rise of finance that causes the decline of wages but, to the contrary, the rise of uninvested profits that feeds finance. [. . .] Thus, financialization is not an autonomous factor and appears to be the logical counterpart of the decline of the wage share and the growing scarcity of profitable investment opportunities[11].'

Moseley's (2009) view is similar, but the emphasis is placed on the capacity to lend: 'An important further consequence of the higher profits and the continued weakness of business investment was that financial capitalists had lots of money to lend, but nonfinancial corporations did not have much need to borrow. Therefore, financial capitalists went searching for new borrowers.' Lapavistas (2010, p. 3) quite convincingly criticized this viewpoint:

> The literature on financialisation generally links weak production with booming finance; according to some, causation runs from weak production to booming finance [as in Husson, Mohun, Moseley], while for others it runs in the opposite direction. This article argues that there is no direct causation between booming finance and weak production. Rather, financialisation represents systemic transformation of capitalist production and finance, which ultimately accounts for the crisis of 2007–9.

We interpret the simultaneous downward trends of accumulation and the explosion of financial mechanisms as two *consequences* of the specific

---

[10] Kotz (2009, p. 310) points to a phase of 'overinvestment'. The pre-crisis decade must be interpreted as the combination of a 'broad structural crisis' marking 'the end of the ability of the neoliberal form of capitalism to promote profit-making and accumulation,' on the one hand, and a crisis of 'overinvestment' (a shorter term mechanism), on the other hand.

[11] http://hussonet.free.fr/attacris.pdf, p. 3.

rules of functioning properly to neoliberal capitalism. But none caused the other.

5.   A HISTORICAL PERSPECTIVE

Issues such as the trends of the profit rate or financialization can be addressed in an even more general historical perspective than in the previous sections. Below we, first, discuss a number of such approaches retaking the tradition opened by Braudel. Then, we contrast these interpretations to our own analysis of historical transformations. Note that the scope of our investigation is much more limited, since we only begin in the late 19th Century and focus on the United States.

5.1.   The Legacy of Fernand Braudel

A number of analysts, elaborating on Braudel's work, developed a broad historical interpretation of the history of capitalism, now prolonged to the contemporary crisis. This perspective is that of long waves, world-systems, etc. As stated by Arrighi (1999, p. 223):

> As Fernand Braudel observed in *Le temps du monde* (1979), all major expansions of world trade and production have resulted in an over-accumulation of capital beyond the normal channels of profitable investment. Whenever this happened, the organizing centers of the expansion were in a position to reaffirm, for a while at least, their dominance over world-scale processes of capital accumulation through greater specialization in financial intermediation. This has been the experience, not just of Britain in the Edwardian era, but also of Holland in the 18th century and of the Genoese capitalist diaspora in the second half of the 16th century. As we shall see, it has been also the experience of the United States in the Belle Époque of the Reagan era.

All the ingredients of a large set of interpretations are there: the lack of profitable investment opportunities, over-accumulation, and the move toward financial activity. Given, the above, there is no surprise to discover that Arrighi (1999, p. 223) retakes most Braudelian themes:

> At the roots of all these experiences we can detect a double tendency engendered by the over-accumulation of capital. On the one hand, capitalist organizations and individuals respond to the accumulation of capital over and above what can be reinvested profitably in established channels of trade and production by holding in liquid form a growing proportion of their incoming cash flows. This tendency creates an overabundant mass of liquidity that can be mobilized directly or through intermediaries in speculation, borrowing and lending.

This framework of analysis is shared by analysts such as Brenner, Harvey, and Wallerstein. Below we do not repeat the basic interpretations but point to specific aspects.

Concerning, at least, profit rates, Brenner (2006) shares the common perspective of the group, but one important difference is that he engaged into the explicit calculation of profit rates. In the interpretation of the current crisis, the problem in this first respect is the consideration of profits from which only indirect business taxes have been subtracted. The relevant profit rate for enterprises, in particular if the financing of investment is considered, is a measure after all taxes (actually the rate of retained profits). Independently of this misleading calculation, the central issue is the misinterpretation of the historical trends of the profit rate. Brenner (2006) pins the periods of rise and decline of the profit rate on international competition[12]. It is, therefore, not surprising that the central variable in his analysis is the profit rate in the manufacturing sector, since, besides raw materials, mostly industrial goods are the object of international trade. We criticized this view point in other works (Duménil and Lévy 2002). Harvey's (2003) work seems to follow Brenner's analysis and elaborates on the notion of over-accumulation, linked to his own concept of spatio-temporal fix.

Wallerstein retakes Braudel's line of argument within the general framework of Kondratieff's long waves. Neoliberalism is seen as the ultimate phase of capitalism:

> We are clearly, today, in phase B of a Kondratieff cycle that began thirty or thirty-five years ago, after phase A [. . .] (from 1945 to 1975) [. . .]. In phase A, profits are generated by material production, industrial or other; in phase B, in order to continue to generate profits, capitalism must seek financing and take refuge within speculation. [. . .]. We are today in the last section of phase B of a Kondratieff, when the virtual decline becomes real and bubbles burst one after the other: bankruptcies multiply, the concentration of capital increases, unemployment grows, and the economy undergoes a situation of real deflation[13] (Wallerstein 2008, authors' translation).

---

[12] We will not discuss here the relationship between this specific interpretation and the more general Braudelian perspective.

[13] 'Nous sommes aujourd'hui clairement dans une phase B d'un cycle de Kondratieff qui a commencé il y a trente à trente-cinq ans, après une phase A [. . .] (de 1945 à 1975) [. . .]. Dans une phase A, le profit est généré par la production matérielle, industrielle ou autre; dans une phase B, le capitalisme doit, pour continuer à générer du profit, se financiariser et se réfugier dans la spéculation. [. . .] Nous sommes aujourd'hui dans la dernière partie d'une phase B de Kondratieff, lorsque le déclin virtuel devient réel, et que les bulles explosent les unes après les autres: les faillites se multiplient, la concentration du capital augmente, le chômage progresse, et l'économie connaît une situation de déflation réelle.'

And Wallerstein concludes: 'Yes, I think, we, thirty years ago, entered into the terminal phase of the capitalist system[14]' (authors' translation).

In other contexts, the reference to profit rate is explicit. World capitalism must confront three types of rising costs, which necessarily entail the historical decline of the profit rate:

> There are three main types of costs of production: personnel, inputs, and taxation. Each is of course a complex package, but it can be shown that on average, all three have risen over time as percentages of the potential sale prices, and that in consequence there is today a global profit squeeze threatening the ability to continue the accumulation of capital at a significant rate. This is therefore undermining the raison d'être of the capitalist system, and has led to the structural crisis in which we find ourselves (Wallerstein 2006).

Note that these lines were written in 2006, that is prior to the 2008 crisis.

Overall, the Braudelian perspective quite adequately combines two categories of factors: the tendency for the profit rate to fall and the development of financial mechanisms. In the interpretation we gave of the history of capitalism from the late 19th Century to the present, both aspects are also considered, but in a distinct manner. The first disagreement is the interpretation of the current crisis as a profitability crisis. The second divergence relates to the interpretation given of neoliberal decades as a phase B, with the corresponding financial patterns. In our opinion, the turn to financialization in neoliberalism was not a reaction to deficient investment opportunities in the nonfinancial sector, but the manifestation a phase of financial hegemony.

5.2. When Capitalism Sinks – when Capitalism Explodes – when Capitalism Changes

Not only profitability crises are part of Marx's framework of analysis, but also what we denote as 'crises of financial hegemony.' In the *Manifesto*, Marx caricatured capitalist classes as apprentice 'sorcerers' initiating processes that they, later, become unable to control; the ample developments in Volume III of *Capital* concerning fictitious capital prolong this early analysis of the *Manifesto*.

Capitalism underwent four large crises, which we denote as 'structural crises': the crisis of the 1890s, the Great Depression, the crisis of the 1970s, and the current crisis. The first and third ones were profitability crises. The second and fourth crises followed phases of financial hegemony (taking

[14] 'Je pense en effet que nous sommes entré depuis trente ans dans la phase terminale du système capitaliste.'

'Finance' in the sense introduced earlier). During financial hegemonies, capitalist classes attempt to remove all barriers to their power and quest for income. Thus, in the determination of the nature of a structural crisis, not only the trends of the profit rate are involved, but also the mechanisms of the crises themselves. The forms of the crisis are quite distinct. In a profitability crisis, capitalism 'sinks'; in a crisis of financial hegemony, capitalism 'explodes.' The two crises of profitability manifested themselves, respectively, in a crisis of competition (in the 1890s) and a cumulative wave of inflation (in the 1970s), both signaling the pressure on profitability levels. Nothing similar happened before the Great Depression and the current crisis; instead a sequence of phases of explosion of financial mechanisms – notably the dramatic rise of stock-market indices, unsustainable levels of indebtedness, and the involvement in speculative financial investment – and financial crashes was observed.

In various earlier works, we described and attempted to interpret the historical profile of the profit rate in the U.S. economy. The patterns of evolution are shown in Figure 2.9. The variable is the profit rate in the United States since the Civil War, in a measure 'à la Marx' (as defined in Section 3.1). The four segments of the trend line account for the succession of four phases: (1) the first phase of decline to World War I; (2) a lasting recovery, only apparently interrupted by the Great Depression (the

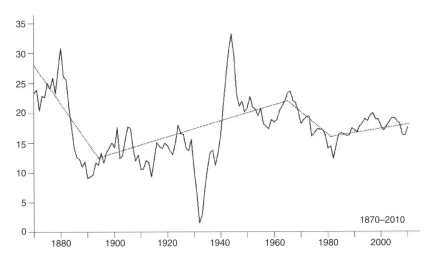

Source: Duménil and Lévy (2011a, p. 270)

Figure 2.9   *The profit rate in the U.S. private economy since the Civil War (percentage, yearly)*

manifestation of the low levels of output); (3) the decline from the mid-1960s to 1980; and (4) a slack recovery during neoliberal decades. The two phases of decline, (1) and (3), led to the two profitability crises. The Great Depression and the current crisis interrupted phases of recovery, what the analysts in the previous section interpret as phase B with declining profitability trends.

The measure in Figure 2.9 is for the total private economy. In this unit of analysis, it is not possible to account for the effects of taxation. Considering a similar measure for the corporate sector, the series are available since 1929. They show the dramatic impact of taxation during World War II. In the after-tax measure, the profit rate during the 1950s was lower than in 1929. All of the additional profits involved in the rise of the profit rate in the upward fluctuation above were transferred to the state, accounting for the 'big' state after World War II (Duménil and Lévy 1996, Chapter 19). The alleviation of taxes during the 1970s must be understood in relation to this earlier increase in taxation.

The existence of phases of recovery of the profit does not contradict Marx's analysis. The 'law' is still there, a crucial component of the dynamics of capitalism. But capitalism must not be understood as a passive victim of the tendency of the profit rate to fall, sliding to the tomb. Strong and meaningful reactions are observed in the history of capitalism, in the continuous transformation of technical/organizational trends and of social and institutional relations, with recurrent major changes – a continuous and active process of the reaction of capitalism to its inner tendencies, with moments of sharp acceleration.

The phase of restoration of profitability levels that occurred during the first half of the 20th Century to the middle of the 1960s is of great interest in the interpretation of these historical dynamics. It was caused by a true 'metamorphosis' of capitalism in which relations of production and class patterns were involved (Duménil and Lévy 1996, 2011a Figure 21.1). Three revolutions occurred: (1) the corporate revolution; (2) the financial revolution (with the emergence of large banks linked to corporations); and (3) the managerial revolution. A new bourgeoisie emerged, at a distance from corporations, whose property was supported by securities, and managerial classes became a crucial actor within social relationships. These three revolutions were prolonged after World War II by the revolution in the management of the macroeconomy, the Keynesian revolution. Neoliberalism stabilized the trends of the profit rate, though without revolutionizing the functioning of capitalism in this respect, and conserved the Keynesian framework of macro policies with new objectives. Despite such dramatic transformations, however, unsustainable trends were, once again, established as a result of the return to the unchecked leadership of capitalist classes in neoliberalism.

REFERENCES

Arrighi G. (1999), 'The global market,' *Journal of World-Systems Research*, **5** (2), 217–51.

Braudel F. (1979), *Le temps du monde*, Le Livre de Poche, Paris: La Librairie générale française.

Brenner R. (2006), *The Economics of Global Turbulence*, London: Verso.

Duménil G. and D. Lévy (1996), *La dynamique du capital: Un siècle d'économie américaine*, Paris: Presses Universitaires de France.

Duménil G. and D. Lévy (2002), 'Manufacturing and global turbulence: Brenner's misinterpretation of profit rate differentials,' *Review of Radical Political Economy*, **34** (1), 45–8.

Duménil G. and D. Lévy (2011a), *The Crisis of Neoliberalism*, Cambridge, MA: Harvard University Press.

Duménil G. and D. Lévy (2011b), *The Crisis of the Early 21st Century: A Critical Review of Alternative Interpretations*, Paris: CNRS.

Gowan P. (2009), 'Crisis in the heartland. Consequences of the New Wall Street System,' *New Left Review*, **55** (January–February), 5–29.

Harvey D. (2003), *The New Imperialism*, New York: Oxford University Press.

Husson M. (2009), *La crise et les marxistes* (available at: www.npa2009.org/content/la-crise-et-les-marxistes-par-michel-husson).

Husson M. (2012), 'Le néolibéralisme, stade suprême?' *Actuel Marx*, **51**, 86–101.

Kotz D. (2009), 'The financial and economic crisis of 2008: A systemic crisis of neoliberal capitalism,' *Review of Radical Political Economics*, **41** (3), 305–17.

Lapavistas C. (2010), *Financialisation and Capitalist Accumulation: Structural Accounts of the Crisis of 2007–9*, Research on Money and Finance Discussion Paper n. 16, School of Oriental and African Studies, University of London.

Maki D. and M. Palumbo (2001), *Disentangling the Wealth Effect: A Cohort Analysis of Household Saving in the 1990s*, Washington: Federal Reserve.

Marx K. (1885/1978), *Capital, Volume II*, New York: Vintage Books.

Mohun S. (2013), 'Rate of profit and crisis in the US economy: A class perspective,' in L. Taylor, A. Rezai and T. Michl (eds), *Social Fairness and Economics: Economic Essays in the Spirit of Duncan Foley*, London and New York: Routledge, pp. 171–98.

Moseley F. (2009), 'The US economic crisis: causes and solution,' *International Socialist Review*, **64** (on-line).

Shaikh A. (2011), 'The first Great Depression of the 21st Century,' *Socialist Register*, **47**, 44–63.

Sierminska E. and Y. Takhtamanova (2007), 'Disentangling the wealth effect: Some international evidence,' *FRBSF Economic Letter*, **2**, 1–3.

Valle A. (2008), 'La crisis estadounidense y la ganancia,' *Razón y Revolución*, **18**, 79–93.

Wallerstein I. (2006), *European Universalism: The Rhetoric of Power*, New York: New York Press.

Wallerstein I. (2008), 'Le capitalism touche à sa fin,' *Le Monde*, 11 October (on-line).

3. Marx, Keynes and Hayek and the Great Recession of 2008

Meghnad Desai

1. INTRODUCTION

The recession which began in 2008 started as a financial crisis of a depth not seen before since perhaps the stock market crash of 1929 and the collapse of the Kreditanstalt in 1931. That shock was called the Great Depression and lasted from 1929 till 1940 in the USA (various other dates for European economies) as the recovery in 1937 was short lived. US GDP in nominal terms was $103.6 million ($976.1 million in 2005$) in 1929 and did not exceed that level till 1941, when it was $126.7 million ($1365 million in 2005$). It was during that crisis that the new theories of Keynes won over the economics profession as well as policy makers and the ideas of Hayek and, to some extent, Marx (about economic cycles at least) were discredited or at least devalued.

This time around the recession of 2008 onwards has raised questions about whether Keynesian theories and policies can explain what happened or whether we need the devalued ideas of Marx and Hayek to come back into play (Desai 2008a, 2008b, 2009a, 2009b). The latest recession is as severe as the Great Depression. UK GDP dropped by 7 per cent within 12 months after the start of the recession in 2008, while in the earlier case GDP dropped from £4692 million (£216 946 million in 2005£) in 1929 to a low of £4223 million – i.e. by 10 per cent by 1932 but recovered to £4720 million (£232 855 million in 2005£) – by 1935. The UK cycle, lasting six years, was shorter than the USA, which lasted eleven years because the UK went off the Gold Standard in 1931, i.e. devalued and imposed tariffs by using Imperial Preference. Of the three post-war recessions – the 1973–76 (first oil shock), the 1979–83 (second oil shock) and the 1990–93 recessions – even the most severe one in 1979–83 saw only a 6 per cent drop in GDP and a recovery back to normal within 48 months. The other two post-war recessions were milder and lasted only around 36 months before output returned to the pre-recession normal. This time around, even after 42 months GDP remains 4 to 5 per cent below the pre-recession level.

The latest recession has been characterised by certain features which set it apart from previous recessions. Thus, governments in the USA and the UK, along with many Eurozone countries, have a high Debt to GDP ratio as well as high current budget deficits. Households have also been highly indebted, with their principal asset – houses – depreciated in value, and thus face negative equity. Banks have needed recapitalisation in the USA and the UK and will do so in the Eurozone countries. There are global imbalances, with many 'Emerging' Economies having large surplus foreign exchange reserves and the developed countries, especially the USA, indebted to them.

There has been a lot of debate as to whether the weak recovery is due to the cautious fiscal response on the part of governments as they are wedded to cutting budget deficits rather than boosting fiscal spending. The UK economy is now committed to eliminating the budget deficit of around 10 per cent of GDP completely in five years – by 2015 (extended recently to eight years – 2018 – due to global slowdown). The USA has had a large fiscal boost ($800 billion in 2009), but it has proved inadequate. Even three years after it was launched, the recovery has been feeble and there has been a budget deadlock between the Congress and the President. Central Banks in the USA and the UK have embarked upon an aggressive monetary expansion by buying bonds – Quantitative Easing (QE) as it is called. Even that has had a limited effect thus far, except perhaps in fuelling inflation in raw material markets and setting off outward capital flows, which has led to the appreciation of many foreign currencies such as the Brazilian Real. Keynesians have been arguing the case for a strong fiscal response, spending the economy out of recession now and worrying about the debt deficit issues later on (Skidelsky 2009, 2011).

Against that, it is possible to argue that this recession is not a Keynesian one, which typically arises from a collapse of effective demand due to over-saving. This recession was caused by over-spending by governments and households, thanks to cheap credit fuelled by the global imbalances. This is the sort of recession predicted by Hayek in his work during the 1930s. The failure of Keynesian policies undertaken so far – fiscal spending and monetary expansion (QE) – may be due to the need on the part of households to deleverage and for governments to guard their triple A rating in bond markets.

The severity of the present recession may be due to the confluence of a longer, Kondratieff type cycle beginning in the 1970s along with a shorter twenty year cycle. The longer cycle needs a Marxian explanation in terms of the crisis of profitability in Developed Economies (DEs) which caused the irreversible outward migration of manufacturing to the 'Emerging' Economies (EEs). It was at the very outset of the 1970s that Glyn and

Sutcliffe (1971) explained the crisis of profitability in the DEs in terms of a rising share of wages in total income and the consequent fall in the share and the rate of profit. The emergence of China and other Asian industrialised economies during the subsequent decades has altered the nature of inflation and set up the global imbalances. It has also slowed the growth of wage incomes in the DEs and deepened the long run unemployment situation. The DEs responded by liberalising their capital markets and encouraging flows overseas. There was a growth of services which partially replaced manufacturing as sources of employment. Financial services grew, but employed mainly skilled workers, and public services expanded to absorb the semi-skilled and unskilled manual workers. Private services, such as retailing and hospitality, also absorbed workers, but at wages lower than what they earned in manufacturing. In the USA, where the expansion was less in public services and more in private ones, average wages stagnated. Elsewhere, many DEs also carried a large proportion of their labour force as long term unemployed or economically inactive. Welfare states expenditures expanded to take up the burden of these unemployed.

A second cycle was set off by the collapse of the USSR and a significant acceleration in the process of globalisation. The World Trade Organization (WTO) was established, capital flows to developing economies accelerated, and many governments began to borrow on global financial markets. Activities on the financial front exploded as many new stock markets opened up and many instruments were innovated – credit default swap (CDS) and collateralised debt obligation (CDO) being lately the most notorious. But much of this was the consequence of the pioneering work of Black and Scholes (1973) on options. Hedge funds and many other institutions of what became known as the shadow banking structure also proliferated. Transactions on the foreign exchange markets reached a level of trillions of dollars.

The so-called Emerging Economies were able to benefit from the increased flow of foreign capital, which was used to further manufacturing industry in the EEs. The WTO allowed greater exports from the EEs to the developed countries' markets. But, at the same time, the free flow of capital and the flexible exchange rates systems proved too risky for some EEs. A result was the Asian crisis of 1997, in which many of the EEs of Asia suffered from sudden capital outflows which emptied their foreign exchange reserves. The International Monetary Fund (IMF) failed to help them in a creative way. This led to the Asian economies adopting the strategy of under-consumption and over-saving, accumulating large foreign exchange surpluses.

The counterpart of this over-saving was the long boom in the DEs, which lasted from 1992 to 2007 (with a short setback during the collapse of the dotcom boom), during which over-consumption became the norm. This dual matching of Western over-consumption and Asian under-consumption fed a debt fuelled boom in the developed countries with persistent under-saving. An additional cause of the persistence of such under-saving was the sophistication of financial markets, which were able to build ever taller inverted pyramids of debt on a small base of cash. When the bubble burst, it was a double crisis of solvency and liquidity for the banks and other financial intermediaries, leading to the collapse of Lehman Brothers in September 2008.

In what follows, I will briefly outline the three approaches to understanding the causal explanation and the policy cures proposed by Marx, Keynes and Hayek. While much of the ground is familiar, I will highlight those features which are most germane to the present argument.

2. GRAMMAR, MODEL AND TOOL KITS OF THREE ECONOMISTS

Marx was the first major Classical economist to point out the regular nature of cycles in capitalist economies (strictly speaking Engels should have priority as he mentioned cycles in his first essay on *Political Economy* in 1844, published in Deutsch-Franzosiche Jahrbucher edited by Marx). Marx developed a theory of crises and cycles (Hollander 2008). As against the debate between Ricardo and Malthus about the possibility or otherwise of a 'glut', an argument which Malthus lost to Ricardo, Marx showed the empirical fact of ten-year cycles in Part VII of Volume 1 of *Capital*. He also provided an explanation in terms of the interaction between the pressure on wages during the boom, which finally threatens profit rate, and the reaction of capitalists who move on to more capital-intensive techniques and make workers redundant. Soon accumulation speeds up and wages start rising again. Goodwin (1967) gave an exact mathematical formulation of this theory in a predator–prey model of the Lotka–Volterra type (see also Desai 1973). Marx used his *grammar* of surplus value, organic composition of capital, rate of profit and rate of exploitation to *model* the crisis ridden nature of capitalism. He did not, however, offer any *tool kit* or policy solution to avert crises.

Much more debate surrounded Marx's Scheme of Expanded Reproduction in Volume 2 of *Capital* in which he showed a balanced growth possibility for a two sector model. Lenin, Bukharin and Rosa Luxemburg, among many others, challenged this conclusion and tried to extract a crisis story by varying the parameters of the original model.

Luxemburg (1913/1951), in particular, influenced Michał Kalecki, among others, to see a proto-Keynesian message of likely over-production as a problem for capitalism, for which a solution had to be found in a 'Third Department' to dispose of surplus output. She also put Marx's closed economy model in a global perspective (Desai 1979).

Keynes gave economics a new *grammar* of macroeconomics, a *story/ model* of the reasons why market economies were susceptible to underemployment equilibria, and a *tool kit* to tackle problems of underemployment which he demonstrated could be endemic to a free market system. The grammar is what we all use – concepts such as Consumption Function, Marginal Efficiency of Capital, Liquidity Preference and the more exotic notions of animal spirits and uncertainty. Keynes's grammar created the language of macroeconomics. His model was not taken up as he had originally proposed with Aggregate Demand and Supply Curves defined in terms of total revenues and costs deflated by a wage unit plotted against total employment. The curves were non-linear and illustrated the possibility of an underemployment equilibrium (Desai 2002). This way of telling the story did not catch on. It was translated early on by Hicks in a much more familiar version of general equilibrium. Hicks's IS–LM diagram (IS–LL in the original article) took the exotic bits of Keynes's model away – Aggregate Demand and Supply Curves, etc. Hicks's IS–LM diagram is an analogue of a demand and supply diagram. He shows that there could be an equilibrium which could be short of full employment. He also showed how comparative static analysis could be carried out to point out that policy would shift the equilibrium towards full employment (Hicks 1937). Disagreements about Hicks's simplification of Keynes's model were rampant during the 1960s and 1970s, with many economists arguing that the IS–LM approach distorted the original message of Keynes's *General Theory* (Leijonhufvud 1968).

Yet, there was much less disagreement about the policy effectiveness of Keynes's policy nostrums or rather nostrums derived from his message by civil servants and Treasuries around the world though more in Anglo-Saxon economies than in continental European ones. Keynes's version of the Bretton Woods system may not have been accepted in its entirety, but the structure of fixed exchange rates in a Dollar Exchange Standard, limited capital movements and the relaxed attitude about budget deficits and public debt allowed the Western economies to have twenty-five years of steady growth with only a few shallow recessions.

The Achilles heel of Keynesian policy was inflation, which became a problem increasingly in the 1950s and 1960s. Keynesian models neglected prices, as they downplayed the role of money. The inflation gap in the Keynesian theory was filled by Phillips's work on wage inflation and unemployment. The counterattack, when it came from Milton Friedman and Chicago, concentrated on the fragility of the Phillips Curve (and its inconsistency with Neoclassical Homogeneity Postulate) and the superior explanation provided by the movements in money stock. By the end of the 1960s the hegemony of Keynesian economics was challenged. Desai (1981) summarises this debate and gives a detailed bibliography of the issues.

Monetarism derived much of its grammar from the Cambridge Equation of Money Demand, on which Keynes had done much work before he wrote the *General Theory*. By shifting the policy focus away from fiscal policy and towards money supply and linking the budget deficits with loss of control over money supply, Monetarism undermined the twin pillars of Official Keynesianism (Desai 2002). Budget deficits were no longer benign and inflation rather than underemployment was the principal problem market economies had to tackle.

Parallel with this shift from Keynes to Monetarism were the breakdown of the Bretton Woods arrangements, when, in August 1971, America abandoned its commitments under the Dollar Exchange Standard, and the quadrupling of oil prices in 1973. Fixed exchange rates were replaced by flexible exchange rates and the sole anchor for the international monetary system was the dollar. This gave enormous seigniorage privileges to the USA. The 1970s introduced the world to the concept of *stagflation*, an idea which the Phillips Curve version of Keynesianism could not accommodate. It was in this decade that the ideas of Hayek came back into fashion and there was also a revival of Marxian notions.

New Classical economics was fashioned by Lucas along with Sargent, and Prescott. It re-established the idea that the market economy would be in full employment equilibrium, except when it was disturbed from that position due to unexpected shocks. Agents had Rational Expectations (risk but no radical uncertainty) and had a knowledge of how markets worked. The Dynamic Stochastic General Equilibrium (DSGE) model replaced the Keynes–Hicks schema as econometrically calibrated by Lawrence Klein in a series of models as the staple of macroeconomics (Lucas 1981).

3. HAYEK

Hayek is a part of the tradition of the Austrian School, which was the least well known of the three schools of the Marginalist Revolution – of Walras in Lausanne, Switzerland, Jevons in Manchester, England, and Menger in Vienna, Austria. The Austrians adhered to the notion of free market equilibrium along Walrasian lines, but they had a distinctive capital theory.

While Walrasian theory was a static one, the Austrians were interested in mapping the growing economy. Böhm-Bawerk pioneered the capital theory in which the period of production between the initial input and eventual output became an index of productivity.

Neither Neoclassical nor Classical economics had a theory of cycles. Marx was the first major, albeit heterodox, economist to deal with cycles. Wicksell took on the task of modelling cycles within the orthodox theory. He innovated the notion that it was the gap between the market rate and the natural rate of interest which generated cycles. The natural rate was the rate at which real savings and real investment were in equilibrium. The market rate was the rate at which banks lent money. There is no reason why they should be in equilibrium, but, if they were, you would have a zero inflation equilibrium. Money would be neutral (Wicksell 1898/1936).

Since banks were creatures of habit, they did not change their interest rate frequently. But innovations could shift the natural rate. If the natural rate was above the market rate, then there was an upswing since investors were willing to borrow on the confidence that they would make profits. This cycle over-reached itself and, when the reversal came, banks would raise their market rate abruptly and the crash would follow.

Mises integrated Wicksell's theory with the Austrian theory. He made a distinction between investors in consumer goods industries with a short input–output gap and investment industries with a longer period of production. But low market rate encouraged the investment industry entrepreneurs to borrow more aggressively than the consumer goods ones. Again, when the crisis came, it was the investment goods entrepreneurs who suffered.

Hayek began his career with an abiding interest in understanding why cycles occurred despite the obvious truth of Walrasian Equilibrium theory. He went to America in the early 1920s to visit Columbia, where Wesley Mitchell was pioneering the measurement of business cycles. Hayek came back to Europe to head the Research Institute on Business Cycles at Vienna. He began with the idea that to understand cycles you had to investigate the one element which was missing from Walras's theory: money. He wanted to integrate money into general equilibrium (Desai 1982).

In 1931, Hayek gave five lectures at the London School of Economics (LSE), which were published as *Prices and Production* (Hayek 1931). This was Hayek's model of why cycles occurred in a free market economy. The causal model was a Wicksell–Mises theory of the gap between the natural rate and the market rate. The reason was cheap credit, i.e. the market rate was too low – it was below the equilibrium natural rate. Entrepreneurs who have long dated projects are encouraged to borrow and embark upon their projects. This diverts resources from the existing production which leads to wage and price inflation. The upswing can be sustained till banks can go on supplying credit. But soon the banks panic (due to outflow of gold) and sharply put up the market rate. This causes the abandonment of many long dated projects before completion. There is unemployment of labour and capital simultaneously. Mal-investments by the entrepreneurs caused by cheap credit are at the root of the crisis.

Hayek's model was vitiated by his exotic grammar. He assumed a vertically integrated economy producing a single good. This economy could progressively move towards another economy with a longer period of production as long as there were enough voluntary savings. This smooth traverse could be disrupted if the expansion was financed not by voluntary savings but by cheap credit with consequent inflation and hence forced savings. The traverse is disrupted and this leads to a crisis (Hayek 1931).

Hayek's exotic grammar attracted much attention in the early 1930s with young economists such Nicholas Kaldor, Evan Durbin, Hugh Gaitskell (later Leader of the British Labour Party) and Ragnar Nurkse all debating Hayek's model. It was only when Keynes burst on the scene that Hayek was abandoned and Keynes became the leader of young economists. It was then said that Hayek's model did not fit the facts. What was more of a problem was that Hayek did not have any policy solution. Indeed, he believed that any attempt to reflate the economy would be counter-productive. All that was required was to wait till the normal gradient prices (short term interest rates as against long run ones for example, undistorted by inflation and cheap credit) had been restored. Keynes won not just because of a superior theory but because he was proposing a solution to cure the problems rather than suffer patiently.

During the 1930s Hayek tried subsequently to elaborate and adapt his model to the new grammar of macroeconomics. His lectures, collected as *Profits, Interest and Investment*, failed to win back any adherents. Many of his former admirers, Kaldor and T.M. Wilson among them, criticised him for inconsistency. Hayek's insight that cheap credit led to mal-investments which in turn led to a crisis was not to find favour till inflation became a problem again in the 1970s (Hayek 1939, Desai 1991). Marx, Keynes and Hayek are thus three economists who studied the nature of capitalism and tried to chart its course. Of the three, Marx admired but did not love capitalism while the other two, liberals in their own ways, did. But it is the understanding they yield which is of relevance today.

4. WHICH MODEL EXPLAINS THE CURRENT CRISIS?

It is necessary to embed any explanation of the 2008 crisis and subsequent Great Recession in the longer run cyclical context of what has happened since 1971. What began as a crisis driven by the decline in profitability in Western economies caused their relative de-industrialisation as manufacture of mature products migrated to poorer, labour rich countries. Hence the rise of the Asian Tigers or later EEs is a mirror reflection of the search for profitability on a global scale. Marx's model in Volume 1 of *Capital* was a single country model. The recourse for capitalists was to increase the capital intensity of their production to pull up the profit rate. But in a global context, capital could migrate to the periphery to restore profitability. Indeed, with the innovations in transport (container ships) and communications (COMSAT, IT), it became possible to fragment production in different regions, whereby skilled labour could work in the metropolis and cheap labour in the periphery, their work being coordinated by computer aided design and management (CAD/CAM).

What Marx added later on in Volume 2 of *Capital* was a two sector model in which the surplus output of the investment goods sector (Department 1) had to be absorbed by itself and by the consumer goods sector (Department 2). Marx found an arithmetical schema which solved the problem of over-production so perfectly that the economy would be in balanced growth equilibrium free of cycles. Luxemburg argued that this was fortuitous, as Marx had neglected the monetary dimension of the issue. She predicted that the surplus production of Department 1 would not be automatically absorbed and the capitalists may have to set up a new Department 3 to absorb the surplus. This could be a luxury goods or armaments sector or it could be colonies where the surplus could be dumped.

It would be possible, in a stylised way, to apply the Luxemburg insight to what happened in the 1971–2011 long cycle. In the first phase (1970s onwards) the DEs, faced with an outmigration of manufacturing and a declining profit rate, shift up the value chain to high tech manufacturing and to the service sector, which is less capital intensive and where there are political pressures on trade unions to become weaker. A slew of inventions in IT have the effect of cheapening capital and, thus, the organic composition of capital goes down, restoring the profit rate. These are hypotheses and need empirical verification. But something of the sort must have happened with manufacturing declining in terms of share of GDP and of employment. In the USA, at least, wages stagnated since the welfare state did not take so many out of the labour market as it did in the

European countries. But everywhere the public finance position worsened since the economy had a narrower productive base. American seignior-age privilege allowed it to maintain a sustained balance of trade deficit and a budgetary deficit through much of the forty-year period (except for the last two years of the Clinton Administration when the budget was balanced).

In the second phase (1990s onwards), one could say that the over-saving and over-production in the EEs had to find an outlet, which it did in the DEs via exports of manufactures. Asian countries, especially China, could sustain an aggressive accumulation programme thanks to an outlet which would absorb their surplus product. To facilitate this absorption, the EEs also lent back their surplus foreign exchange reserves to the DEs, thus providing both the goods and the money to buy them. The global imbal-ances were thus crucial to the maintenance of a growth equilibrium in the global economy. The manufacturing exports of the EEs also reduced the threat of inflation, as their prices were lower compared to what the DEs were supplying themselves at during the 1960s.

It should be noted that since we are in an open economy context, the over-saving of the EEs does not cause a Keynesian style depression. Indeed, it caused a long boom from 1992 to 2007, but it was unsustainable. The matching of the DEs' over-consumption and the EEs' over-saving was unsustainable because, eventually, the debts have to be paid back. The DEs' households had been encouraged to borrow by the banks; especially the households which had incomes which would not qualify them as bor-rowers in normal times (sub-prime). Much money was borrowed to buy houses which everyone hoped would inflate in price to generate equity gains and validate the debt. The bubble burst when inflation threatened in raw materials markets, as a consequence of the rapid accumulation in the EEs. This led to a reversal of the gap between the market rate and the natural rate in the DEs à la Wicksell.

Keynes's model involves a flow equilibrium at an underemployment level from where an autonomous (i.e. not driven by market expectations of profit) flow of spending can jack the economy up back to full employment. The extra flow has to come from government. Keynes's model has few stock variables. Capital stock is held constant and money is the only other stock whose supply is exogenously determined by the authorities (some Keynesians argue that the stock of money in circulation is demand deter-mined). Public debt does not figure as a constraint on public spending, because the notion is that public debt is what the economy owes to itself. The rentiers, who hold the debt, can be squeezed to accept very low inter-est rates – euthanasia of rentiers – because the threat to the economy is over-saving and the rentiers do not perform a useful function. Keynesians believe that any addition to debt will be self-liquidating as it will increase income which will help service the debt. Debt does not matter.

Keynes's model also has a passive role for money and interest rates. In his *Treatise on Money* (1930) Keynes did explore a Wicksellian model, but in the *General Theory* (1936) he abandoned it. The marginal efficiency of capital can be deemed to be a surrogate natural rate, which has to equate with the rate of interest in equilibrium. But the equilibrium can be at less than full employment, because of uncertainty or lack of animal spirits. Yet, the equilibrium is static and the return to full employment is given by a comparative static analysis. We are not told what would happen if the two rates do not match. There is much dynamic movement in Keynes's theory (in the prose) but not formally as part of his model. Thus Keynesians had some difficulty getting a cycle out of his model. Samuelson's model based on an interaction of multiplier and accelerator became the basic cyclical framework. He obtained a second order difference equation from the parameters of the two equation system and examined it for the likely size of roots which may help generate a cycle. But the scheme had no role for money or interest rates or prices. Hicks also tried to get a cycle out of Keynes but did not succeed. Klein built a series of econometric models, based on the Samuelson schema, but as later research showed, the model could not by itself generate cycles; stochastic shocks had to be added to generate cycles in the Klein type Keynesian models (Samuelson 1939, Hicks 1950, Klein 1950, Klein and Goldberger 1955, Adelman and Adelman 1959).

The lack of stocks and the closed economy vision of debt are two features which make the Keynesian model unsuitable as a guide to understanding the current crisis. In a globalised world, even the Nation State is not an autonomous borrower which can dictate its terms. The holders of the debt may be spread worldwide. Even if the debt is held by nationals, they do have the freedom to invest their money elsewhere. Since some of the rentiers may be pension funds, there is an inter-temporal aspect to the desire for the borrower maintaining a good credit rating.

It is these aspects which constrain the DEs' governments from using the Keynesian policy instruments. In any case, the crisis did not arise from over-saving in the EEs but under-saving in the DEs. The EEs have suffered a growth shock, but are not in recession by any description. The under-saving problem reduces the multiplier since, even when incomes are lower than before, households are concerned with servicing the debts, especially if non-payment may entail loss of their principal asset – the house. Faced with negative equity, households have to increase their savings and not their spending. This has been the reason why stimulus programmes such as the US $800 billion of 2009 have not delivered expected results.

Hayek's schema has not been developed very much beyond what he wrote (see, however, Desai and Redfern 1994). Nor has anyone formulated it mathematically and tested it statistically. But its non-equilibrium properties relying on a Wicksellian mechanism of the divergence of the natural rate and the market rate, plus the idea that entrepreneurs are tempted by low interest rates to indulge in 'mal-investments', and that the boom collapses when banks shift their interest rates sharply up, are relevant to the current crisis. They also explain why the crisis is so difficult to get out of. The adjustment of flows is quicker but the adjustment of stocks to their desired levels will take longer. It is this that we are experiencing in the current recession.

Hayek's abstruse grammar forbids any extensive use of his model. He envisages the economy as a fully integrated single firm producing a homogenous product. He does not express it like this, but he does use the device of a triangular input–output table (one of the first such used after Quesnay) to illustrate his theory in *Prices and Production*. Cheap credit encourages entrepreneurs to embark on a new integrated economy, which is longer in terms of the period of production and will be more productive. In Austrian theory, there is no fixed capital since all capital is made from land and labour in a series of stages. As the new economy is built up from scratch, it takes inputs away from the existing economy. Since credit is being issued and the output of the existing economy begins to shrink due to lack of inputs, there is inflation. But the credit keeps on expanding to further the new economy. If the expansion had been sustained by real savings, the entire process would end with the traverse from the old economy to the new one. But, since the source is credit, the expansion stops short of completion and is aborted when the banks panic and sharply raise their interest rate. The new economy is abandoned unfinished. The inputs employed in it are wasted as they cannot be shifted to the old economy (Hayek also failed to clarify this assumption of non-shiftable capital). Once a crisis takes place, there is no quick cure. We have to wait till the interest rate is back in equilibrium with the old natural rate. Thus any reflationary spending will be counter-productive according to Hayek. The correct gradient of prices, i.e. the ratio between present and future goods, will have to be re-established so that investment becomes profitable once again.

Hayek's grammar is unfamiliar and difficult and his policy prescription is almost non-existent. The market has to restore equilibrium at its own pace. Nothing can be forced. The contrast with Keynes is stark. Yet, in the present recession, it is Keynesian policies which are failing to generate a revival. The answer of the Keynesians is of course that the effort should be doubled. But it is also likely that the logic of spending to cure recession is not appropriate for the present crisis.

Hayek's insight about the traverse can be applied to what is happening in the EEs. Here there is plenty of real voluntary savings and these economies are traversing to a 'longer' (in the Austrian sense), more capital-intensive phase. But even as they grow at a fast pace, the natural rate remains higher than the market rate, which is biased towards higher savings and few other avenues of spending for the households. This is a cumulative disequilibrium situation, but the boom has so far continued – in China, for example, for nearly two decades. The boom will end – perhaps with a soft landing – when the interest rate catches up with the natural rate.

It is difficult to speculate whether the same logic applies to the DEs. But let me try a preliminary sketch. Here, thanks to Silicon Valley innovations, the economy was traversing to a stage when capital is more productive but less costly. It is a traverse to a 'shorter' economy which is still productive (contrary to the Austrian theory). The collapse of the *dotcom* boom was a sign that that particular cycle was over. It was replaced by no new productive innovation, but investment in housing which had a natural rate inflated by expectations of rising house prices. When those expectations were belied, the boom collapsed.

Perhaps the Marxian model is more appropriate. The profit rate was high while the dotcom boom was ongoing, thanks to the Silicon Valley innovations. Now once again the profit rate in the DEs has shrunk, despite wages being moderate and unemployment high. High profit rates prevail in the EEs. Capital may continue flowing towards the EEs and away from the DEs. The way out would be a new wave of innovations in the DEs, which would raise the natural rate again. At the same time the EEs would have to consume more and lower their natural rate. Either way this re-equilibrating process would take a long while. We are going through simultaneously the long recovery phase of a Hayek cycle and the slow upturn from a Kondratieff cycle.

5. CONCLUSION

This Great Recession has raised questions about the validity of economic theories. But while many have criticised the mainstream DSGE (Dynamic Stochastic General Equilibrium) type models with Rational Expectations, the debate on recovery has focused on the revival of Keynesian explanations. This essay has argued that it is not Keynes, but other theorists (Marx and Hayek), who offer better explanations of the depth and persistence of the recession. Much more theoretical and empirical wok is required to validate the hypotheses advanced in this essay, but the first step is always to get the theory right.

REFERENCES

Adelman, F. and I. Adelman (1959), 'The dynamic properties of the Klein–Goldberger model', *Econometrica*, **27** (4), 569–625.

Black, F. and M. Scholes (1973), 'The pricing of options and corporate liabilities', *Journal of Political Economy*, **81** (3), 637–54.

Desai, M. (1973), 'Growth cycles and inflation in a model of the class struggle', *Journal of Economic Theory*, reprinted in Desai (1995), pp. 1–19.

Desai, M. (1979), *Marxian Economics*, Oxford: Blackwell.

Desai, M. (1981), *Testing Monetarism*, London: Pinter.

Desai, M. (1982), 'The task of monetary theory: The Hayek–Sraffa debate in modern perspective', in M. Baranzani (ed.), *Advances in Economic Theory*, Oxford: Blackwell, pp. 149–70, reprinted in Desai (1995), pp. 39–60.

Desai, M. (1991), 'Kaldor between Hayek and Keynes: or did Nicky kill capital theory?', in E. Nell and W. Semmler (eds), *Nicholas Kaldor and Mainstream Economics*, London: Macmillan, pp. 53–71, reprinted in Desai (1995), pp. 255–73.

Desai, M. (1995), *Macroeconomics and Monetary Theory: The Selected Essays of Meghnad Desai Volume.1*, Aldershot, UK and Brookfield, VT, USA: Edward Elgar Publishing.

Desai, M. (2002), 'The nature of equilibrium in Keynes's General Theory', in P. Arestis, M. Desai and S. Dow (eds), *Methodology, Macroeconomics and Keynes: Essays in Honour of Victoria Chick, Volume 2*, London: Routledge, pp. 15–25.

Desai, M. (2008a), 'Saving capitalism from its friends', *The Guardian*, 19 September.

Desai, M. (2008b), 'Who'd be a Keynesian?', *The Guardian*, 22 October.

Desai, M. (2009a), 'Keynesianism isn't working', *The Guardian*, 16 February.

Desai, M. (2009b), 'Hayek: another perspective', in R. Skidelsky (ed.), *The Economic Crisis and the State of Economics*, London: Centre for Global Studies, pp. 61–6.

Desai, M. and P. Redfern (1994), 'Trade cycle as frustrated traverse: An analytical reconstruction of Hayek's model', in M. Colonna and H. Hagemann (eds), *Money and Business Cycles: The Economics of Hayek Volume 1*, Aldershot, UK and Brookfield, VT, USA: Edward Elgar Publishing, pp. 121–45.

Glyn, A. and R. Sutcliffe (1971), 'The critical condition of British capital', *New Left Review*, **1** (66), 3–33.

Goodwin, R.M. (1967), 'A growth cycle', in C. Feinstein (ed.), *Capitalism, Socialism and Economic Development. Essays in Honour of Maurice Dobb*, Cambridge: Cambridge University Press, pp. 54–8.

Hayek, F.A. (1931), *Prices and Production*, London: Routledge.

Hayek, F.A. (1939), *Profits, Interest and Investment*, London: Routledge.

Hicks, J.R. (1937), 'Mr. Keynes and the Classics: A suggested interpretation', *Econometrica*, **5** (2), 147–59.

Hicks, J.R. (1950), *A Contribution to the Theory of Trade Cycle*, Oxford: Clarendon.

Hollander, S. (2008), *The Economics of Karl Marx: Analysis and Interpretation*, Cambridge: Cambridge University Press.

Keynes, J.M. (1930), *The Treatise on Money*, London: Macmillan.

Keynes, J.M. (1936), *The General Theory of Employment, Interest and Money*, London: Macmillan.
Klein, L.R. (1950), *Economic Fluctuations in the United States, 1921–1941*, New York and London: Cowles Foundation and Wiley & Sons.
Klein, L.R. and A.S. Goldberger (1955), *An Econometric Model of the United States 1929–1952*, Amsterdam: North Holland.
Leijonhufvud, A. (1968), *Keynesian Economics and the Economics of Keynes*, New York: Oxford University Press.
Lucas, R. (1981), *Studies in Business Cycle Theory*, Cambridge, MA: MIT Press.
Luxemburg, R. (1913/1951), *The Accumulation of Capital*, London: Routledge & Kegan Paul.
Samuelson, P.A. (1939), 'Interaction between the multiplier analysis and the accelerator principle', *Review of Economics and Statistics*, **21** (2), 75–8.
Skidelsky, R. (2009), *Keynes: The Return of the Master*, London: Penguin.
Skidelsky, R. (2011), *Economic Crisis and the State of Economics*, London: Centre for Global Studies.
Wicksell, K. (1898/1936 German original translated by R.F. Kahn), *Interest and Prices*, London: Macmillan.

4. Fictitious capital in the context of global over-accumulation and changing international economic power relationships

François Chesnais

1. INTRODUCTION

From early August 2007 onwards, the immediate overriding concern of Western governments and Central Banks was that of fighting off the potential effects of a global financial crisis of potentially unprecedented dimension on banks, investment funds and, more broadly, all owners of financial assets. In September 2008, Wall Street was the eye of the cyclone of the crisis, the failure of Lehman Brothers bringing the global financial system close to a collapse. 'Save the banks' became more than ever the watchword of Western governments and Central Banks. In 2010 the hurricane zone moved to Europe. Residential mortgage-backed, collateralized debt obligations and other species of asset-backed securities (RMBSs, CDOs and ABSs) ceased to be viewed as the most highly vulnerable form of assets in the portfolios of banks and financial investment funds. Their place was taken, notably in the case of European banks, by government bonds of Eurozone member countries considered liable to default, many of which had become highly indebted largely on account of the amount of public money put into saving banks, automobile firms and building corporations in 2008. Greek government bonds led the way, but the contagion of investor qualms fueled by the Credit Rating Agencies spread suspicion about the solvency of other countries, primarily those grouped by traders under the unmistakable aphorism PIGS. In this second major phase of overt financial crisis, which began in early 2010 and worsened continually during 2011, Eurozone banks have become the weakest link in chains of financial operations marked by very high levels of leverage and an important dependency on interbank loans. The financial interests and social position of interest-bearing capital with *rentier* traits are threatened by the possibility of a chain process of bank failures. The political reach of the organizations and institutions which represent them is such that the lower classes are called on to shoulder the burden of public debt. The method used by European governments for ensuring that the default of the weaker countries is avoided and that the servicing of debt and the payback of bonds take place on time is that of increasingly harsh fiscal austerity, drastic cuts in social expenditure and further privatizations. The effect of these very strongly pro-cyclical policies is to increase the need by governments to float bonds and thus to worsen indebtedness.

The contemporary sway of finance capital is lodged in very powerful socio-political institutions and rooted in the fetishistic illusion, nourished by financial organizations and conveyed to a large part of society, that money can beget money through the 'shortened' M . . . M' cycle (Marx, *Capital*, Volume III, Chapter 24). At some point this fetishistic illusion must necessarily run up against reality. This is the case now. Today, the beneficiaries of financial income, notably in Europe, are in fact confronted by the clear reassertion of two major facts. The first is that the payment of dividend and interest depends on the successful closing of the full accumulation cycle, M . . . C . . . P . . . C' . . . M'. Second, given the strong oligopolistic rivalry prevailing in the world economy between firms and governments some degree of direct control over value and surplus-creating investment and production matters. Hence the shallow talk in France and even in the United Kingdom about 'reindustrialization.' The focus on the issue of public and private debt by European banks and insurance companies and the governments that bow to them, mirrors a fall in the mass of value and surplus produced by European capital or appropriated globally and the increasing difficulties that the owners of claims on current and future production foresee in pocketing the financial income they consider due to them. This process also concerns the United States, but not as acutely as for Europe. But large industrial corporations are bent on value for shareholders and are rapidly shifting investment and production to Asia and South America. In many core European countries the working class is facing the consequences of fiscal and social austerity along with the effects of the migration of large firms.

As of January 2012, many countries in the European Union have entered into recession, because of the inherent strongly pro-cyclical nature of the policies chosen, but also on account of the situation of the world economy, which is one of a huge over-accumulation of capital in the form of industrial capacity and so of an equally massive overproduction of commodities. The need for a proper understanding of the nature and role of interest-bearing and fictitious capital means that this chapter starts with these. All ambiguity concerning the nature of the world crisis must, however, be dispelled. Viewed from the standpoint of the 'world market,' the crisis is an *economic* and *not* simply a financial crisis. It is a crisis of over-accumulation and overproduction. This characterization is all the more important that the international context of massive overproduction is also one of a major global shift in the economic power relationships between the countries classified as 'industrial' and 'emerging' economies. The fact that, in the former group, policies have consistently been focused primarily on addressing the financial, rather than on the economic dimensions of the crisis has accelerated changes previously under way. We are living in an acute situation of degeneration of the 'political economy of the Western and notably the European rentier,' to coin the title of an erstwhile well-known book by Nikolai Bukharin (1927/2011)[1]. As a result of the unresolved ideological and political crisis of the Left, and in many cases its outright subordination to the policies quite clearly dictated by finance, the working class is being taken in its fall.

2. THE NOTIONS OF INTEREST-BEARING AND OF FICTITIOUS CAPITAL

The hypertrophy of the financial sector has increasingly attracted the attention of heterodox economists. The term financialization has come to be widely employed over the last six or seven years even if each author generally gives his own nuance to the term. My use of the term dates back to the mid-1990s. In work undertaken in debate with the French École de la Régulation, I defined the accumulation regime successor to 'Fordism' as a 'finance-dominated' one, (Chesnais 1996, 1997, 2006a). But to understand the significance of finance one must really go back to Marx (Chesnais 2006b) and use the categories and notions laid out in Part V of Volume II of *Capital*. The first is that of interest-bearing money capital, which also includes dividend-bearing money capital (this extension of the category of interest-bearing capital is in line with Marx's analysis, notably the account he gives of the division between managers and the owners of the means of production). This capital reaps a part of profits in the form of interest and dividends. As soon as it gains a strong position vis-à-vis industrial capital and puts pressure on borrowers (small industrial capitalists) or on managers (joint-stock companies), it will force industrial capitalists to increase the rate of exploitation further than that required by the sole effect of competition. Wages grow slower and slower in relation to productivity. Marx stresses that interest and dividend-bearing money capital is in a

---

[1] The English edition uses the softer term 'leisure class.'

position of 'exteriority' to production, a fact that reacquired increasing significance in the 1990s giving rise to the term 'short-termism' and all the effects on corporations in terms of organization and management that radical Anglo-Saxon industrial economics has identified as going with it (Lazonick and O'Sullivan 2000). This part of the Marxian theory of interest-bearing capital is compatible with Keynesianism and was best expressed by the place attributed by *rentiers* in Michał Kalecki's growth models (see, *inter alia*, Kalecki 1943). Despite this affinity, many contemporary Marxo-Keynesian economists have downplayed surprisingly the role of the division between profit and interest and its effect on the rate of accumulation. However, the theory of money capital has further dimensions or extensions with which even the most radical Keynesian economists, but also many Marxist ones, have great difficulty in getting to grips. The most important one concerns money fetishism. Once financial markets have been in being for some time and thus become 'naturalized' (Paulani 2010), a situation sets in where interest which 'is only a portion of the profit, *i.e.*, of the surplus-value, which the functioning capitalist squeezes out of the laborer, appears now, on the contrary, as though it were the typical product of capital,' as though 'the primary matter, and profit, in the shape of profit of enterprise, were a mere accessory and by-product of the process of reproduction' (Marx, *Capital*, Volume III, Chapter 14).

Recourse to the notion of fictitious capital which is to be found in Marx alone also sharpens the analysis of the financial dimensions of the ongoing crisis. Banks which are now, since the deregulation of the 1980s and 1990s, very big, highly diversified and internationalized financial service corporations have been at the heart of the crisis since its start in August 2007. They have extended bank credit and bought debt in an ever growing relationship with what is defined as their own 'capital,' which consists almost completely of financial assets in the form of the steadier, most trustworthy claims on production. The hypertrophic growth of debt and the vulnerability of the base which sustains them are best captured analytically by the notion of fictitious capital developed by Marx in Volume III of *Capital*. After the publication of Volume III of *Capital* by Engels it received little attention. The discussion of fictitious capital by Hilferding (1910/1981) only bears on stock and bonds. He does not recognize bankers' credit as being fictitious capital, nor does he analyze the composition and vulnerability of bank assets (Chesnais 2006b). Prior to the mid-2000s, practically the only Marxist academic scholar to have recognized and worked on this category was Harvey (1982/2006). Marx (*Capital*, Volume III, Chapter 29) uses the term with reference to two different types of claims on value and surplus and then to banking operations *in toto*.

The use of the term fictitious is first of all an attempt at pinpointing the different meanings of the term capital, notably in relation to long term accumulation. What may seem to be 'capital' when viewed from the standpoint of financial investors or households with savings has no such status from that of accumulation and production. This is first discussed by Marx with reference to shares. Here he stresses the opposition between the accumulation of stock and genuine accumulation, for example investment in means of production.

> The stocks of railways, mines, navigation companies, and the like, represent actual capital, namely capital invested and functioning in such enterprises [. . .]. *This capital does not exist twice* (author's stress), once as the capital-value of titles of ownership (stocks) on the one hand and on the other hand as the actual capital invested in those enterprises. It exists only in the latter form, and a share of stock is merely a title of ownership to a corresponding portion of the surplus-value to be realized by it (Marx, *Capital*, Volume III, Chapter 29).

The issue is then taken up in relation to loans made to the State. Marx refers to the capital in the form of government bonds as being both fictitious and illusory. The capital is fictitious in so far that, 'not only the amount loaned to the state no longer exists, but it was *never intended that it be expended as capital* (author's stress), and only by investment as capital could it have been transformed into a self-preserving value' (Marx, *Capital*, Volume III, Chapter 29). It is illusionary in that the bonds issued by governments can become 'unsalable':

> To the original creditor A, the share of annual taxes accruing to him represents interest on his capital, just as the share of the spendthrift's fortune accruing to the usurer appears to the latter [. . .]. The possibility of selling the State's promissory note represents for A the potential means of regaining his principal. As for B, his capital is invested, from his individual point of view, as interest-bearing capital. B has simply taken the place of A by buying the latter's claim on the State's revenue. No matter how often this transaction is repeated, the capital of the State debt remains purely fictitious, and, as soon as the promissory notes become unsalable, the illusion of this capital disappears (Marx, *Capital*, Volume III, Chapter 29).

This, of course, is what banks and Hedge Funds fear today in the face of potential insolvencies and default.

Moving to banking operations, the term fictitious capital is used two different ways, which help to clarify major issues pertaining to bank credit. When banks create credit in the form of loans to industrial capitalists, these supplement the funds that firms set aside on their own for investment aimed at producing value and surplus-value. In this sense fictitious capital is created. However, this trait will disappear if the loan is used for genuine investment, if it produces value and surplus and is paid back without the start of debt self-reproducing mechanisms of the type experienced by governments and households. It is the fictitious character of bank capital *per se* which creates insoluble problems for capitalism. As carefully analyzed by Harvey (1982/2006, Chapter 9), Marx stresses in his treatment of interest-bearing capital both the crucial importance of the credit system for the flexibility of capitalist production and its capacity to expand and the fictitious nature of the banks' own capital, the consequences of which are revealed completely in times of crisis. Loans are made in conditions where 'the greater portion of banker's capital is purely fictitious and consists of claims (bills of exchange), government securities (which represent spent capital), and stocks (drafts on future revenue)' and also where

> all the deposits, with the exception of the reserve fund, are merely claims on the banker. Apart from the reserve funds, every deposit is nothing but a debt on the banker. It is not truly there on deposit. As far as the funds are acting in transfer operations, they perform the function of capital for the bank when the banker lends them' (Marx, *Capital*, Volume III, Chapter 29).

In order to reap profit in the form of interest, banks extend credit to industrial capitalists beyond their capacity to produce and sell commodities. They can also devise 'financial innovations' (in Marx's time the 'cavalier' operations he is so ironic about). Chains of debt and claims and interbank lending result from this: 'With the development of interest-bearing capital and the credit system, all capital seems to double itself, and sometimes treble itself, by the various modes in which the same capital, or perhaps even the same claim on a debt, appears in different forms in different hands' (ibid.). On account of the very long period over which the accumulation of capital at world level developed without any real break, and so of the unprecedented size of the 'accumulation of the actual money-capital,' the need and the opportunity for financial innovations grew accordingly. Indeed in the United States and Europe they belong to the specific set of factors which prolonged unbroken accumulation during fifteen years or so prior to 2007.

3. THE IDIOSYNCRATIC FEATURES OF THE CONTEMPORARY WORLD CRISIS

Every capitalist crisis has had idiosyncratic features in terms of the length of the phase of accumulation leading up to the crisis, its duration, its politico-spatial scope and, of course, its ways out and political outcomes. A theory of long term capital accumulation is required if one is to understand these differences, set each great crisis in its historical setting in more than an anecdotal, superficial way and assess, however tentatively in the midst of a given crisis, its possible length and other related features, today notably the shift in economic power within the world economy.

Very briefly sketched out, the starting point of the theoretical model underpinning my remarks lies in Chapter 4 of Volume I of *Capital*, at the point where money becomes capital and where a process begins where the circulation of money as capital 'becomes an end in itself,' where money as capital is bent on expanding 'without end or limits' and also, of course, without experiencing major breaks or caesura. In the course of this process, capital runs up against barriers: 'immanent barriers,' barriers arising from 'capital itself' from the fact that 'capital and its self-expansion appear as the starting and the closing point, the motive and the purpose of production; that production is only production for *capital* and not vice versa, the means of production are not mere means for a constant expansion of the living process of the *society* of producers' (Marx, *Capital*, Volume III, Chapter 15, stress in the original). 'Capitalist production seeks continually to overcome these immanent barriers, but overcomes them only by means which again place these barriers in its way and on a more formidable scale' (Marx, *Capital*, Volume III, Chapter 15). The specific character of these means and their degree of success will command the length of the phase of 'accumulation without major break or caesura.' They will also shape the conditions in which capital again finds these barriers in its way, on a more formidable scale, and thus the idiosyncratic features of the crisis which, however long it is delayed, necessarily breaks out at a given moment.

The period of accumulation of unprecedented length dates back to 1942 in the United States and around 1948 in the case of Europe and Japan, once the most basic industries and communication systems had been made to work again. The United States experienced a very short crisis in 1952 before launching its arms industry again and expanding through multinational corporate investment. It was only in 1973–75 that the United States, Europe and Japan really ran up again against capital's immanent contradictions. However, despite very strong working class and student action, it did so in historical conditions which allowed it to readjust strategically fairly quickly and easily. The 1973–75 period sees the start of long term slowdown of GDP growth and investment in the industrialized countries. But there is no true break in accumulation. In the mid-1990s the slowdown in the Triadic countries starts to be offset by investment and growth in the Asian 'emerging countries.' Once the Asian crisis is overcome and China is admitted to the World Trade Organization (WTO), from 2002 onwards the offsetting effect reappears strongly.

Three main means can have been seen as having been used by capital to prolong accumulation until 2007–08, albeit at a slower rate. Although there are considerable overlaps between them, it is easiest for the sake of clarity to list them separately. The first was the neoconservative revolution planned by Friedrich Hayek and Milton Freidman and led by Margaret Thatcher and Ronald Reagan, which organized the liberalization, deregulation and globalization of finance, trade and foreign direct investment (FDI), with the North American Free Trade Agreement (NAFTA), the Washington Consensus, the Treaty of Maastricht and the Treaty of Marrakesh as the key landmarks. The second was the rise in the United States, later spreading to other industrialized countries, of the 'debt economy' on a totally new scale and in a domestic configuration as distinct from the previous dominant pattern of foreign debt. It represented, and continues to represent, the response of finance capital to the weakening of effective demand as a result of the increasingly strong shift in income distribution between capital and labor as a result of globalization and the growth of financial markets. 'Debt-led,' or better 'debt-driven,' growth was the response given by finance to the 'immanent barriers' to accumulation rebuilt by the neoconservative revolution after a period during which liberalization and deregulation had seemed to have successfully overcome them. The third way chosen by capital to overcome these barriers and prolong accumulation was, as mentioned, from 1992 onwards the successful politically managed reintroduction of capitalist production in China, its incorporation into the world market, and its cooption into the WTO in 2002, this process taking place alongside the acceleration of liberalization and deregulation by India initiated by the 1992 economic reforms.

These three main means, by which capital overcame temporarily its immanent barriers, now find themselves again 'in its way and on a more formidable scale.' As an outcome of the first and third responses, the ongoing great crisis has novel global spatial and politico-institutional features. The space in which it is being played out is the 'world market' in conditions nearer the full sense of the term hypothesized by Marx that the world economy has ever known. The configuration of this space is totally new, since as a result of successful counter-revolution within the national liberation and anti-colonial and anti-imperialist movement of the 1950s and 1960s, followed by their full incorporation into the world economy after 1992, China and India are now simultaneously mainstays of world capitalism and very uncomfortable rival-cum-partners of the United States and Europe in the G20. This world space, finally, is characterized by the almost complete destruction of the social institutions and policy instruments devised during the Great Depression of the 1930s and the post WWII period and their non-replacement. The 'anarchy of capitalist production' and the 'blind forces of capitalist competition' have an almost total free play. Following the full flowering of the new 'debt economy' of the 1990s and the almost total reliance after the Nasdaq 2001 crash on 'debt-led growth' based on mortgage and securitization, the second response has resulted in the consolidation by finance capital of politico-institutional power-positions, leading, *inter alia*, to the establishment of debtor–creditor subordination relationships between finance capital and governments. The existence, despite the 2008 crisis, of a largely undented mass of claims on current and future production in the form of bonds and shares and the flowering of derived forms of fictitious capital, contain the threat of new episodes of major worldwide financial crisis.

4. OVER-ACCUMULATION AT THE LEVEL OF THE WORLD ECONOMY

Overhanging the world economic situation as a whole is the scale, and also the precise location, of over-accumulation of industrial capacity and overproduction. In the industrialized countries over-accumulation and overproduction are lodged in specific industries (automobiles) and sectors (real estate, housing and construction). From the standpoint of the world economy as a whole, the cornerstone of overproduction is in far-East Asia, where it concerns a wide spectrum of industries. This follows from the full reincorporation of China and India in the world economy and subsequently the call on them, in particular China, to prevent the collapse of world production and trade in late 2008. What started off as a major means, possibly the most decisive one, for prolonging the duration of accumulation by extending its space, has transformed itself into a presently almost formidable barrier. In the industrialized countries, the crisis was largely allowed to exercise its classical destructive function in the sphere of industrial production in late 2008 and 2009 – not of course, as just stressed, in that of finance. Quite the opposite has taken place in China.

Since mid-2011 the process of capacity destruction has launched at full speed again in much of Europe, and in the United States new investment is very low. Over the whole period beginning in 2008, the destruction of means of production unprofitable at prevailing rates of profit has been offset by the pursuit of Chinese capacity creation. In China, over the whole of the first decade of the 21st century, extended reproduction as laid out in Volume II of *Capital* has been marked by very strong differences between the rates of growth of sector I and that of sector II. Relative to sector I, sector II has grown very slowly. Investment has grown fast while private consumption has fallen as percentages of GDP. The existence of large overcapacity is recognized by China[2]. The difficulty in curbing it is a consequence of China's particular socio-political traits at the point now reached in its history (see, *inter alia*, Gaulard 2009). On the one hand, the communist-cum-capitalist elites entrenched in large cities and provinces are engaged in deep competition with one another, the result of which is the multiplication of investment in plant. On the other, workers are refused the right to build independent trade unions of their own, since the concession of this right by the Chinese Communist Party (CCP) would open the door for the building of independent political organizations. An increasing number of workers now organize local industrial actions of different types, including strikes, but the working class does not exist as a force capable of weighing on the overall pattern of income distribution. The central leadership of the CCP is committed to growth. It is better than nothing if this is the result of accumulation internal to sector I. It has been all the less prone to put a break on investment by municipalities and provinces that it has been in a position to sell abroad.

Hence over-accumulation is as rife as ever in the world economy. On account of the specificity of the European Union as a peculiarly vicious engine of liberalization and privatization and of destructive intra-European competition, its effects are hitting many European countries, and none, even Germany, will be immune as the crisis lasts. After calling on China to avert a full-scale slump in late 2008, G7 governments are asking it to abandon its control over the exchange rate. But the weight of Chinese competition and the attractiveness of China as the terrain of new investment by major industrial corporations make the subordination of governments to finance all the more perilous. Among the many consequences of 'honoring' Sovereign debt whatever the social but also the economic costs, deindustrialization is one of the most serious. This is the case in many European countries where the pro-cyclical dimensions of austerity are leading to quasi-irreversible structural changes.

---

[2] The website of the English edition of the CCP's daily newspaper gives examples continually: http://english.peopledaily.com.cn/. See also the report made for the European Chamber of Commerce: www.rolandberger.com/media/pdf/Roland_Berger_Overcapacity_in_China_20091201.pdf.

5. FIFTY YEARS OF ACCUMULATION OF INTEREST-BEARING CAPITAL AND ITS RECENT OFFSPRING

In my approach, the cornerstone of an analysis of contemporary capitalism is the unprecedented dimension of the accumulation of money capital as distinct from 'actual accumulation' (Marx, *Capital*, Volume III, Chapter 31). In a little quoted passage of Chapter 1 of Volume II of *Capital*, Marx has, at the height of the Industrial Revolution, enough evidence to write that for interest-bearing capital 'the process of production appears merely as an *unavoidable intermediate link*, as *a necessary evil* (author's stress) for the sake of money-making. All nations with a capitalist mode of production are therefore seized periodically by a feverish attempt to make money without the intervention of the process of production.' What was still a periodical fever took on structural features from the 1990s onwards. Following a multi-source process of centralization of money capital over two decades and the parallel play of 'snowball' mechanisms leading to an ever greater accumulation of money capital, the intent to make money without the intervention of the process of production became a permanent pathological state. It has played a central role in the outbreak and progression of the ongoing crisis. Some key moments in the process of the 'actual accumulation of money-capital' as distinct from genuine capital accumulation can usefully be briefly recalled.

The reemergence of 'idle funds' seeking to beget money outside production in the form of dividend, interest and gains from speculation is closely interconnected with the length of the period of accumulation without a break and the amount of capital not reinvested in production. The major initial cause of the reappearance of large-scale interest-bearing capital at the end of the 1960s was the decline in profitable investment opportunities for US multinational enterprises (MNEs). For this mass of capital not to remain 'idle,' it was necessary for it to have the opportunity of transforming itself into loan capital. This function was performed by the City of London's Eurodollar offshore loan capital and money markets. The next step was also initiated by banks located in the City. Following the 1973 jump in oil prices, it consisted of the recycling of rent from oil (the so-called Petrodollars) in the form of syndicated bank loans to Third World governments made at variable as opposed to fixed interest rates. The ground for the first major large-scale self-reproducing debt process was set. In the wake of financial liberalization by the United States and the jump in US interest rates, the Mexican debt crisis of 1982 marked the start of the Latin American 'lost decade' and a reversal of financial flows from South to North. At the same moment, the new method introduced for the financing of the Federal budget through the auction of Treasury Bonds subsequently negotiated on secondary financial markets marked the start of an even larger source of financial accumulation. Investors, notably at that time Pension Funds and incipient Mutual Funds, became the beneficiaries of a massive domestic transfer of value and surplus through the serving of Government debt. The US example was quickly followed by other OECD countries. Governments could borrow from the wealthy rather than tax them. A major mechanism behind the growth of Sovereign debt was launched, followed by a second. Whenever GDP growth rates fell below interest rates, as they did significantly from 1992 to 1996 in a large part of the OECD, the cost of the servicing of Sovereign debt increased and an ever higher fraction of fiscal revenues had to be earmarked for this purpose. Barring the servicing of financial-market-based retirement schemes, the wealthiest strata of society, and indeed the wealthiest among the wealthiest, enjoyed a rapid growth of financial revenues, till the present situation, 'We are the 99%,' was reached. The process is a global one. It concerns the 'South' as much as the 'North.' It has had strong benefits for rentier social classes enjoying rent from oil (the Gulf States) or from raw materials, often in combination with domestic financial appropriation (Brazil's domestic real interest rate was circa 10 percent over nearly two decades).

The continuous strengthening of financial investors and the need for them to diversify their portfolios made them turn to traditional stock markets and the ownership of shares. A new pattern of manager–owner relationship set in from the mid-1990s onwards under the name of corporate governance. The fund representatives sitting on corporate boards have undoubtedly focused on the production of value and surplus in keeping with the full accumulation cycle, M. . . C. . . P. . . C'. . . M'. The second half of the 1990s saw a sharp increase in the rate of exploitation reflected in figures of the recovery of the profit rate in the United States and other OECD countries. Backed by the globalization of the industrial reserve army, flexibilization of hiring and work, large-scale resorting to out-sourcing, new forms of computer-based work control, and so on, were enforced. They continue to be so today, probably, however, with diminishing returns because none of these methods can wrench surplus beyond certain limits. A large part of profits were not reinvested and were instead turned over to financial managers within holding company corporate structures. Purely financial 'profit centers' grew until they became in many cases the most lucrative ones within industrial and service corporations. This financialization of corporations increasingly fed into, merged with and fueled the new processes of fictitious capital 'accumulation' devised at a rapid rate by 'financial innovation.' The final complete repeal in 1999 of the 1933 Glass–Steagall Act marked the triumph of financial conglomerates (notably those that continue to be named banks). In the years leading up to the 2000–01 crash on the Nasdaq, finance capital, in Hilferding's meaning of the term, despite its new configuration, was increasingly overshadowed by the ever growing strengthening of the organizations exclusively involved in making money through the 'shortened' M . . . M' cycle. The growing dearth of value and surplus despite the increase in the domestic rate of exploitation and the flows back to home countries of profit by MNEs, notably the United States (Duménil and Lévy 2004), meant that in the case of the United States in particular, interest from mortgages became, notably from 2002 on, a key source of surplus appropriation by banks. Workers became ever more subordinated to capital as borrowers and debtors as much as wage-laborers, leading to 'the real subsumption of labour to finance' (Bellofiore and Halevi 2010). But this could not have occurred without the accelerated growth of securitization. Derivatives and even more highly fictitious types of over-the-counter (OTC) assets became the 'initial and terminal points of an M . . . M' form of circulation' seemingly delivering 'profits' to traders and the banks that employ them. I have named assets, offspring of the cardinal forms of claim on value and surplus (interest and dividends), 'fictitious capital in the nth degree.' The use of the term 'notional' in financial reports is a form of recognition of this. Naming them 'fictitious profits' is a way of pointing to the ambiguities of financial profits as calculated by national accounts, but this does clarify their economic status[3]. It is not that of interest and dividend. Derivatives and OTC assets represent a circulation within the sphere of financial markets of 'notional' sums corresponding to unceasing re-divisions of the total amount of value and surplus already extorted from production and successful commercialization.

6. TWO COMPLEMENTARY INTERPRETATIONS OF THE CONTEMPORARY POWER OF FINANCE

From 2003 on, the course towards the subprime crisis was set. In its 2005 Global Stability Report, the International Monetary Fund (IMF) even described households as the global financial market's 'shock absorber of

---

[3] Carcanholo and Nakatani (2007) name them 'fictituous profits.' The article is stimulating. However, it is impossible to follow the authors when they write that these profits have been 'a new and powerful factor against the tendency of the rate of profit to fall.' Only factors that can increase the rate of exploitation or lower the price of the constituent elements of constant capital can do that. Fictitious profits are an expression of financial hypertrophy.

last resort'[4]. Yet, riskier and riskier housing loans were offered and then sold off in the bundles of assets which finally proved in 2007 to contain un-payable mortgage debt. Recourse by banks to leverage skyrocketed and increased qualitatively their dependence on interbank loans. The debt of financial institutions outstripped in size and rate of growth that of governments, households and firms[5]. Yet, we are faced with a situation where the financial crisis has left the power of finance largely unscathed. Lehman Brothers has been up to now the only major casualty of the 2008 critical episode. Market-based pension schemes suffered quite significantly and never totally recouped the heavy losses experienced in 2008[6]. This is but another expression of capital's present capacity to make workers shoulder the burden of its difficulties. Data is not yet available for 2011, during which the Eurozone public debt and banking crisis troubled financial investors a little. But for the three previous years, figures show that total value of the world's financial stock, comprising equity market capitalization, bonds and loans (e.g. 'true claims on surplus'), increased from $175 trillion in 2008 to $212 trillion at the end of 2010, surpassing the previous 2007 peak[7]. This mirrors an effective increase in the rate of exploitation. However, the growth of the notional value of 'fictitious capital in the nth degree' has been more spectacular still. The total combined notional amount outstanding of interest rate, credit and equity derivatives stood at 30 June 2007 at $412.6 trillion and at 30 June 2010 at $466.8 trillion[8]. Estimations of the notional value of global OTC derivatives are still more spectacular. According to estimations by the International Bank of Settlements (BIS), in June 2001 the aggregate stock of contracts outstanding stood at nearly $100 trillion. Ten years later, notional amounts outstanding of OTC contracts in all risk categories rose by 18 percent to $708 trillion at the end of June 2011, well above the previous $673 trillion peak in mid-2008[9].

An attempt must be made at explaining the largely unscathed power of finance. Two avenues seem worth exploring, state capture and money fetishism, as having become fairly deeply rooted. In his chapter on finance capital, Harvey (1982/2006) places particular emphasis on the relationship

---

[4] I am indebted to Bryan, Rafferty and MacWilliam (2010) for this quotation.
[5] See figures 1 and 5 in McKinsey Global Institute (2011).
[6] See Keeley and Love (2010). 'After a partial recovery between late 2009 and early 2011, pension funds are hit again by the 6.3 trillion erasion of stock value experienced over a large part of 2011' (*The Financial Times*, 30 December 2011).
[7] McKinsey Global Institute (2011).
[8] International Swaps and Derivatives Association (ISDA) (2011).
[9] Data from Bank of International Settlements publications. For 2001 *Regular OTC Derivatives Market Statistics*, December 2001; for 2011 *BIS Quarterly Review*, December 2011 at www.bis.org.

between this capital, more precisely the organizations in which it is lodged, and the State. The outcome of 1929 and the years that followed was the destruction of much fictitious capital and the record is one of fairly antagonistic relationships between finance and the State during the New Deal and the post WWII period. Hence Harvey's assessment: 'No matter what the circumstances, the state can never be viewed as an unproblematic partner of industrial and banking capital within a dominant power bloc' (1982/2006, p. 323). The situation more than four years after the Lehman crash is extremely different, with shadow banking untouched and governments heavily indebted and, in many cases, as in the Eurozone, totally in the hands of finance. This is the subject of several essays, notably by Gowan (2010), and also of critical literature by American authors. There one finds an adaptation of the notion of 'state capture' to account for the situation fully revealed during Henry Paulson's tenure of the US Treasury Department, in particular over the year 2008.

The notion of 'state capture' was developed in the World Bank and the IMF during the 1990s in particular with respect to Russia and other States born as a result of the breaking up of the USSR. Hellman and Kaufmann (2001) define it 'as the efforts of firms to shape the laws, policies, and regulations of the state to their own advantage by providing illicit private gains to public officials.' On returning to academia, Johnson, former chief economist at the IMF, examined the US situation and found that with one major difference, possessing, however, possibly even more serious implications, the definition could be applied to the United States (and by extension to other countries with large financial industries). The difference is that in the United States bribes are unnecessary:

> the American financial industry gained political power by amassing a kind of cultural capital – a *belief system* (author's stress). Once what was good for General Motors was good for the country. Over the past decade, the attitude took hold that what was good for Wall Street was good for the country. The banking-and-securities industry has of course become one of the top contributors to political campaigns, but it does not have to buy favors the way, for example, the tobacco companies or military contractors might have to (Johnson 2009).

Since the start of the 1990s, a major channel of influence has obviously been the 'Wall Street–Washington Corridor,' the to and fro of high ranking officials between bank directories and government. Robert Rubin, erstwhile co-chairman of Goldman Sachs, served as Treasury secretary under Clinton, and later became chairman of Citigroup's executive committee. Henry Paulson, CEO of Goldman Sachs during the long boom, became Treasury secretary under George W. Bush. John Snow,

Paulson's predecessor, left to become chairman of Cerberus Capital Management, a large private-equity firm. Alan Greenspan, after leaving the Federal Reserve, became a consultant to Pimco, one of the largest Mutual Funds. This two-way flow has also taken place intensively at lower levels of administrative responsibility. The role of banks, notably Goldman Sachs, in selecting high level officials, has extended to the European Union, as recent very high level European Central Bank (ECB) and government nominations have highlighted. But the analysis cannot stop here. This anecdotal evidence reflects essentially the exploitation by finance in its own interests of the 'belief system' that took root deeply in US society from the 1980s onwards.

One of the important foundations of this 'belief system' is that ordinary people, among them workers with market-based retirement schemes, have been led, indeed forced, to interiorize, in differing degrees, the illusion that money can beget money. Money fetishism has plunged its roots in a large part of Western society. What are simply claims on production seem to them as being 'capital,' a 'capital' of their own, the 'fruitfulness' of which affects their material conditions to a higher or lower degree. Since this illusion depends on the stability and profitability of financial markets and the 'capital' which people not understood to be fictitious is in the care of the banks, these possess indeed a huge 'cultural capital.' Another key dimension has been the wide dissemination that homes are not just dwellings but also assets, 'capital.' The call for households to use finance to secure their own future well-being is said by Martin *et al.* (2008) to illustrate 'the ontological nature of financialization.' My preference goes to the approach adopted by Paulani (2010), the cornerstone of which is the process of autonomization of money inherent in capitalist production and money fetishism. 'Social processes set in' she writes, which 'naturalize the fictitious processes of formation and valorisation of capital' and create a situation where what seems to 'really matter are "the markets", their moods and idiosyncrasies.' This explains the current situation in the Eurozone in which Presidents and Prime Ministers can address citizens in solemn and dramatized ways and call on them to bow to the injunctions of 'markets' and 'honor' the payment of public debt to quite identifiable financial investors whatever the individual and collective human costs entailed. Western society in its entirety is in the throng of what Marx named 'the perversion and objectification of production relations to their highest degree.' How can one begin to counteract the immense pressure of finance? One avenue is to scrutinize the growth of debt in general (Graeber 2011) and of public debt in particular (CADTM 2011, ATTAC 2011, Chesnais 2011), to question its legitimacy and to fight politically for its repudiation. As aptly put by Graeber (2011, p. 391) in the last page of his book: 'The sacred principle that "we must all pay our debts" has been exposed as a flagrant lie. As it turns out, we don't "all" have to pay our debts. Only some of us do.' The challenge is to help hundreds of thousands of people to understand this and to deny all political legitimacy to those that destroy in the name of the 'morality of the payment of debt.'

REFERENCES

ATTAC (2011), *Le piège de la dette*, Arles: Editions Les liens qui lient.

Bellofiore, R. and J. Halevi (2010), 'Magdoff–Sweezy, Minsky and the real subsumption of labour to finance,' in D. Tavasci and J. Toporowski (eds), *Minsky, Crisis and Development*, Basingstoke: Palgrave Macmillan, pp. 77–89.

Bryan, D., M. Rafferty and S. MacWilliam (2010), 'Foreclosing or leveraging labor's future,' in M. Konings (ed.), *The Great Credit Crash*, London and New York: Verso, pp. 353–69.

Bukharin, N. (1927/2011), *The Economic Theory of the Leisure Class*, New York: Monthly Review Press.

CADTM (2011), 'Break the chains of debt' (available at: www.cadtm.org).

Carcanholo, R. and P. Nakatani (2007), 'Capitalismo espectulativo y alternativas para America Latina,' *Herramienta*, n. 35 (available at: www.herramienta.com.ar).

Chesnais, F. (1996), *La mondialisation financière. Genèse, coûts et enjeux*, Paris: Editions Syros.

Chesnais, F. (1997), *La mondialisation du capital*, Paris: Editions Syros.

Chesnais, F. (2006a), 'The special position of the finance-led regime: how exportable is the US venture capital industry?' in B. Coriat, P. Petit and G. Schméder (eds), *The Hardship of Nations, Exploring the Paths of Modern Capitalism*, Cheltenham, UK and Northampton, MA, USA: Edward Elgar Publishing, pp. 37–67.

Chesnais, F. (2006b), 'La prééminence de la finance au sein du "capital en général", le capital fictif et le mouvement contemporain de mondialisation du capital,' in Séminaire d'Etudes Marxistes (eds), *La finance capitaliste*, Actuel Marx Confrontation, Paris: Presses Universitaires de France, pp. 91–6.

Chesnais, F. (2011), *Les dettes illégitimes. Quand les banques font main basse sur les politiques publiques*, Paris: Editions Raison d'Agir.

Duménil, G. and D. Lévy (2004), 'Le néolibéralisme sous hégémonie étatsunienne,' in F. Chesnais (ed.), *La finance mondialisée: racines sociales et politiques, configuration et conséquences*, Paris: La Découverte, pp. 90–92.

Gaulard, M. (2009), 'Les limites de la croissance chinoise,' *Revue Tiers Monde*, n. 200, December.

Gowan, P. (2010), 'The crisis in the heartland,' in M. Konings (ed.), *The Great Credit Crash*, London and New York: Verso, pp. 47–71.

Graeber, D. (2011), *Debt: The First 5000 Years*, New York: Melville House Publishing.

Harvey, D. (1982/2006), *Limits to Capital*, London and New York: Verso.

Hellman, J. and D. Kaufmann (2001), 'Confronting the challenge of state capture in transition economies,' *Finance and Development*, **38** (3) (available at: www.imf.org).

Hilferding, R. (1910/1981), *Finance Capital*, London: Routledge and Kegan Paul.

International Swaps and Derivatives Association (2011), www.isda.org/statistics.

Johnson, S. (2009), 'The quiet coup,' *The Atlantic*, May.

Kalecki, M. (1943), 'Political aspects of full employment,' *Political Quarterly*, **14** (4), 322–30.

Keeley, B. and P. Love (2010), 'Pension and the crisis,' in *From Crisis to Recovery: The Causes, Course and Consequences of the Great Recession*, OECD Publishing.

Lazonick, W. and M. O'Sullivan (2000), 'Maximizing shareholder value: a new ideology for corporate management,' *Economy and Society*, **29** (1), 13–35.

Martin, R., M. Rafferty and D. Bryan (2008), 'Financialization, risk and labour,' *Competition and Change*, **12** (2), 120–32.

Marx, K. *Capital* (available at: www.marxists.org).

McKinsey Global Institute (2011), *Mapping Global Capital Markets* (available at: www.mckinsey.com/Insights/MGI/Research/Financial_Markets/Mapping_global_capital_markets_2011).

Paulani, L. (2010), *The Autonomization of Truly Social Forms in Marx's Theory: Comments on Money in Contemporary Capitalism*, Paper presented at the Conference Marx International VI, Nanterre, September (available at: http://actuelmarx.u-paris10.fr).

5. Conventions and disruptions
Christian Marazzi

1. INTRODUCTION

The Keynesian concept of 'convention,' which appears for the first time in Chapter 12 of *The General Theory*, is a major contribution to the analysis of the functioning of financial capitalism in recent years. Along with the theory of regulation, the economics of convention, which has been developed in France since the 1980s thanks to the work of, among others, Aglietta and Orléan (1982), allows an interpretation of the formation of financial bubbles starting from the issue, central in finance theory, of uncertainty. Given that knowledge of the future cannot be objective, but is irreducibly subjective, it follows that the opinion of the multiplicity of traders plays a key role in determining the prices of securities. Consequently, the concept of the bubble, itself defined as a persistent gap between the value of the security and the price observed, loses its meaning. The theory of convention considers the financial market as a 'cognitive machine,' whose function is to produce a reference opinion, perceived by all operators as an expression of 'what the market thinks.' This is because of the self-referential nature of speculation, where each individual makes up his mind according to what he anticipates the majority opinion to be (the famous 'beauty contest model' used by Keynes 1936). The market price, as the expression of a salient opinion which imposes itself on agents, can therefore be considered as a convention. The representation of the future, as the result of a self-referential process of shared beliefs, is historically and socially constructed, but from an observer's point of view, it may appear to be chosen because of its objectivity. My analysis traces the development of financial capitalism over the last thirty years, using the concept of 'collective convention' as well as the mimetic behavior of agents operating in the market. I explore the question of the origin of conventions, primarily of money as the 'absolute convention,' as a transposition of social violence on the institutional level. From this point of view, money is the principle of sovereignty and at the same time a vehicle of potential violence, which may erupt in various forms: as hyperinflation, deflation, or crisis. The governance of the financial crisis, which broke out in 2007–08 with the creation of the bubble of sovereign debt on a global scale, jeopardizes basic social rights and access to common goods, and represents a critical test of the theory of convention.

2. THE SOVEREIGNTY OF PUBLIC OPINION

> The extraordinary surge of stock market volatility during the past month cannot be explained by conventional means. Yes, hundreds of scholarly papers have tried to predict the size of such swings, and whole markets – like those for futures and options – thrive on these movements. Yet we still do not have a clear, mathematical understanding of volatility's source (Shiller 2011).

Robert Shiller, Professor of Economics at Yale University, is referring to the extreme volatility which has characterized the financial market since the beginning of August 2011. On Thursday, 4 August, Wall Street fell almost 5 percent, as measured by Standard & Poor's 500-stock index. The next day was quiet, but the following Monday, the index dropped almost 7 percent. In successive days, it rose 4.7 percent, fell 4.4 percent, and rose 4.6 percent. During the months of September and October, bigger-than-normal changes persisted, though they were not quite as drastic. 'The kind of volatility we have just seen comes along only every five years or so, although there was an even more extreme episode at the peak of the financial crisis of 2008' (Shiller 2011).

To be sure, two important events explain, at least partially, market volatility: the unprecedented downgrading of U.S. long-term debt by the rating agency Standard & Poor's after the close of the market on 5 August, which connected the United States to the sovereign debt crisis already under way in Europe, and, four days later, the promise by the U.S. Federal Reserve to keep short-term interest rates near zero for two more years. Since then, a series of news events, from the risk of default by Greece to the imminence of the 'double-dip recession,' have continued to destabilize financial markets. May we then conclude that recent market volatility has been the consequence of rational behavior in response to these news events? Not at all, Shiller answers, because if so we should have to ask ourselves, 'Why did investors react so strongly to the rating change, which, after all, was merely the opinion of a few analysts on a committee' and 'Why did the market swing so much day to day, even when there was no significant news?'

We are in the middle of the debate between proponents of the neoclassical hypothesis of market efficiency and those, like Shiller and a growing number of economists, who, inspired by the theory of *behavioral finance*, go so far as to theorize the complete self-referentiality of financial markets. At stake is the analysis of the formation of financial bubbles, the dynamics of the crisis, and the impact of processes of financialization on the real economy. More precisely, it is the *relationship* between finance and the real economy that emerges as a theoretical problem, since in the last thirty years, the classic distinction between the financial sphere and the sphere of the real economy has failed, giving rise to financial capitalism, or 'money manager capitalism.'

> The incorporation of families into financial capital and the reduction of wages, have led to very concrete and radical transformations in production structure, increasing unused production capacity. The new capitalism has been able to solve this problem, at least temporarily and partially, ensuring that businesses find demand and funding, although allowing for the circuitous course of the private debts of families who have sustained consumption separated from income. A sort of mechanism that has made it impossible to separate 'bad' finance and 'good' real economy[1] (Bellofiore 2009, p. XLI, author's translation).

It is, therefore, in the light of transformations in the real economy, of the relationship between capital and labor, and of the role of the state in the new financial capitalism, that it is necessary to study the functioning of financial markets and the logic of the behavior of investors in a climate of increasing uncertainty, such as that which has arisen starting from the 2008 crisis.

According to Orléan (2004a), it is from the way in which *financial rationality* is conceived that it is now possible to characterize the three most important theories of finance, namely the neoclassical theory of market efficiency, behavioral finance, and the theory of self-referential, 'conventionalist' finance. If the first is still dominant to this day, the second is well represented in the academic world, while self-referential finance, which is directly inspired by the work of Keynes, is definitely in a minority position.

> For efficiency, fundamentalist rationality dominates because the purpose of finance is to make the best assessment of the most fundamental values. For

---

[1] 'La incorporazione delle famiglie nel capitale finanziario e la riduzione della quota dei salari, insomma, hanno determinato trasformazioni ben concrete e radicali nella stessa struttura produttiva, aumentando la capacità produttiva inutilizzata. Il nuovo capitalismo è stato in grado di risolvere almeno temporaneamente e parzialmente questo problema, facendo sì che le imprese trovassero domanda e finanziamento, sia pure per il giro traverso dell'indebitamento privato delle famiglie che ha sostenuto un consumo sganciato dal reddito. Una sorta di meccanismo unico che ha reso impossibile separare finanza "cattiva" ed economia reale "buona."'

behavioral finance, the rational investor is essentially a strategist. He doesn't limit his field of vision to only fundamental values, but fully integrates into his analysis the fact that ignorant investors are present in markets, and the ways in which their presence hinders assessment. Behavioral finance differs strongly from fundamentalist rationality because it does not believe in the efficiency of financial markets. This is an essential point with respect to the central role played by the hypothesis of efficiency in economics. But these two approaches meet again in the fact that both adhere to the idea of an objectively definable *ex ante* fundamental value[2] (Orléan 2004a, p. 268, author's translation).

Before describing the characteristics of self-referential finance, let us pause a moment on an aspect of the difference between the theories of efficiency and behavioral finance, namely the fact that markets are *not* efficient *because of* the presence of 'ignorant' investors, that is, investors who ignore the fundamental values of securities. In the theory of behavioral finance, this introduces a radical *uncertainty* into markets, impeding investors from making rational investment decisions solely on the basis of the fundamental value of listed securities. As is known, it is this characteristic which led Keynes, in *The General Theory of Employment, Interest and Money*, to describe markets as a 'beauty contest' in which 'the best strategy is not to pick the faces that are your personal favorites. It is to select those that you think others will think prettiest. Better yet,' he said, 'move to the "third degree" and pick the faces that you think that others think that still others think are prettiest' (Shiller 2011). If, in the view of the theoretical efficiency of markets, investors calculate an optimal portfolio on the basis of a rational statistical analysis of fundamental economic data, for supporters of behavioral finance one wins not by picking the most sound investment, but by picking the investment that others, who are playing the same game, will soon bid higher for. Behavior is, therefore, rational in so far as it is strategic, and is strategic to the extent that it assumes that, ultimately, it is the collective opinion which decides.

So far, this is the main difference between theories of efficiency and those of behavioral finance. But it is what the two views have *in common* that causes problems. For both theories, the irrationality of investors stands out as a cause of inefficiency in prices. Thus, in both cases, the *starting*

---

[2] 'Pour l'efficience, domine la rationalité fondamentaliste car le but de la finance y est d'évaluer au mieux les valeurs fondamentales. Pour la NTA, l'investisseur rationnel est essentiellement un stratège. Il ne limite pas son champ de vision aux seuls fondamentaux. Il intègre pleinement à son analyse le fait que des investisseurs ignorants sont présents sur les marchés et la manière dont cette présence perturbe l'évaluation. Ce dernier courant se distingue fortement du précédent en ce qu'il ne croit pas à l'efficience des marchés financiers. C'est là un point essentiel eu égard au rôle central que joue l'hypothèse d'efficience en économie. Mais, ces deux courants se retrouvent dans le fait que tous deux adhèrent à l'idée d'une valeur fondamentale objectivement définissable ex ante.'

point is the fundamental values of securities. For theories of efficiency, deviations from fundamental values cancel each other because irrational investors, acting at random, are not correlated. For behaviorists, however, deviations from fundamental value are amplified because the behavior of poorly informed investors is *correlated* around the same error.

As mentioned by Shleifer (2000), empirical studies show very precisely that people do not deviate from rationality randomly, but rather that most deviate in the exact same way. However, a similar correlation around the same mistake, such that it produces real bubbles, is anything but easy to explain, all the more so if we hypothesize, as does behavioral finance, the existence of perfectly rational investors alongside ignorant or misinformed investors. Not only this, but the same empirical studies mentioned by Shleifer show that a bubble can arise, even in the absence of a general blindness, which irreversibly disrupts the fundamentalist assessment of investors. That is, speculative bubbles are also compatible with a (hypothetically) perfect knowledge of the core data!

What happened in August 2008 in part confirms the thesis of theories of behavioral finance. On the one hand, the best explanation for the market's back-and-forth swings is that each day we are conducting a Keynesian beauty contest and reassessing what others, and still others, are thinking. Therefore, markets are not efficient because individual choices, whatever they may be, are conditioned by strategic rationality which has nothing to do with the fundamental values of listed securities. But the example of market volatility in the month of August leads us to believe that a more correct explanation of the functioning of markets presupposes the non-validity of the hypothesis of the existence of a fundamental value which is objectively definable and knowable by all those acting within the market. Let us remember that Standard & Poor's downgraded U.S. long-term debt after the close of the market on 5 August, that is, on a Friday. Over that weekend, there was widespread speculation that the downgrade would have pushed interest rates way up. But on 8 August, even *before* the Fed issued its decision to keep short-term interests near zero for two more years, ten-year Treasury yields began to drop, not rise, so that many people had to start reassessing what other people were thinking. It is clear that economic rationality based on the fundamental value of the securities, in this case U.S. Treasury bonds, is purely a scholarly construction. In fact, this economic rationality does not exist because of the simple fact that the values and prices that represent it are not objective, but are the result of a process of assessment by collective opinion.

The French economist André Orléan (1999, 2010), one of the most important representatives of the theory of self-referential finance, has pushed the critique of neoclassical finance even further than the behavioral theorists. In the wake of the teachings of J.M. Keynes, and on the basis of the experience of actual market operators like George Soros and Pierre Balley, Orléan submits that it is in the *nature itself* of financial markets to function on the basis of the herd behavior of the mass of investors, and that is why communication is a fundamental ingredient of market functioning.

At odds with those who believe that 'the minute by minute television coverage of Wall Street distorts the workings of the market, transforming a group of thinking investors into a herd that thinks as a single animal: sell or buy, all together' (Surowiecki 2004, quoted in Marazzi 2008, p. 24), Orléan demonstrates how the mimetic behavior of investors is not a value-distorting factor. The herd behavior that reveals itself through the acceptance by millions of investors of symbols and signs that each of them recognizes as the legitimate expression of wealth, is instead *intrinsic* to the concept, so central in financial markets, of *liquidity*.

Liquidity, even prior to its being a concrete monetary function, is a concept. It arises from the need for securities, in which people have invested their savings, to be rapidly exchangeable. If securities were not liquid, that is to say negotiable, the propensity to invest would be strongly inhibited.

> The objective is to transform what amounts to a personal wager on future dividends into immediate wealth here and now. To this end, it is necessary to transform individual, subjective evaluations into a price everyone can accept. Put another way, liquidity requires the production of reference value that tells all financiers the price at which the security can be exchanged. The social structure which permits the attainment of such results is the market: the financial market organizes the confrontation between the personal opinions of investors in such a way as to produce a collective judgment that has the status of a reference value. The figure that emerges in this manner has the nature of a consensus that crystallizes the agreement of the financial community. Announced publicly, it has the value of a norm: it is the price at which the market agrees to sell and buy the security in question, at a certain moment. That is how the security is made liquid. The financial market, because it institutes collective opinion as the reference norm, produces an evaluation of the security unanimously recognized by the financial community[3] (Orléan 1999, p. 32, author's translation).

[3] 'Il s'agit de transformer ce qui n'est qu'un pari personnel sur des dividendes futurs en une richesse immédiate hic et nunc. Pour ce faire, il faut transformer les évaluations individuelles et subjectives en un prix accepté par tous. Autrement dit, la liquidité impose que soit produite une évaluation de référence qui dise à tous les financiers le prix auquel le titre peut être échangé. La structure sociale qui permet l'obtention d'un tel résultat est le marché: le marché financier organise la confrontation entre les opinions personnelles des investisseurs de façon à produire un jugement collectif qui ait le statut d'une évaluation de référence. Le cours qui émerge de cette façon a la nature d'un consensus qui cristallise l'accord de la communauté financière. Annoncé publiquement, il a valeur de norme: c'est le prix auquel le marché accepte

In financial markets, speculative behavior is rational because the markets are self-referential. Prices are the expression of the action of collective opinion, so the individual investor does not react to information but to what he believes will be the reaction of the other investors in the face of that information. It follows that the values of securities listed on the stock exchange make reference to themselves and not to their underlying economic value. This is the self-referential nature of financial markets, in which the dissociation between economic value and exchange value is symmetrical to the dissociation between individual belief and collective belief.

The theory of self-referential finance reveals the centrality of communication, not only as a vehicle for transmitting data and information but also as a creative force. Communicative action is at the origin of the *conventions*, of the 'interpretive models,' that influence the choices and the decisions of the multitude of players operating in the markets. For companies listed on the stock exchange, the centrality of communication certainly leads to economic distortions, in that the self-referentiality of the markets exposes them to the risks of volatility in the markets, originating from factors which have nothing to do with productive rationality.

It must be understood, however, that a convention (for example, an average return of 15 percent on capital invested in securities) is not right or wrong by virtue of its being a good or bad representation of objective reality, but by virtue of its public force. It is the *public* nature of conventions that must be explained because it is on this basis that financial markets work. In Keynesian terms,

> The concept of self-fulfilling prophecy breaks with this [the neoclassical theory of prices based on the scarcity of goods] naturalist epistemology. It proposes a radically new idea: beliefs have a creative role. What the actors think, the way they represent the world, has an effect on prices and, therefore, on the relationships that economic actors weave among themselves. This concept profoundly alters our analysis of the crisis and of the way to overcome it. For Keynes, the obstacle to full employment is not the objective scarcity of capital, but the way in which individuals themselves perceive the normal value of interest rates. They believe in a value that's too high to permit full employment. The obstacles between people and their happiness are no longer exogenous natural constrictions but their own beliefs[4] (Orléan 1999, p. 85, author's translation).

de vendre et d'acheter le titre considéré. C'est ainsi que le titre est rendu liquide. Le marché financier, parce qu'il institue l'opinion collective comme norme de référence, produit une évaluation du titre reconnue unanimement par la communauté financière.'
[4] 'Le concept de prophétie autoréalisatrice rompt avec cette épistémologie naturaliste. Il met en scène une idée radicalement nouvelle: les croyances ont un rôle créateur. Ce que les agents pensent, la manière dont ils se représentent le monde a un effet sur les prix et, donc, sur les relations que les agents économiques nouent entre eux. Cette conception modifie en profondeur notre analyse de la crise et des moyens pour en sortir. Pour Keynes, ce qui fait obstacle

The conventions work and, historically, they change because they act as cognitive constrictions on the multiplicity of players operating in the markets. The recurrence of conventions over the course of certain historic periods is such that their *conventional* nature is almost always forgotten, so that most people end up believing them to be conventions rooted in the *nature* of things.

3. FINANCIAL INSTABILITY AND CRISIS OF ACCUMULATION

The theory of self-referential finance allows us to define these crises as originating within financial cycles, that is, they are *inherent* to the very functioning of finance. After Keynes, it is Hyman P. Minsky who has contributed the most to proving not only the inherent instability, but also the cyclical nature of financial crises. Structural financial instability can be explained through two basic considerations. Firstly, as mentioned by Aglietta (2010), market prices of financial assets are not formed in the same way as they are in markets for ordinary commodities. Secondly, money being a public asset, behavior toward it can be collective and, possibly, violent: 'Money plays a vital role in crises. In order to make the most of financial assets, they are transformed into money, and financial crises in their turn cause a shortage of liquidity'[5] (Aglietta 2010, p.11, author's translation).

In markets of ordinary products, when prices rise or fall, after some time the demand for goods decreases or increases. Price plays a role of adjustment, that is, if demand is too strong, price increases, lowering demand and increasing supply. The reverse occurs if demand is weak. In the world of financial assets, however, things do not work at all in the same way. Here, when asset prices rise, demand also increases: 'Paradoxically, increase in value creates global demand. There is no market glut in abstract enrichment, that of pure value'[6] (Aglietta 2010, p.12, author's translation). The price of assets is a function of the anticipation of their rise in value, so much so that they always attract new buyers. To the extent that the acquisition of financial assets is carried out mainly by means of

au plein-emploi, ce n'est pas la rareté objective du capital, mais la manière dont les individus se représentent la valeur normale du taux de l'intérèt.'

[5] 'La monnaie joue un rôle essentiel dans les crises. Pour pouvoir se valoriser, en effet, les actifs financiers se transforment en monnaie, et la crise financière entraîne une pénurie de liquidité.'

[6] 'Paradoxalement, la valorisation fabrique globalement de la demande. Il n'y a pas de saturation dans l'enrichissement abstrait, celui de la valeur pure.'

credit, it follows that the stronger the credit, the more asset prices rise, and the more buyers are encouraged to go into debt because they can insure their credit in increasingly expensive assets. In the financial universe, supply and demand are growing functions of the rise in asset prices. Both are pulled upwards by the increase in the price of assets, these in turn being pushed upwards by the growth and abundance of credit, which explains why the process cannot but go to extreme limits. It follows that

> the cause of financial turmoil is found in the very instability of financial markets, that is, in their inability to act in such a way that price developments are kept within reasonable limits, both in rise and decline. In other words, we return to the central theoretical question, that of the efficiency of financial markets. The heart of the problem is here, not in the appearance of greedy or irrational behavior. *The crisis is not due to the fact that the rules of the financial game have been circumvented, but to the fact that they have been followed*[7] (Orléan 2010, p. 31, author's translation).

For theories of the efficiency of financial markets, however, turmoil and financial crises are attributable to disturbing *exogenous* forces. In the case of the subprime crisis, it is *securitization*, poorly done and lacking transparency, which has hampered the smooth functioning of financial markets. In the case of the sovereign debt crisis, it is excessive public spending that impedes the realization of an effective allocation of capital.

Strictly speaking, according to the argument of endogenous instability, financial crises can develop *independently* of the appearance of specific conventions, from that of Mexico in the 1980s to the Asian Tigers, from that of the Internet and subprime lending to the sovereign debt. According to this theory, in fact, money is the 'absolute convention,' the original convention, the mother of all conventions. Given the extension of primacy accorded to financing in markets, the physical nature of credit – real estate, assets, gold, or dollars – is of no importance, because the only requirement is that of self-reference in monetary terms. In point of fact, conventions impress time and manner upon the process of financialization, because conventions are an expression of how the financial community represents wealth from *concrete, historically determined* processes of the accumulation of capital.

---

[7] 'la causa dei disordini si trova nell'instabilità propria dei mercati finanziari, cioè nella loro incapacità di fare in modo che le evoluzioni dei prezzi siano mantenute in limiti ragionevoli, al rialzo come al ribasso. Questa crisi è dunque, a nostro parere, endogena. Detto diversamente, si tratta di ritornare alla domanda teorica iniziale, quella dell'efficienza dei mercati finanziari. E' qui il cuore del problema e non nella pretesa apparizione di comportamenti cupidi o irrazionali. *La crisi non è dovuta al fatto che le regole del gioco sono state aggirate ma dal fatto che sono state seguite.*'

The current crisis, which began in August 2007 and is still ongoing, is the result of a process of financialization that has its roots in the crisis of the Fordist model of accumulation which took shape during the 1970s. Like its predecessors, this financialization begins from a block of accumulation (over-accumulation) understood as the non-reinvestment of profits in directly productive processes (constant capital, that is, instrumental goods and variable capital, or wages). In those years, there were all the premises of a repetition of classical financialization based on the dichotomy between real (industrial) and monetary economies, with the consequent shifting of profit quotas to financial markets to ensure profitable growth without accumulation. In the beginning of the 1980s, the primary source of financial bubbles was the trend of the growth of non-accumulated profit, growth caused by a double movement: on the one hand, a generalized decrease in wages and, on the other hand, the stagnation – that is, the decrease – of the rate of accumulation, despite the reestablishment of profit rate. Accumulation rate indicates the net growth of the amount of net capital, while profit rate means the relationship between profits and capital: the divergence between the two rates starting in the 1980s represents one of the many certain indicators of financialization. Other sources of accumulation of financial capital are gradually added to the non-reinvested industrial profits. In particular, financialization involved a process of banking disintermediation, but it also involved a process of multiplication of financial intermediaries resulting from the deregulation and liberalization of the economy.

The transition from the Fordist mode of production to post-Fordist 'money manager capitalism' is, in fact, explained by the drop in profits between the 1960s and the 1970s, due to the exhaustion of the technological and economic foundation of Fordism, particularly by market saturation of mass consumption goods, the rigidity of production processes, and the 'downward rigidity' of wages. At the height of its development, Fordist capitalism was no longer able to suck surplus-value from living labor.

> Hence, from the second half of the 1970s on, the primary propulsive force of the world's economy was the endless attempt of capitalist companies – under the demand of their owners and investors – to bring the profit rate back up, using various techniques, to the highest levels of twenty years before[8] (Gallino 2005, p. 35, author's translation).

We know how it went: reduction in the cost of labor, attacks on unions, automatization of labor processes, delocalization to countries with low

---

[8] 'Pertanto, fin dai secondi anni '70 la principale forza propulsiva dell'economia mondiale è stato l'incessante tentativo delle imprese capitalistiche – sollecitato dai loro proprietari e investitori – di riportare, con differenti mezzi, il tasso di profitto ai maggiori livelli di vent'anni prima.'

wages, precarization of labor, and financialization, or profit increases not as excess from sales over costs (that is, not in accordance with manufacturing-Fordist logic) but as excess value in the stock market at the time t_2 with respect to t_1 – where the gap between t_1 and t_2 can be a few days or, indeed, a few seconds.

> As Greta Krippner has shown on the basis of a thorough analysis of the available evidence, not only had the share of total U.S. Corporate profits accounted for by finance, insurance and real estate (FIRE) in the 1980s nearly caught up with and, in the 1990s, surpassed the share accounted for by manufacturing: more importantly, in the 1970s and 1980s, *non-financial firms themselves* sharply increased their investment in financial assets relative to their investment in plants and equipment, and became increasingly dependent on financial sources of revenue and profit relative to that earned from productive activities. Particularly significant is Krippner's finding that manufacturing not only dominates but *leads* this trend towards the financialization of the non-financial economy (Arrighi 2007, p. 140).

This is enough to discard the distinction between real (industrial) and financial economies, distinguishing industrial profits from 'fictitious' financial ones, as well as to stop identifying capitalism with industrial capitalism (as Arrighi writes, a typical act of faith of orthodox Marxism that does not merit a justification).

In the post-Fordist configuration of financial capitalism, where wages are reduced and investments in capital stagnate, the problem of *realization* of profits (that is, the sale of surplus-value) leads to the role of consumption by means of *non-wage incomes*. The reproduction of capital is carried out partly thanks to the increase in the consumption of rentiers and partly thanks to the indebted consumption of wage earners. It is legitimate to affirm that, parallel to the reduction of the redistributive function of the welfare state, there has been a kind of privatization of Keynesian deficit spending, that is, the creation of additional demand by means of private debt.

Financialization is the other side of the post-Fordist capitalism coin, its 'adequate and perverse' form. Maintaining that financialization is consubstantial to the new processes of capital accumulation means going beyond the 20th Century idea that there exists a good real economy and a bad financial economy – two conflicting worlds where finance works 'against' the real economy, ripping capital from its productive use, the creation of employment and wages. Certainly, the way the logic of finance works, along with the succession of speculative bubbles which increase private and public debt, there is an impact on the real economy, provoking ever more frequent recessions. The problem is that, with financial capitalism on a global scale, it is extremely difficult to overcome the crisis by de-financializing the economy, that is, by reestablishing a more balanced relationship between the real and financial economy, for example by increasing investments in the industrial sector or, as in the 1930s in the United States, investing in the construction of the social security.

By now, finance permeates the circulation of capital from beginning to end. Every productive act and every act of consumption is either directly or indirectly tied to finance. Debt–credit relationships define the production and exchange of goods, according to a speculative logic which transforms the use value of goods (theoretically all-produced or to-be-produced goods) into veritable potential financial assets that generate capital gains. The demand, and the indebtedness it implies, for a financialized use value, as happened with housing during the subprime bubble, induces further increases in demand by virtue of the increase in the price of a given product. After the ascendant phase of the economic cycle, when the inflated prices of financialized goods begin to diminish for lack of new buyers (caused by price inflation), the contradiction between debt levels (fixed in nominal terms) and prices of financial assets (which, instead, can both increase and decrease) violently explodes. This triggers a selloff of financial assets, in order to be able to cover the debt contracted, a selloff which in turn causes a further reduction in prices and therefore more selling (this spiral is called a 'debt deflation trap').

The debt crises that have characterized businesses, consumers and states for nearly 30 years are based on carry trade, that is, borrowing at a low cost to invest in higher yielding bonds. As such, the debt crisis is, as was theorized years ago by the American economist Hyman P. Minsky, inherent and cyclical to financial capitalism. In the ascending phase of the cycle, in times of prosperity, businesses, consumers, and states are encouraged to assume more and more risks, thereby going into debt. Initially, such speculation is profitable and encourages more and more new subjects to go into debt, as a consequence of the increase in the price of financial assets. This inclusive process works as long as the capacity to repay the debt is guaranteed by new cash inflows, but ends in flipping over into its opposite, that is, into crisis, when the difficulty of repaying debt first begins to show, thus triggering a selloff of assets and an increase in interest rates.

In global financial capitalism, the margin of flexibility in interest rates, used by monetary authorities, is very limited. This is due to investment fluxes in state bonds, in particular in American T-bills, which lengthen the expansive phase of the debt spiral, despite the increases in interest rates decided on by central banks in order to contain speculative bubbles. Today, more than interest rates, which are, in fact, close to zero, it is the interbank market (the wholesale market that banks use for their account activities) that is responsible for rationing credit to the real economy. In order to save the financial-banking system from collapse with injections of liquidity, public intervention, be it national or supranational, reveals two things: firstly, the necessity to plug up the surplus-value, produced in the expansive phase of the cycle through debt, with added demand (to prevent a crisis of over-production); secondly, the determination of a process of exclusion from access to goods produced in the ascending phase through layoffs and the worsening of living conditions. It is during this phase that we see a selloff of excess produced goods coupled with processes of industrial and bank capital concentrations.

Overcoming the subprime crisis caused the shift of debt from private to public sectors, but the public debt, increasing vertiginously, is the result of the socialization of financial capital made with taxpayers' money and the creation of liquidity by monetary authorities. This is a kind of communism of capital where the state, or the collectivity, caters to the needs of 'financial soviets' – banks, insurance companies, investment funds, and hedge funds – thereby imposing a sort of market dictatorship over society. The 'communism of capital' is the result of a historical process, beginning with the recourse to pension funds to finance the public debt of New York in the mid-1970s and, following this, the transformation of new productive processes, which have changed the basis of the creation of wealth and the very nature of labor.

There is something Luxemburghian about financial capitalism that, between one bubble and the next, colonizes more and more common goods.

> Rosa Luxemburg wrote her study on capital accumulation, where she maintained that capitalism cannot survive without 'non-capitalist' economies: it is able to progress, following its own principles, as long as there are 'virgin lands' open to expansion and exploitation; but as soon as it conquers them to exploit them, it takes their pre-capitalist virginity away from them and [thus] exhausts the sources of its own nourishment[9] (Bauman 2009, p. 7, author's translation).

The imperialistic accumulation cycle was characterized by a precise relationship between center and periphery, development and underdevelopment. The center exported the surplus it could not sell internally,

---

[9] 'Rosa Luxembourg aveva scritto il suo studio sull'accumulazione del capitale, dove sosteneva che il capitalismo non può sopravvivere senza le economie "non capitalistiche": esso è in grado di progredire, seguendo i propri principi, fintanto che vi sono "terre vergini" aperte all'espansione e allo sfruttamento; ma non appena le conquista per poterle sfruttare, le priva della loro verginità precapitalistica e così facendo esaurisce le fonti del proprio nutrimento.'

due to lack of demand, to the pre-capitalist countries of the periphery. In order to allow poor countries to import capitalist goods, the creation of external demand was based on a 'debt trap,' a device by which the banks of the North created the demand necessary for selling surplus through the indebtedness of importing countries. This mechanism forced peripheral countries both to destroy the natural local economy in favor of imported capitalist goods, and to export as much of their raw materials as possible at prices determined by capitalist markets in order to be able to honor the debt. The *destructuration* of common goods, of the local natural resources essential for the capitalist development of countries in the North, had to come about without the *restructuration* of the local economy, that is, without the possibility for poorer countries to escape poverty and their dependency on rich Northern countries, unless they suffer the same problem of selling surplus on a greater scale. The dependency between rich and poor countries was sealed by the relationship of debt–credit.

This scheme of imperialistic relations has historically gone into crisis when peripheral countries have matured forms of political autonomy capable of setting their indigenous development strategies against their dependence on the predatory development strategies of Northern countries. This is the historical result of the struggles for national liberation, struggles which have transformed underdeveloped countries into new developing countries.

Today, the same logic of dependent relationships between the centre and the periphery is found *inside* the global capitalist economy. The hidden face of financialization, of the recurrent production of 'debt traps,' as happened with the subprime bubble, is constituted by the expropriation of public goods, that is, the destructuration-without-restructuration of the welfare state.

4.   UNCONVENTIONAL FINANCIAL CAPITALISM

For the first time one is able to depress wages without reducing the consumption of wage earners, through what Bellofiore (2009) defines as 'financial Keynesianism, which for the first time one is able to depress wages without reducing the consumption of the wage earners.' The reasons for the crisis lie in '"an interaction between restructuring of the processes of the extraction of surplus value, on the one hand, and the subordinate inclusion of families within capital, on the other". This integration has enabled first a drugged growth, then a return to instability, and finally the crisis of this model'[10] (Bertorello and Corradi 2011, p. 38, author's translation).

From the bankruptcy of Lehman Brothers in the Fall of 2008 until 2011, the crisis of financial capitalism has deepened and become ever more complicated. In three years we have gone from state bailouts of banks, insurance companies, financial institutions and entire industrial sectors to the so-called crisis of sovereign debt. This latter is the result of states taking responsibility for salvaging banks, the massive de-fiscalization of capital, the high incomes of the last fifteen years, the reduction of fiscal revenue typical of recessions, the increase in costs tied to social welfare, and the interest on debt paid to Treasury bond holders.

In the same period, we have seen a process of economic and political concentration and reinforcement of the banks bailed out by the state, which have exploited low interest rates to increase profits by directly and almost exclusively investing in the stock market and in state bonds. This has allowed banks to pay back the aid received in the heat of the crisis, thus freeing them from any political interference and putting them back into a position of dictating the conditions for recovery. Three years from the subprime bust, the political power of banking institutions has grown to such a point as to mitigate and slow down the application of the most urgent legislative reforms in the sector, in particular the separation of commercial and investment banks (following in the footsteps of the Glass–Steagall Act of 1933) found in the 'Dodd–Frank U.S. Financial Regulation,' voted on in June 2010, with the result that the financial-banking system will continue to be 'too interconnected to let it fail' for a long time to come.

The banks, both public and private, highly exposed to debt – and still holding toxic bonds inherited from the speculative wave of subprime mortgages – in countries like Greece, Portugal, Spain, Ireland, and Italy, are at the origin of the financial aid of the EU and the International Monetary Fund (IMF) to 'peripheral' countries and the severe austerity measures imposed on their governments. The aid provided to indebted states actually constitutes measures to bail out major European banks, in particular German and French ones. It is masked 'recapitalization' in a phase in which, just as during the American subprime crisis, banks no longer trust one another because of the opacity of their accounts, the interbank market is practically blocked, and the threat of selling off public bonds – urged on by the devaluation of the Euro – is provoking the fall of

---

[10] '"un'interazione tra ristrutturazione dei processi di estrazione di plusvalore, da una parte, e inclusione subalterna delle famiglie dentro il capital, dall'altra". Interazione che ha consentito prima una crescita drogata, poi un ritorno dell'instabilità e infine la crisi di questo modello.'

those same bonds, thereby increasing interest rates. These, in turn, further burden the most indebted countries with the cost of debt and the deficit.

The net result of this 'financial Keynesianism,' in which central banks monetize the growing demand of the financial-banking sector at the expense of investment aid to growth and employment, constitutes the continuing crisis. The 'real subsumption of public debt under finance' (Bellofiore and Halevi 2010) prevents financial Keynesianism from carrying out the function of creating additional demand which, in the course of thirty years of the crisis of accumulation, has allowed capital to increase profits without increasing wages or investment in capital goods. We have, in fact, entered a *crisis* phase of financial Keynesianism, a crisis in which the policies of 'quantitative easing,' the creation of liquidity through the purchase of Treasury bonds by the central banks, on the one hand, and austerity measures with the aim of reducing public debt in order to avoid the devaluation of 'toxic' government securities held by European banks, on the other, are unable to overcome the crisis by re-launching economic growth. The result of this monetary management of the crisis is increasing unemployment and poverty and the preparation of a new financial crisis, similar to that which erupted in 2008, but with the difference that this time the states no longer have the same leeway for saving the banking and financial system from bankruptcy.

The same function of conventions in the self-referential theory of finance seems to have fallen into crisis. In this new stage of financial capitalism,

> Almost every asset class seems to be fraught with danger. Equities have suffered two bear markets in just over a decade and remain vulnerable to a rich-world recession; government bonds offer little protection against a resurgence of inflation; commodities are volatile and hostage to a possible drop in Chinese demand; property is still suffering from indigestion after the past decade's boom[11].

The emergence of a unanimously shared belief starting from the imitation of the majority choice of financial investors, in other words, the election of a convention capable of 'pulling' markets in a given direction, is the problem that financial capitalism faces today. In the absence of a convention which can mobilize a wave of investment, whether in Treasury securities, certain equity securities, or emerging countries, the risk of a normalization of the crisis and its self-referentiality can only increase.

[11] *The Economist*, 15 October 2011.

REFERENCES

Aglietta, M. (2010), *La crise. Pourquoi en est-on arrivé là? Comment en sortir?*, Paris: Michalon.

Aglietta, M. and A. Orléan (1982), *La violence de la monnaie*, Paris: Puf.

Arrighi, G. (2007), *Adam Smith in Beijing: Lineages of the Twenty-First Century*, London: Verso.

Bauman, Z. (2009), *Capitalismo parassitario*, Roma: Laterza.

Bellofiore, R. (2009), 'Introduzione,' in Hyman P. Minsky, *Keynes e l'instabilità del capitalismo*, Torino: Bollati Boringhieri.

Bellofiore, R. and J. Halevi (2010), 'Magdoff–Sweezy, Minsky and the real subsumption of labour to finance,' in D. Tavasci and J. Toporowski (eds), *Minsky, Crisis and Development*, Basingstoke: Palgrave Macmillan, pp. 77–89.

Bertorello, M. and D. Corradi (2011), *Capitalismo tossico. Crisi della competizione e modelli alternativi*, Roma: Alegre.

Gallino, L. (2005), *L'impresa irresponsabile*, Torino: Einaudi.

Keynes, J.M. (1936), *The General Theory of Employment, Interest and Money*, London: Macmillan.

Marazzi, C. (2008), *Capital and Language. From the New Economy to the War Economy*, Cambridge, MA and London: MIT Press.

Orléan, A. (1999), *Le pouvoir de la finance*, Paris: Odile Jacob.

Orléan, A. (2004a), 'Efficience, finance comportamentale et convention: une synthèse théorique,' in R. Boyer, M. Dehove and D. Plihon (eds), *Le crises financières*, Rapport du Conseil d'Analyse Economique, pp. 241–70.

Orléan, A. (2010), *Dall'euforia al panico. Pensare la crisi finanziaria e altri saggi*, Verona: Ombre corte Uninomade.

Shiller, R. (2011), 'Wall Street in the "beauty contest" rut,' *International Herald Tribune*, 3–4 September (on-line).

Shleifer, A. (2000), *Inefficient Markets. An Introduction to Behavioral Finance*, Oxford: Oxford University Press.

Surowiecki, J. (2004), *The Wisdom of Crowds*, Garden City: Doubleday.

6. Debt, class and asset inflation

Jan Toporowski

1. INTRODUCTION

The mainstream view of household consumption and saving is based on the idea of a 'representative' household endowed with more or less perfect foresight, according to whether the theory is New Classical or New Keynesian. The traditional Keynesian view had household saving and consumption determined by income, with Post-Keynesian innovations in the form of differentiated propensities to consume on the part of workers or capitalists and, following Minsky, increasing indebtedness of firms (Minsky 1978). The analysis below in Section 4, based on the theories of Kalecki and Steindl, bears some relationship to the financial accelerator theory of Bernanke and Gertler, in using a similar 'net worth' factor in the analysis. However, it should be pointed out that Bernanke and Gertler do not provide any rationale for changes in net worth other than the observed fluctuation in net worth over the business cycle (Bernanke and Gertler 1989).

In the twenty-first century, in particular following the financial crisis that broke out in 2007, more radical economists have tried to link financial instability with inequality of incomes. A number of studies (e.g. those of Duménil and Lévy 2011, Brenner 2006) have argued that the crisis is the outcome of rising household indebtedness at a time of stagnating or falling wage income, combined with a rising share of profits being paid to financial intermediaries. The increased share of profit paid to financial intermediaries is supposed to squeeze investment and inhibit the economic growth necessary to generate the incomes needed to service debt.

Implicit in this approach is a view of saving that may be regarded as 'Ricardian' in at least three senses. In the first place, the criticism of the rising share of profits being paid to financial intermediaries echoes the critique of usury in the era of mercantile capitalism. At the time, capitalist traders regarded the interest that they paid to inactive partners who financed their cargoes as a deduction from profits, rather than recognising the expenditure out of that interest income of rentiers as contributing to profits. Secondly, the analysis presupposes that debt may only be serviced out of income. This too is a feature of the critique of usury in the seventeenth and eighteenth centuries. The flaw here is that it does not allow for the servicing of debt from inflation of asset values, where assets may be traded in markets to generate capital gains that may be used to service debt that is usually fixed in money terms. Behind the notion that debt may only be serviced out of income is a crude notion of credit that involves the lending out of commodity money, rather than the modern practice of credit that involves creating new credit against assets. Finally, the approach is Ricardian in the sense that the authors classify incomes solely into those of capitalists, rentiers and workers, corresponding to the three great classes of David Ricardo's analysis, the capitalists, the landowners and the workers. It is inadequate for the purposes of analysing the modern capitalist economy in which the middle class, broadly defined as the members of the free professions, public services and financial and managerial bureaucracies, now constitute a large proportion of households, even the majority of them in, for example, the United States and the United Kingdom.

The failure of economic theory to give a distinctive analysis of the role of the middle class is an important lacuna in macroeconomics. Not only does this class account for the majority of household consumption and saving but the incomes of this class are also largely independent of industrial conditions, including the distribution of industrial income between wages and profits. The Ricardian approach is, therefore, thoroughly inadequate for the analysis of the modern capitalist economy in which the expenditure of the middle class makes up the bulk of household consumption and the saving of the middle classes makes household saving impervious to the business cycle affecting industry. More striking is the failure of any major macroeconomist, with the exception of Joseph Steindl, to theorise adequately the middle class in the modern economy.

A feature of the modern middle class is its distinctive contribution to inequalities of income and wealth. The second part of this chapter puts forward an analysis of how such inequalities are intrinsically linked to asset inflation. The third part of the chapter shows how asset inflation combines with debt to produce a new political economy of the middle classes. The fourth part of the chapter argues that this new political economy generates a new industrial cycle driven not by changes in distribution between wages and profits in industry, or innovation or new opportunities in industry, or even by the rising indebtedness of firms, as supposed by many Post-Keynesians, but by the net saving of middle class households.

2.   ASSET INFLATION AND INEQUALITY

Asset inflation and income and economic inequalities are intimately linked. Asset inflation means rising values of financial assets and housing. Such inflation allows owners of such assets to write off debts against capital gains, buying an asset with borrowed money and then repaying that borrowing together with interest and obtaining a profit when the asset is sold. Hence, active trading in assets held by middle class households supports the proliferation of borrowing by households and consumption ultimately financed by debt. When the asset is housing, its inflation leads to a very particular social and economic pathology. The profit that accrues to the owner of an asset from the appreciation in its value depends to a great extent on how long that asset has been owned. The older owners, therefore, benefit most from an appreciation. The housing market then redistributes income and wealth from young people earning less at the start of their careers and indebting themselves hugely in order to get somewhere decent to live, to people enjoying the highest earnings at the end of their careers. But housing inflation is also like a pyramid banking scheme because it requires more and more credit to be put into the housing market in order to allow those profiting from house inflation to be able to realise their profits.

Nevertheless, even those entering the system with large debts hope to be able to profit from it. In the period before the financial crisis broke out in 2008, governments and society in general became dependent on asset inflation: governments because it facilitated the sale of public assets and of public debt, regarded as 'risk-free' in portfolios containing inflating (and hence 'risky') assets. The prevailing political consensus became 'intensely relaxed' about the regressive redistribution of income that arose from such inflation. That consensus encouraged the belief that the best that young people can do to enhance their prospects is to indebt themselves in order to 'get on the property ladder', that is enrich themselves (or at least improve their housing) through housing inflation, or ingratiate themselves with wealthy elders in their family.

Those at the bottom of the income distribution inevitably suffer most from rising house prices because, living in the worst housing, they have the least possibility to accommodate their house purchase to their income by buying cheaper, smaller housing. Having little other option but to over-indebt themselves in order to secure their housing, default rates among households in this social group are also most likely to rise with house price inflation. This inequality lies behind the problems in the sub-prime market in the United States and the equivalents of that market in the United Kingdom and elsewhere.

Paradoxically, a more equal distribution of income and wealth is more likely to keep the housing market in equilibrium. In a society in which all incomes and wealth are more or less equally distributed, any increase in house prices above the rate of increase in income and wealth results in a fall in demand for housing. The fall in demand for housing brings house prices back down. Where income and wealth are already unequally distributed, and house prices rise faster than incomes, the housing market becomes stratified according to income and wealth. The movement of households between the strata prevents house prices, except those at the bottom of the market, from falling. Thus, if house prices in general rise, a fall in demand from those who can no longer afford a given class of housing is off-set by the increased demand for that class of housing among households that previously could afford better housing. In this way, the redistribution of income and wealth from those with more modest incomes to those with higher incomes also facilitates asset inflation in the housing market.

Thus asset inflation makes inequalities of wealth and income even more extreme, and those inequalities further feed that inflation. Such inflation is, therefore, a self-reinforcing pathology of financial markets and society, rather than, as the economics establishment tells us, a temporary disequilibrium in the markets. It is certainly not a 'bubble' because when the so-called housing 'bubble' burst, it did not do so in that part of the housing market in which market value had risen most (i.e. in the markets for luxury housing), but in that part of the housing market that had risen least, that is in the poorest end of the housing market. Financial stability, therefore, rests not only on sound banking and financial institutions. It also requires a much more equal distribution of income and wealth. In the modern capitalist economy, in which a large asset-owning middle class comes to depend on asset inflation, that dependence needs to be confronted and reduced.

3. THE ASSETS OF THE MIDDLE CLASSES

Since the start of the twentieth century, the central fact of changes in the distribution of income and wealth has been the rise of the middle class, a property-owning class whose members are not strictly capitalists or workers. From the 1970s, the growing prosperity of the middle classes in the 'financially advanced' countries, such as the United States and Britain, was associated with a switch in their asset holdings, from modest holdings of residential property and direct ownership of stocks and shares, to residential property that was increasing in value, and indirect ownership of stocks and shares in the form of funded pension entitlements and insurance policies. In the early 1960s, the majority of stocks and shares in both countries were owned by wealthy private individuals. A decade later, the majority of stocks and shares were owned by pension funds and insurance companies. This does not mean that such funds were not active before the 1960s. They were, but had only a limited market because their use-value was just that they provided pensions and insurance. After the financial crises of the 1970s, financial inflation gave such intermediary funds a new use-value: that of financial enrichment.

Pension funds and insurance policies are relatively illiquid, and the cash flow that they provide is restricted to circumstances provided for in the terms of the policies: pensions in retirement or payments defined by the terms of an insurance policy. However, the long boom in the housing market, with its growing liquidity, allowed additional borrowing against capital gains in that market. In the United States, from the 1970s, so-called 401 pension funds allowed contributors, under certain circumstances, to draw out of those funds before retirement. As credit going into asset markets increases, the values of those assets increases too. The system of secured lending then allows owners of assets to generate cash from the markets. Financial inflation and the conversion of capital gains into income change the credit operations of the middle class. The use of debt by the middle class household becomes more closely linked to transactions in asset markets.

This change in credit operations by the middle class affects not only the frequency and value of tedious banking transactions. The change also changes the way in which capitalism is experienced, and hence the mentalities of those living in that system. That changed experience in turn alters the culture, preoccupations and hierarchy within the propertied classes. The following features have come to dominate the political economy of the middle classes and resulting economic cycle of the economy dominated by those classes.

a) *An enhanced delusion of successful thrift among the middle classes.* In any scientific study of economic behaviour in market economies, it is necessary to distinguish the experiences or perceptions that people may have, from the market process that gives rise to such experiences or perceptions. Individuals who enjoy the benefits of asset inflation only directly experience the purchase of the financial asset which gives them a claim on a capital gain, rather than the money coming into asset markets that allows that gain to be realised. Capital gains are therefore 'naturally' attributed to provident and well-calculated asset purchase, perhaps even to some intrinsic characteristic of a given asset, rather than generalised asset inflation. In this way, the

propertied classes succumb to a comforting illusion, carefully culti-
vated by their financial advisers and intermediaries, that their foresight and financial acumen have secured them their gains. In fact,
the situation is quite the reverse. The benefits which the propertied
classes obtain from inflated property and financial asset markets are
increasingly capital gains on wealth rather than accumulated saving
out of income. As property markets inflate and pension funds mature,
it is the propertied classes who dissipate on their own consumption
the capital gains that they are able to take out of property and financial asset markets, through the enforced saving of the young buying
housing at prices that swallow up most of the incomes of the young, or
lower paid workers obliged to subscribe to pension funds[1]. The delusion of thrift reinforces a growing sense of financial self-reliance and
independence of the state welfare system.

b) *The emergence of inflated property and financial asset markets as a
'welfare state of the middle classes'.* Inflated asset markets act as a
welfare state in that such markets socialise the financial risks of those
owning such assets. Asset markets afford asset owners unconditional
access to money through the sale of an asset typically to another asset
owner with spare liquidity. Inflated asset markets allow owners of
such assets to cross-insure each other in this way against extraordinary liabilities for health care, holidays, school fees, the purchase of
housing or the repayment of inconvenient debt. Such extraordinary
liabilities may be accommodated by taking out of those asset markets
money that is being put into them by those acquiring such assets. The
use of asset markets as a fund to pay for the social welfare expenses of
the middle class alienates that class from the state welfare system. In
most countries, and especially the advanced capitalist ones, the middle
class pays the majority of taxes on households, taxes that support
public consumption financed by the state welfare system. Deriving
little direct benefit from state welfare, middle class taxpayers are more
inclined to demand that the cost of that welfare state is reduced by
concentrating state benefits more narrowly on 'those in need'. This
reduces the benefit that the middle class obtains from the state system
and, since 'those in need' usually pay the least taxes, such concentration reinforces that middle class alienation from the state system. The

---

[1] In the early years of the century, before the financial crisis gripped the United States and
Europe, the households in the United States and Great Britain had reduced their saving virtually down to zero. An implication of this recent zero net saving in the household sector is
that households forced by debt to consume less than their incomes have their counterpart in
households that consume in excess of their incomes.

reduction of state welfare in this way marginalises still further those who do not own assets.

c) *The marginalisation of those without appreciative wealth.* They may be home-owners in places where wealthy property-owners do not wish to buy housing, for example in rural areas far from urban middle class concentrations; or those who do not own inflating assets, such as housing, in places where wealthy property-owners are buying housing. Where property-owners transfer capital into the housing market, the increase in house prices obliges the young and migrant workers to live in over-crowded conditions, because housing has become a perquisite of property-owners, rather than being available to all. Not having property denies marginalised sections of society the opportunity to operate balance sheets actively, and therefore denies them access to that welfare state of the middle class that the housing market becomes when it is inflated. For those without property, debt is more likely to finance current consumption, rather than the acqui-sition of inflatable assets. These are the lower class counterparts of those among the propertied classes whose possession of inflated assets allows them to consume in excess of their incomes. An unequal distri-bution of income is, thus, enhanced by a growing economic, social and political distinction between the 'balance sheet' rich and the 'balance sheet' poor.

d) *State-administered social welfare as a system for prosecuting the poor.* While the official welfare state may provide some minimum income for those without means of support, this is paid for by taxpayers predominantly among the middle classes. Such minimum income is increasingly delivered with a degree of institutional bullying and menaces, designed ostensibly to make welfare claimants more active in securing their financial independence. But, in reality, bullying and menaces are supposed to reassure propertied taxpayers that those claimants are being penalised for their improvidence in not having property to support them. Right-wing politicians and economic advis-ers repeatedly assert that maintaining an unpleasant and inadequate system of income support is necessary as an 'incentive' to keep up the 'willingness to work' of the poor. However, in reality it is their lack of saleable property that is being punished. No one threatens, with removal of their income, the propertied classes for their improvidence in living on unearned income from property or capital gains on that property. The selective penalisation of those without property or income is a natural consequence of a state welfare system that is no longer comprehensive because the middle class is increasingly opting out of it.

4. THE 'POST-MODERN' BUSINESS CYCLE

The 'modern' business cycle is the cycle identified with fluctuations in fixed capital investment, whose theory was developed for the most part in the first half of the last century, from Aftalion and Wicksell, through Hawtrey, Hayek, Schumpeter, Keynes and Kalecki, to Hicks, Samuelson and Kaldor (see Matthews 1964). With the emergence of asset inflation in the 1980s, a new kind of business cycle has appeared, based on a combination of wealth effects, due to asset inflation, stimulating the consumption of the middle classes. The debts incurred as credit is attracted into inflating asset markets, cause debt deflation when asset prices fall. The debt deflation is expressed as rising net saving, which reduces business liquidity and causes industry to go into recession, until middle class consumption can be stimulated again.

The 'post-modern' business cycle is based on an economic and social structure that includes a middle class whose demand for goods and services is large in relation to the economy as a whole. In an economy in which income and wealth are unequally distributed, the share of the middle class in aggregate demand will typically be greater than the proportion of the population that is middle class. The relative demographic size of the middle class will, therefore, underestimate the economic significance of that class.

The economy may, therefore, be divided into two sectors. The first is the industrial sector in which capitalist firms employ workers to produce goods and services that are consumed by all classes. The workers are assumed, as a whole, not to save, that is the saving of those working class households that save is balanced by the dissaving of other working class households. The second sector is the middle class, consisting of those employed in the free professions, public services and the salaried employees of business and financial services. The middle classes own assets, in residential property and financial claims on capitalist firms.

Among the capitalists, a sector of rentier capitalists also own assets in the form of claims on property and capitalist firms. The difference between rentiers and the middle classes is that the rentiers do not work, but live off the revenue from their rents and financial claims. By contrast, the middle classes work, producing professional and other services for each other and for capitalists and workers. Producing professional services, the middle class is isolated from the conditions of distribution and industrial demand that determine returns in industry. The middle classes therefore are not affected by industrial fluctuations. For the middle classes, their income from assets is supplementary to their income from their work. In the case of rentiers, their income from assets represents their only income.

For the economy as a whole, the identities of the circular flow of income apply, that is in a given year, t, total Income (Y_t) minus Consumption must be equal to Total Gross Fixed Capital Formation (I_t) plus the fiscal deficit, plus the foreign trade surplus. If, for the sake of simplicity, it is assumed that the fiscal deficit is balanced by the trade surplus, and further dispensing with time subscripts, we have Income minus Consumption equalling Saving (S) which is equal to Fixed Capital Formation (I). Saving can be divided up into the saving of firms (S_f) plus the saving of rentiers (S_r) plus the saving of the middle classes (S_m). The saving of firms is the retained profits that firms keep after all payments on their financial obligations. The equality of saving and investment may, therefore, be written as:

$$S = S_f + S_r + S_m = I$$

Rearranging this gives the following equation for the retained profits of firms:

$$S_f = I - S_r - S_m \tag{1}$$

This is the Steindl equation showing that firms' total additions to their liquid reserves are equal to firms' investment, minus the saving of rentiers and the saving of the middle classes (Steindl 1982). This means that a portion of firms' investment effectively finances itself through the additions that it makes to firms' retained profits. However, a further portion, corresponding to rentiers and middle class saving requires credit from outside firms, that is the addition of financial obligations of firms to rentiers and the middle classes that corresponds to their saving.

So far the analysis has consisted of definitions and the fundamental macroeconomic principle of the circular flow of income. Some dynamics can be introduced by making some plausible behavioural assumptions about saving behaviour. In the case of rentiers' saving, it is convenient and plausible to suppose that this does not change very much over the cycle[2]. In other words, increases or decreases in rentier incomes are matched by increases or decreases in consumption. This is plausible because at a very high standard of living, it becomes very easy to spend additional income conspicuously on luxuries. If income falls, then more or less the same standard of living may be maintained through consuming the same articles of consumption, but in a less luxurious style or version. In the case of

---

[2] '*Rentiers' saving* is the least elastic of all. . . . rentiers' saving will change only very sluggishly, and will prove completely inelastic below a certain minimum' (Steindl 1952, p. 115).

middle class saving, this may be expected to vary with difference between debt (D) and asset values (A) so that:

$$S_m = \delta\,(D - A)$$

This equation would give negative net saving by the middle class when asset values exceed total debt. This would be because the middle class could extract capital gains from asset markets and use those gains to pay for additional consumption or service their debts. This would correspond to the well-known 'wealth effect' on consumption. By contrast, when the value of a middle class household's debt exceeds the value of its assets, the household would find that further borrowing is restricted by the lack of un-mortgaged security value. In such a situation, assets become less liquid for their owner and less likely to be sold, because such sale would not pay off all the debt, and holding onto the asset at least offers the possibility that in the future its value may exceed the debts held against it. These restrictions on the credit operations and assets sales limit the ability of the middle class household to extract capital gains out of asset markets, forcing that household now to service debt solely out of income. The middle class household in this situation would find its consumption squeezed below its income by debt service payments. Substituting this middle class saving function into equation (1) gives:

$$S_f = I - S_r - \delta\,(D - A) \tag{2}$$

This equation summarises how a post-modern business cycle, that is a business cycle driven by fluctuations in asset values, might work. With capital market or residential property inflation, asset values would rise faster than middle class indebtedness. This would stimulate middle class consumption (the wealth effect) which, for a given value of firms' invest-ment, would result in higher retained profits in non-financial businesses. These in turn would stimulate business investment. The economy would enter a boom phase, with rising middle class indebtedness, to acquire assets and facilitate extraction of capital gains from asset markets. The increase in net credit entering the markets for residential property or financial assets would increase the values of residential and financial assets, stimulating further middle class consumption. The boom would proceed until debt values exceeded asset values. The rise in middle class saving would now result in a fall in firms' saving or their retained profits. With reduced inflow of liquidity, firms will cut back or postpone their investment. In turn this will exacerbate their situation by reducing those retained profits still further.

In small open economies, and in developing economies, the discretionary part of middle class consumption that is stimulated by the 'wealth effect', may have a high import content where foreign exchange controls permit such expenditure. Imported luxury goods, travel abroad, foreign residential property and financial assets, and foreign health and educational services, frequently offer superior quality and bestow distinction upon households otherwise distinguished only by having more income and wealth. In such a situation, a boom based on middle class consumption will result in a rapid deterioration of the foreign trade balance. In such countries the boom is therefore more likely to end in a foreign exchange crisis (this was a feature of the Argentine crisis in 2001).

A decline in middle class consumption of domestically manufactured goods reduces the revenue of domestic manufacturers. If they respond to this by cutting back on production and investment, then this may reduce firms' investment below the threshold ($S_r + \delta [D - A]$) that investment has to exceed if firms are to have a positive cash flow, that is retain profits from their productive activities (see equation (2) above). If firms have negative cash flow, then, they will tend to reduce production and investment further. At this point, the relative inelasticity of middle class saving becomes a factor in exacerbating the industrial situation. Since their incomes are relatively independent of the industrial business cycle, and their saving is determined by balance sheet considerations, the saving of middle class households will not be reduced by an industrial recession. On the contrary, the debts incurred during the previous asset inflation will, when asset prices fall, have to be serviced out of income, causing a rise in household saving (that is the difference between household income and expenditure). The rise in household saving will have its counterpart in the reduced income of those workers made unemployed in industry, and the rise in debt, or reduction in reserves, of industrial firms, forced by their negative cash flow or limited retained earnings to borrow or run down their savings.

5. CONCLUSION

With greater economic inequality and active asset markets, the middle classes come to rely on active asset markets to manage their debts. More active debt management allows property-owners to generate cash flow from inflating asset markets. In turn, this alters the attitudes of even owners of modest property towards public consumption, the state welfare and the taxation that is necessary to support the welfare state. Where asset inflation gives rise to a 'wealth effect' on consumption, this may give rise to a new type of economic fluctuation that does not depend on either the increasing indebtedness of firms or Keynesian speculative bubbles. In a boom, asset inflation allows the middle class to provide a net 'external' market for the output of industry, stimulating industrial output. In a recession, faced with an excess of debt over asset values, the middle classes engage in net saving in order to manage their debts, forcing the industrial sector into financial deficit. This deficit is managed by reducing investment and output. In the traditional Keynesian analysis, unemployment would continue to rise until saving is reduced. However, the middle classes are unaffected by falling output or returns in industry, so that rising unemployment does not reduce their saving that is causing the financial deficit in the industrial sector. Net middle class saving in the form of debt repayment, at the expense of unemployment in industry, continues until the middle classes start borrowing again to invest in assets, causing asset prices to rise again. In this way the working class pays the debts of the middle classes, reinforcing those inequalities of income and wealth that are so congenial to asset inflation.

REFERENCES

Bernanke, B. and M. Gertler (1989), 'Agency costs, net worth and business fluctuations', *American Economic Review*, **79** (1), 14–31.
Brenner, R. (2006), *The Economics of Global Turbulence*, London: Verso.
Duménil, G. and D. Lévy (2011), *The Crisis of Neoliberalism*, Cambridge, MA: Harvard University Press.
Matthews, R.C.O. (1964), *The Trade Cycle*, Cambridge: James Nisbet.
Minsky, H.P. (1978), 'The financial instability hypothesis: a restatement', Hyman P. Minsky Archive, Paper n. 180 (available at: digitalcommons.bard.edu/hm_archive/180).
Steindl, J. (1952), *Maturity and Stagnation in American Capitalism*, Oxford: Basil Blackwell.
Steindl, J. (1982), 'The role of household saving in the modern economy', *Banca Nazionale del Lavoro Quarterly Review*, **35** (140), 69–88.

7. Speculation, financial fragility and stock-flow consistency

Jo Michell

1. INTRODUCTION

Minsky argued that, under the conditions imposed by modern capitalism, it is impossible for households, firms and banks to avoid speculative decision making when financing their expenditures: 'speculation cannot be avoided—to decide is to place a bet' (Minsky 1975/2008, p. 75). Building on the theoretical system of Keynes's *General Theory*, Minsky's analysis incorporates changing perceptions of financial risk into the investment decisions of firms to develop a theory of the business cycle based on financial fragility.

This chapter argues that Minsky's theory relies on the macroeconomic assumption that, during an investment boom, the firms sector as a whole operates with an increasing financial deficit which is matched by the saving of the household sector. Firms' investment in capital goods is thus financed, via the intermediation of the banking system, by household savings. In such a system, the speculative decisions made by each sector are summarised as follows:

> [S]peculation has three aspects: (1) the owners of capital-assets speculate by debt-financing investment and positions in the stock of capital-assets; (2) banks and other financial institutions speculate on the asset mix they own and the liability mix they owe; (3) firms and households speculate on the financial assets they own and on how they finance their position in such assets (Minsky 1975/2008, p. 121).

It is shown that this assumption about the configuration of relative net financial positions of macroeconomic sectors does not match the empirical evidence for the United States in the period preceding the 2007–08 financial crisis. Over this period, the net financial balance of firms was close to zero, while the household sector moved into deficit.

Using a simple stock-flow consistent accounting framework, the implications of different assumptions about macroeconomic sectoral balances are examined. It is shown that situations may arise in which rising asset prices do not lead to inter-sectoral financial flows, presenting difficulties for macroeconomic models based on sectoral budget constraints. The accounting framework is used as the basis for a description of a stylised process of asset inflation, based on the 'post-modern' business cycle theory of Toporowski (2000). In this analysis, the speculative decisions of firms and households result in the redistribution of financial balances *within* sectors. It is demonstrated that such a process can lead to a situation of increasing financial fragility without the need for inter-sectoral imbalances at the macroeconomic level.

2.   A SIMPLE ACCOUNTING FRAMEWORK

In this section, a simple flow-of-funds accounting framework is developed which will be used to analyse the relationships between income distribution, financial operations and macroeconomic balances. The framework is a simple application of the approach developed by Godley and Cripps (1983) and Godley and Lavoie (2007), which has come to be known as the 'stock-flow consistent' approach to macroeconomics. This approach is predicated on the simple assertion that for any model to incorporate considerations of financial structure meaningfully, all flows of funds through those financial structures—and the resulting changes in stocks of financial assets and liabilities—should be explicitly accounted for within models. In such models, each sector of the economy (such as households, firms, and so on) is treated as an economic 'actor' represented by an aggregated balance sheet. Assuming a closed economy, the analysis starts from the standard identities that over any given time period saving, S, must, by definition, be equal to investment, I. Likewise, national income, Y, and national expenditure, E, must also be equal:

$$S = I$$
$$Y = E$$

Abstracting from the government sector, a simple three-sector model can be obtained by allocating these income–expenditure and saving–investment balances across households, firms and a consolidated banking system comprising both commercial banks and the monetary authority. The assumption is made that banks operate costlessly, supplying credit in response to demand from customers, based on their reckoning of the credit-worthiness of borrowers. Banks thus do not directly engage in the real transactions which combine to make up income, expenditure and saving, but act as a pure intermediary, sitting between the household and firms sectors.

Saving can divided between the saving of households, S_H, and the saving of firms, in the form of their retained profits, P_F

$$S = S_H + P_F$$

Investment can be similarly divided between these two sectors. It will be assumed that firms invest in fixed capital, denoted I_F, while household investment is directed towards housing, I_H:

$$I = I_H + I_F$$

Abstracting for now from income arising from holdings of financial assets, such as interest and dividends, total national income can be divided into wages, W, and profits, P_F, while expenditure (which must equal income) is similarly divided between consumption, C, and investment, I:

$$Y = W + P_F$$
$$E = C + I$$

While investment and saving must be equal at the aggregate level, this is not so at the level of the household or firms sector. Each sector may either spend less than the amount received in income, and thus accumulate financial assets, or spend in excess of income, requiring that the sector emit financial liabilities. The difference between income and expenditure for each sector is the *net financial position* (NFP) of the sector. The requirement that $S = I$ at the aggregate level logically implies that the total of all sectoral NFPs be equal to zero. In the case of the simple three-sector system, the implication is that the NFP of the firms sector must have an equal and opposite value to that of the household sector, since the NFP of banks is assumed to be zero.

In order to complete this simple framework, the financial assets and liabilities which are used to accommodate the NFPs of the two sectors are specified. Two types of financial operations are assumed. Firstly, it is assumed that banks interact with both firms and households by issuing loans and 'accepting' deposits from each sector[1]. Secondly, it is assumed that firms can obtain funding by issuing equity, which may be held either by households, or by other firms.

---

[1] The terminology of banks 'accepting' deposits is problematic in a pure credit framework in which banks create deposits when they issue new loans.

Table 7.1 Transaction flow matrix for speculation, financial fragility and stock-flow consistency

	Households	Firms (cur)	Firms (cap)	Banks	Total
Consumption	$-C$	$+C$			0
Investment	$-I_H$	$+I$	$-I_F$		0
GDP		$[Y]$			
Wages	$+W$	$-W$			0
Profits		$-P_F$	$+P_F$		0
Net fin. position	$[S_H - I_H]$	$[0]$	$[P_F - I_F]$	$[0]$	$[0]$
Chge in Deposits	$-\Delta D_H$		$-\Delta D_F$	$+\Delta D$	0
Chge in Loans	$+\Delta L_H$		$+\Delta L_F$	$-\Delta L$	0
Chge in Equities	$-\Delta e \cdot p_e$		$+\Delta e \cdot p_e$		0
Total	0	0	0	0	0

These assumptions result in a notional aggregate balance sheet for the economy as a whole. The balance sheet of the household sector will contain housing, bank deposits and equities on the asset side and bank loans on the liability side. The balance sheet of firms will comprise fixed capital and bank deposits on the asset side and bank loans and equities on the liability side. In addition, it is assumed that firms may hold shares in other firms, so that equity will also enter the firm's balance sheet as an asset.

The relationships between the stocks held on this balance sheet and the accounting assumptions already described can be combined and summarised in the form of a 'transactions flow matrix', as shown in Table 7.1. In this matrix, each column represents one sector of the economy, while each row represents a flow of money, resulting either from real expenditure (in the top half of the Table), or changes in the net holdings and outstanding issuance of financial assets and liabilities (bottom section)[2]. The firms sector is sub-divided into a 'capital account' and a 'current account' such that all income and expenditure takes place on the current account while asset transactions take place on the capital account[3].

In this matrix, sources of funds are denoted as positive values and uses of funds as negative values. Thus, household expenditure on consumption is denoted as a use of funds, $-C$, in the household column and as a source

[2] The organisation of the flow table is such that each row and column sums to zero, so that an identity may be obtained by extracting each row or column and setting it equal to zero.
[3] The advantage of this form of representation is that firms' expenditures on investment in fixed capital, and saving in the form of retained earnings, can be explicitly included as flows between the current and capital account of the firms sector.

of funds, $+C$, in the current account of the firms sector. The same notation is used in the case of financial assets and liabilities, so that deposits are a *use* of funds for households and a *source* for banks. For the sake of simplicity, the current flows associated with each type of financial asset are not explicitly shown in the matrix, but it should be assumed that deposits and loans result in interest flows between sectors, while equities lead to dividend payments. Finally, it should be noted that prices are not included explicitly in the flow matrix other than in the case of equities, for which the flow is shown as change in volume of equity held multiplied by the price.

So far, the framework is composed of a set of pure accounting identities. These represent the flow relationships of the system which are required, given the assumptions made about the structure of balance sheets, for the system to maintain internal consistency. In order for these relationships to provide anything other than a set of *ex post* truisms, this accounting framework must be supplemented by behavioural assumptions about the way that the variables of the system interact. One way in which these behavioural assumptions are often presented is in the form of explicit algebraic relationships between variables, resulting in a set of simultaneous equations composed of accounting and behavioural assumptions. Instead, the approach taken here is to use the accounting identities implied in the table as a framework in which to conduct a 'thought experiments' about different possible configurations of the evolution of stocks and flows under various behavioural assumptions. One key assumption, which will be maintained throughout the remainder of the discussion, is that the banking system acts as a 'manufacturer' of purchasing power. Following the theoretical line of the post-Keynesians and the *circuitistes*, it is assumed that the banking system creates deposits *ex novo*, when it issues loans to firms or households[4]. The result is that the banking system is not a passive channel, transferring purchasing power between savers and borrowers, but has the power to actively redistribute resources within the economic system. This leads to the possibility that borrowers may violate their budget constraint and spend in excess of their income, without a corresponding decision to 'not-spend' elsewhere in the economy.

Investment spending which is financed by new borrowing will therefore result in a corresponding increase in saving. While this saving may be unexpected, whether or not it is 'forced' will depend on whether spare

---

[4] The function of banks as creators of new money, and thus as initiators of fresh circuits of economic production, originates with Hartley Withers' *The Meaning of Money* (1920), and was subsequently developed by Keynes (1930/1971); Keynes (1937); Hayek (1933/2012); and Schumpeter (1938/2008).

capacity exists in the economy. In the case where unutilised productive capacity does exist, the result of such credit-financed investment will be an increase in output, such that some or all of the additional output will accrue as 'unplanned' savings, either in the form of profits or house-hold savings. In general, this is the situation that will be assumed in the subsequent analysis[5].

The introduction of money into the theoretical system in this way has the important result that planned and actual outcomes may differ. The desired, or *ex ante* saving of any given sector may thus differ from the actual, or *ex post* amount realised. As a result, the financial balances—and thus the stocks of financial assets and liabilities—of each sector will not be under the direct control of those sectors. What firms and households *do* determine directly are their own expenditure decisions and financial portfolio allocations. The realised balances at the end of any period thus result from the combined expenditure and portfolio decisions of all agents within the system.

3. DEBT, SAVING AND DISTRIBUTION

Given the identity that total saving is composed of the sum of households' saving and firms' retained profits, two possible 'edge-cases' exist. Firstly, that in which household saving is zero and, secondly, that in which firms' retain zero profits. Consideration of these two edge-cases provides insights into the relationship between the saving–investment mechanism and the distribution of income. In the first case, in which households do not save, all fixed capital investment must be financed out of the retained profits of the firms sector, while in the latter case all fixed capital investment will require firms to issue financial liabilities, such that the counterpart assets are accumulated by households.

Taking the first of these two cases, the assumption is made that house-holds consume all income from wages and firms re-invest all retained profits. This leads to the well-known Kaleckian aphorism that 'the workers spend what they get and the capitalists get what they spend' (Robinson 1969, p. 260). As such, the investment decisions of capitalists will determine the profits received by the firms sector. Assuming, for the moment, that investment in housing is zero, financial structure becomes

---

[5] The alternative possibility is that in which the economy is already producing output at a maximum or equilibrium level, so that credit-financed expenditure leads to 'forced saving', usually as a result of increases in the price of consumer goods. This mechanism is associated in particular with the business cycle theories of Hayek (1935/2012) and Schumpeter (1938/2008).

irrelevant—the real expenditure of each sector will exactly match the level of income: $W - C = 0$ for households and $(C + I) - (W + I) = 0$ for firms. As a result, the net financial position of both sectors is zero and no inter-sectoral financial flows occur. An economic system of this type is thus referred to by Kahn as a 'non-monetary economy' (quoted in Kregel 1989–90, p. 232).

Nonetheless (and assuming that investment is the determinant of output growth), in order for there to be a positive growth rate of output, in each period firms will need to spend on investment an amount which exceeds the profits retained in the previous period. Thus, firms will need access to bank credit in order to finance expenditure on wages and capital goods. But, at the end of each time period, in the absence of household saving, all of this borrowed income will have been spent on consumption and capital investment, so that firms' sales receipts will equal the amount borrowed. Saving, in the form of retained earnings, will thus have increased to match the increase in credit-financed investment, and bank loans can be repaid at the end of the period: '[I]f additional investment is financed by bank credit, the spending of the amounts in question will cause equal amounts of saved profits to accumulate as bank deposits' (Kalecki 1954/1965, p. 244).

The opposite extreme case is that in which it is assumed that firms do not retain any profits, either because receipts are only just sufficient to cover costs, or because whatever remains of firms' revenues after the payment of wages is distributed as dividends. Firms are thus reliant on the issuance of financial liabilities to cover the costs of investment. Given an intended level of expenditure on investment by the firms sector, it can be assumed that firms initially borrow from banks to cover total expenditures (investment, I, plus wage payments, W). If households are willing to hold their savings as shares, and purchase equity of an amount equal to new investment, firms will once again find that at the end of the period they are able to use the proceeds of equity issuance to pay off all of the loans that were taken on to cover expenditures.

In the case of any discrepancy between the desired increase in equity holdings by households and desired investment, the additional deposits borrowed by firms will be held by households at the end of the period. The quantity of deposits held by households in this case may be not be that which they *intended* to hold at the beginning of the period. In the extreme case in which households intended to use all saving for the purchase of equity, the difference between households' desired saving, and firms' credit-financed investment accrues as the additional deposits of households. Since the assumption has been made that the economy is operating below full capacity, and thus that additional demand is accommodated by increases in output, these extra deposits will comprise additional 'unintended' saving of households out of unanticipated additional wage income.

These examples may be used to shed some light on the role that leverage ratios play over the course of the business cycle. The fundamental mechanism in Minsky's theory of the cycle is that of an investment boom, with rising investment in fixed assets financed by increased borrowing, leading to an increase in debt to equity ratios. At the level of the individual firm, investment demand for capital assets is determined by the interaction of two curves: a demand curve derived from the expected discounted yields of new capital assets and a supply curve derived from the cost of production of new capital assets. Assuming competitive markets, this supply price will be perfectly elastic, regardless of the scale of investment. Likewise, if all yields on capital assets were fixed and certain, the expected capitalised yields of investment would similarly be constant. Finally, with an unlimited supply of credit at a fixed rate of interest, the capitalised cost per unit of debt-financed investment will also be constant. Then, so long as the expected capitalised yields from investment are greater than the expected capitalised cost of financing that investment, there will exist no limit to the desired scale of investment for the firm:

> in an abstract hypothetical world in which the supply of finance is infinitely elastic, in which all prices and yields are independent of the firm's own scale of operation, and into which the realities of risk and uncertainty never intrude, if the cash flows . . .on the debts necessary to finance the acquisition of a unit of capital are less than the prospective yields, then a firm, with such prospects, would want to buy an unlimited—nay—infinite amount of capital assets (Minsky 1975/2008, p. 107)[6].

In reality, Minsky argues that the uncertainty of expected yields on capital implies that beyond a certain point, expected capitalised yields begin to fall. Likewise, as lending to an enterprise increases, the lender faces increasing risk, either as a result of 'moral hazard' or project failure. As a result, the 'supply price' of capital rises. Thus, beyond the point at which projects are internally financed, 'supply' and 'demand' curves are no longer horizontal: capitalised returns start to fall and the cost of credit increases. Thus, a limit is set to the level of investment by the degree of 'borrowers' risk' and 'lenders' risk'.

However, since both of these evaluations are based upon judgements

---

[6] This quote anticipates the modelling approach used in many New Keynesian dynamic stochastic general equilibrium (DSGE) models (e.g. Woodford 2003), in which 'perfect capital markets' are assumed, implying that credit may be obtained without limit by the representative agents which populate such models.

about an uncertain future, they are subjective, and thus liable to undergo shifts over time. Minsky argues that, due to the increasingly optimistic views of businessmen regarding the potential yields of their investments, perceived 'borrowers' risk' falls and thus the demand price for capital assets will rise over the course of a boom. At the same time, the interest rates charged by lenders will fall due to their increasingly sanguine views on the degree of 'lenders' risk' that they face. For Minsky, it is this increasing willingness of both lenders and borrowers to increase credit-financed investment over the course of a boom that results in increasing financial fragility.

Minsky projects his analysis from the level of the individual firm to the economy as a whole, to draw the conclusion that, at the macroeconomic level, firm leverage increases over the course of the cycle. Following a period of 'tranquil growth', expectations of profits increase and perceived risk decreases, leading to a greater willingness to take on credit on the part of firms, and to extend credit on the part of banks and bond holders. It has been argued by a number of authors that, in extrapolating the results of his microeconomic analysis of the firm's speculative decisions to the macro arena, Minsky succumbs to a fallacy of composition (for instance, Lavoie and Seccareccia 2001; Toporowski 2008b; Bellofiore *et al.* 2010). The two cases described above can be used to illustrate this.

The first case illustrates the point that under the classical assumption that households consume all of their income and thus save nothing, the volume of retained profits will be exactly equal to investment expenditures. With positive saving in the household sector, only a proportion of this investment expenditure will be realised as profits, requiring that firms must issue financial liabilities in order to finance those expenditures. Increasing gearing for the firms sector as whole implies that the NFP of the firms sector must be negative. For gearing to rise *as a share of output* rather than just in absolute terms, the NFP of the firms sector must be negative and rising in absolute terms as a share of output. The implication, in the simple three-sector framework, is that household saving is rising as a share of output. This could be interpreted either as a fall in the marginal propensity to consume, or a redistribution of income within the household sector from those with a high propensity to consume, such as workers, to those with a low propensity to consume, such as rentiers[7].

In fact, the macroeconomic implications of changes to the total leverage of firms as a result of investment spending by firms are not entirely overlooked by Minsky. He notes that:

---

[7] It is the rigidity of the saving of monopolistic firms and wealthy households which gives rise to the 'enforced indebtedness' of firms in Steindl's (1952) analysis.

In fact, . . .as this excess investment leads to a higher than anticipated aggregate income, it will also lead to a flow of internal funds [for firms] which is greater than anticipated. As a result, after the event, the internal cash flows are such that . . .the improvement of realized profits partially frustrates the planned debt-financing of firms and simultaneously reinforces the willingness of firms and bankers to debt-finance further increases in investment (Minsky 1975/2008, p. 112).

Similarly, he observes that attempts to reduce leverage by cutting back on investment expenditures during the downturn will tend to be partially frustrated by the consequent reduction in retained profits. What is not explicitly considered is the possibility of zero net household saving, as discussed above, so that the liquidity of the firms sector does not suffer as a result of investment expenditure. This point can be taken further by considering the possibility that the net financial position of the firms sector becomes *positive* or that of the household sector becomes *negative*. In such a situation, the firms sector would essentially be 'lending' to the household sector. How could such a situation arise?

In the simplest case, household income would be insufficient to cover household expenditure on consumption and housing, $W - (C + I_H) < 0$. Households would need to fund expenditure in excess of wage income either by running down bank deposits, or by obtaining financing from the firms sector. This could take place in two ways: firstly, households could borrow from banks, to cover excess expenditures, such that the deposits created in the process would accrue as retained profits in the firms sector. The other option is that firms could use internal liquidity from retained earnings to engage in share buy-backs. The money households received from the sale of equity would then be used to support consumption, without requiring an increase in the indebtedness of households[8].

4.   US FINANCIAL BALANCES 1980–2010

The sectoral financial balances, which form the basis of the theoretical framework introduced above, are now examined for the empirical case of the United States in the decades preceding the financial crisis of 2007–08. Figure 7.1 shows the NFP of the firms, household and financial business sectors of the US economy from 1980–2007. In the first decade of the period shown, the pattern displayed conforms broadly to the 'standard' pattern, in which household saving funds investment by the firms sector: the household sector runs a surplus averaging around 5 per cent, while the firms sector

[8] A further possibility is the direct granting of consumer credit by the firms sector, a possibility which is precluded by the simple structure of the accounting model used here.

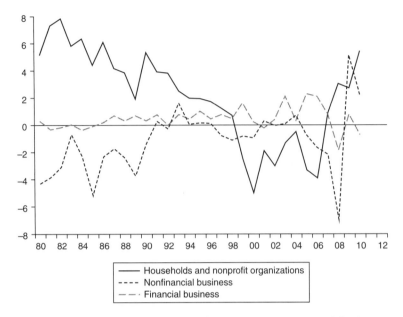

Figure 7.1   US net financial position by sector, percentage of GDP

(non-financial business on Figure 7.1) runs a deficit of similar proportions. Over the next decade, the household surplus steadily declines until 1999, at which point the net financial position of the household sector turns negative. In the late 1980s, the deficit of the firms sector falls, so that from 1991 until the crisis in 2007–08, the firms sector is essentially self-financing. Finally, in the case of the financial business sector, the balance initially remains close to zero, as would be expected from a sector for which the primary role is that of intermediation. From the late 1990s, however, the financial sector increasingly tends to run a net financial surplus, until the crisis of 2007.

It should be noted that the three series in Figure 7.1 do not provide a complete picture of the saving–investment balances of the US economy, since the government and foreign sector are missing. For the sake of completeness, these are shown in Figure 7.2, with the three balances of the previous figure combined into the 'private sector'. The expanded picture demonstrates the additional influence of the US trade deficit in 'funding' the government and private sector deficits[9].

---

[9] Even the 'complete' picture shown in Figure 7.2 is subject to statistical error; this introduces a discrepancy which means that the three balances do not sum to zero. In general, this discrepancy is small, but in the case of 2008, it is significant.

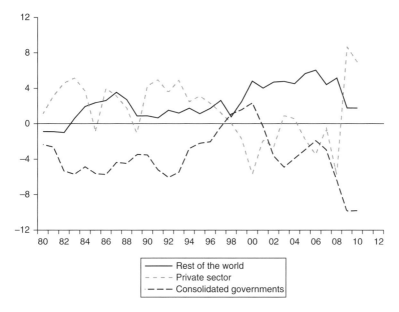

Figure 7.2   US net financial position by sector, percentage of GDP

It is clear that the period in the run up to the crisis of 2007–08 does not fit the standard Minskian story of increasing gearing of the firms sector. Instead, it is the household sector which operates in deficit, while the firms sector is self-financing for most of the period immediately preceding the crisis. As shown in Figure 7.2, the net deficit of the household sector finds much of its counterpart in the deficit on current account.

The financial flow operations of the firms sector are shown in figures 7.3 and 7.4. These figures show a subset of the financial flow operations which combine to produce the NFP for the non-financial firms sector. Figure 7.3 shows three net flows: bank loans, bond issuance and net equity issuance. The figure shows the increasing reliance on direct capital market funding through the issuance of bonds, *vis-à-vis* bank credit. The outstanding feature of the figure, however, is the series for the net issuance of equity. The series shows that for almost the entire time period, net equity issuance has been negative: the volume of equity retirement has exceeded the volume of new issues. An alternative view is shown in Figure 7.4. In this figure, the bank debt and bond issuance series of Figure 7.3 have been combined, along with other types of debt such as mortgage lending, to give a 'total debt' series. In addition, the total acquisition of liquid assets by firms is also shown. These liquid assets include bank

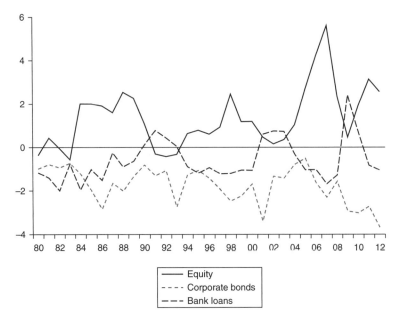

*Figure 7.3   Financial operations of US non-financial firms sector,
            percentage of GDP*

deposits, Treasury bills, shares in money market mutual funds, and so on[10].

The two figures show a firms sector behaving in a way which is hard to reconcile with the standard Minskian story of reliance on increasing volumes of debt to finance investment during boom periods. Rather, the picture is that of a firms sector in which the falling saving of the household sector (along with the government and foreign deficits) leads to retained profits sufficient to finance investment. But instead of this leading firms to refrain from operating in financial markets, the firms sector has continued to issue debt, using the proceeds to accumulate liquid financial assets and to retire equity.

[10] In neither of the two figures do the series sum to the NFP of the firms sector shown in Figure 7.1. This is due, in large part, to the inclusion of a large 'miscellaneous' item in the financial operations of non-financial firms in the US flow-of-funds figures.

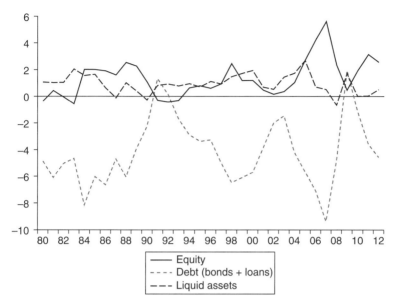

Figure 7.4   Financial operations of US non-financial firms sector, percentage of GDP

5.   ASSET PRICING AND SPECULATION

Nothing has yet been said about the role of equity financing. The assumption that runs through most of Minsky's analysis is that equity financing, along with retained profits, is a source of internal funding for firms. As such, financial fragility is associated primarily with changes in the debt position of firms relative to equity[11]. Thus, in Minsky's analysis, the only material difference between direct ownership of capital goods and the ownership of equity in firms is that equity also implies 'ownership' of the debt liabilities that are 'bundled' with capital assets in firms. Equity prices will thus reflect both the expected yield of capital assets *and* the fixed cash liabilities associated with debt financing. As such, following successful debt-financed investment, perceived borrowers' risk will decline, and the market price of equity shares in the successful company will rise.

---

[11]   There is a degree of ambiguity in Minsky's analysis—at some points, issuance of new shares is classed as a form of external finance: 'Typically, additional capital assets are acquired partially by own funds and partially by borrowed or outside funds, new-share capital being one class of outside funds' (Minsky 1975/2008, p. 105).

On precisely what determines the market price of equities, there are ambiguities in Minsky's exposition. At times Minsky appears to consider the price of equities to be identical to the demand price for capital assets: 'Two market-determined prices are dimensionally equivalent to the capitalised value of [future yields on capital]: the market price for items in the stock of capital assets and the price of equity, of shares' (Minsky 1975/2008, p. 99); while, at other points, it is clear that the price of equities is affected by factors other than the expected yields on capital assets, such as the case in which bank credit is used to purchase shares: 'A revision by bankers of their views about the appropriate leverage to use in financing positions in capital assets will not necessarily cause an immediate revision in the market value of these assets. . . But such a revision of bankers' views can have a strong impacts on equity prices' (Minsky 1975/2008, p. 117).

Thus, although acknowledging that share prices may diverge from the prices of capital assets, for the majority of his analysis Minsky maintains the assumption that the price of capital goods and the price of equities are equivalent. If equity prices and capital asset prices are together determined by the expected yield on capital assets, periods in which share prices are rising should be associated with high investment—rising equity prices signify expectations of rising yields on capital assets: 'a high quotation of existing shares involves an increase in the marginal efficiency of the corresponding type of capital' (Keynes 1936, p. 151). Any discrepancy between the valuation of equities and the market price of capital goods will be eliminated by firms taking money out of the capital markets by issuing new shares and using the proceeds to purchase new capital assets. Conversely, a low market valuation of shares and thus a low demand price for capital assets should lead to a curtailing in the production of new capital goods: instead of buying shares, purchases of capital goods will be confined to secondary markets purchases or merger and acquisitions activity.

An alternative view is that equity represents another class of outside financing, and associated with this financing is a liability rather than a share of ownership. Toporowski argues that this is the only valid interpretation of the role of equity capital in a modern financial system: 'In effect, equity finance is not a substitute for internal finance because it is a capital market liability rather than a liquid asset. . . Minsky's Financial Instability Hypothesis only stands up to empirical scrutiny if debt and equity are regarded as liabilities of companies, in contrast to the legal fiction that equity is equivalent to entrepreneur's capital' (Toporowski 2000, p. 27)[12].

---

[12] Toporowski argues that this view is supported by 'the degree to which companies continued to pay dividends on their equity even when making a loss during the slump of the 1930s,

Toporowski's analysis posits a much weaker link between the cash flow of companies—the margin between the yield on investment and the financial commitments of those companies—and the market prices of securities issued by those companies than that which is explicitly shown in textbook theories of corporate finance and implicit in Minsky's analysis. A secular process is described in which a steady inflow of funds into equities markets raise valuations while those excess funds continue to circulate within the markets. As a result, the possibility arises 'that a regime of growing excess financial inflows into capital markets, or capital market inflation, may create an apparent abundance of liquidity and rising values in the markets, which would not be applied to companies' real investment in fixed capital' (Toporowski 2000, p. 49).

This opens up the possibility that movements in the prices of securities may become 'decoupled' from investment activity. The capital markets then take on a quite different role in the mechanism of capitalist accumulation than that of intermediation between firms' investment and households' saving. The key factor in the determination of the prices of securities thus becomes the relative sizes of the flows of money out of and flows of money into the equities market. In addition to their effect on the role of capital markets in transferring balances *between* macroeconomic sectors with differing surplus and deficit positions, such processes of 'asset market inflation' take on significance as a mechanism for the distribution of net financial positions *within* sectors.

Such processes present problems for macroeconomic models based on sectoral budget constraints, such as the accounting framework used in this chapter. All such models treat each macroeconomic sector of the economy as an 'individual' actor with an income, expenditure and implied budget constraint. Processes of price inflation or deflation in asset markets occur as a result of flows *within* sectors that are 'invisible' within the taxonomy of the model, so long as they do not result in flows *between* sectors.

In particular, redistribution of an asset of particular class within a single sector may have potentially significant macroeconomic implications, without leading to changes in the variables of a sectoral macro model. For example, an increase in the prices of equities may arise from excess demand leading to buying and selling purely within the household sector. Such a process will result in a redistribution of the ownership of shares and bank deposits within the household sector, but will not necessarily lead to inter-sectoral money flows. It is usually assumed that such processes are of secondary importance to the structural relationships that lead to flows

and the economic recessions of the early 1980s and the early 1990s, [confirming] that modern corporations in effect regard the shares that they issue as a liability' (Toporowski 2000, p. 21).

between sectors. However, over an extended period of capital market inflation, such processes may come to play an important role in determining the behaviour of the system as a whole[13]. The extent to which such processes will condition the systemic behaviour of a system will depend, in part, on what proportion of the agents that make up any given sector are involved. These intra-sectoral reallocations of financial assets, and hence bank deposits, if we assume that bank deposits are used to purchase shares, may also occur among a small subset of a particular sector. However, the changes in valuation to these assets affect the balance sheets of all those who hold assets. This point was made by Keynes in the *Treatise on Money*:

> For the value of a security is determined, not by the terms on which one could expect to purchase the whole block of outstanding interest, but by the small fringe which is the subject of actual dealing; just as current new investment is only a small fringe on the edge of the totality of existing investments. Now this fringe is largely dealt in by professional financiers—speculators you may call them—who have no intention of holding the securities long enough for the influence of distant events to have its effect; their object is to re-sell to the mob after a few weeks or at most a few months (Keynes 1930/1971, p. 311).

In such a case, periods of excessive asset price inflation or disinflation may be relatively short-lived and volatile, since all that is required for a reversal is a change of heart on the part of a small number of speculators. However, in the case that the buying and selling of assets becomes 'institutionally' entrenched by involving large proportions of the agents that make up sectors, the degree of upwards momentum may become more significant. This will be the case, for example, when large institutional investors such as pension funds channel the saving of households into the equities markets, or when a country with a high degree of home ownership experiences a housing price boom.

6. ASSET INFLATION AND MACROECONOMIC BALANCES

This section uses the accounting framework developed in Section 2 as the basis for analysing a stylised process of secular asset price inflation. The

---

[13] This also presents difficulties for models in which flows are determined by behavioural assumptions specifying portfolio preferences as functions of expected yields on financial assets, proxied, for example, by past pay-outs. Whilst past dividend pay-outs may be a reasonable proxy on which to base expected yields in the face of an uncertain future, this ties the price of financial assets to the expected yield on physical capital as before, therefore precluding the potential for buying of securities in the hope of speculative gains due to rising prices.

implications for both balance sheets and sectoral flows at the macro level, and the distributional implications at the micro level, are analysed.

In the Minskian analysis, prices of equities can increase in response to successful debt-financed investment. This leads to a fall in the perceived 'borrowers' risk': leverage is lower than was anticipated relative to yields, leading to an increase in the desire to hold equities by households. Following the corresponding adjustment of portfolios, firms may take advantage of rising equity prices by engaging in new issues, serving to temper price rises. However, once price rises set in, expectations of further increases—raising the possibility of speculative gains—may tempt further reorganisation of household portfolios. At the same time institutional changes, such as the reorganisation of pension systems, may lead to large institutional players also entering the market, further increasing excess demand for equities.

If such a process of capital market inflation becomes entrenched, rather than transitory, a mechanism is introduced in which a share of wage income is directed towards the purchase of securities. But how could such a process occur without total household net saving becoming positive? As is shown in the above, the net financial position of the household sector was negative in the period preceding the crisis. One possibility is that there is a corresponding outflow arising as a result of other households choosing to realise capital gains and selling shares in order to spend the proceeds on consumption. But in this case, for net saving to equal zero, outflows would have to equal inflows, so that net excess demand would likewise be zero, precluding price rises. However, if some households take on debt in order to engage in speculative equity purchases, the price of equities will continue to rise, without the need for positive net household net saving. In this case, ΔD_H and ΔL_H will be positive, while $S_H - I_H$ remains zero or negative. New debt liabilities taken on by those purchasing securities will be partially offset by repayments by those realising capital gains, but at the level of the household sector, total gross debt will be rising.

These price rises in equities will be reinforced if firms engage in share buy-backs. As shown in Section 4, such buy-backs occurred on a very large scale in the period preceding the 2007–08 crisis. By reducing the supply of equity, firms reinforce upward movements in shares, redistributing income from the wage income of those purchasing new equity to those already holding it. Given rising equity markets, the credit-worthiness of firms will be strong, allowing access to the capital markets. The firms sector as a whole can thus engage in debt financing, by issuing bonds in order to fund share buy-backs.

Another mechanism by which share capital can be retired is as a result of 'leveraged' mergers and acquisitions activity in which debt is used to finance the purchase of companies: in such cases the debt used to make corporate acquisitions may subsequently be partially or fully repaid using cash reserves held by the purchased company. So long as the company that is purchased has a lower debt–equity ratio than the purchaser, the gearing of the new combined company will be lower than that of the purchasing company, while leverage of the firms sector as a whole may rise[14]. In Minsky's analysis, a result of such operations is to locate and activate any idle reserves of purchasing power, resulting in an increase in net indebtedness, measured as the difference between gross debt and liquid financial assets: 'Thus the progress of a boom sees liability experimentation on three levels. Firms engage more heavily in debt-financing, households and *firms cut their cash and liquid asset holdings* relative to their debt, and "banks" increase their loans at the expense of holding securities, especially government debt' (Minsky 1975/2008).

This is not what has been observed in recent years, as was shown in Figure 7.4. Over the course of asset market inflations, firms have increasingly issued securities for the apparent purpose of holding increasing volumes of liquid balances. Rather than running down cash in order to fund investment, firms have eschewed investment and used capital market operations to maintain increasing stocks of cash reserves. This behaviour on the part of firms is referred to by Toporowski (2008a) as 'over-capitalisation' of firms, defined as 'the holding of financial liabilities in excess of those needed to undertake production' (p. 3).

With ready access to capital markets during a period of rising asset prices, firms can speculate on price rises using funds raised by issuing securities. The balances obtained as a result of this borrowing will circulate within the firms sector as the buying and selling of securities takes place. Firms which have succeeded in speculating in this way may find themselves in possession of large cash stocks, without corresponding financial liabilities. Such liquid balances then provide firms a certain way of funding investment or current operations in the future without recourse to the securities markets.

Such a process will exhibit the characteristics of a 'real' boom—a rising stock market and increasing firm indebtedness—without any change in the pace of real investment. So long as the net financial positions of the firms and household sectors remain balanced, the level of investment may

---

[14] 'The money that is used in such deals often comes from borrowing and from the "excess" money of either the buying or the bought firms. Examples exist in which the "cash" in the purchased firm's balance sheet was used, by the buyer, to well-nigh pay for the purchase' (Minsky 1975/2008).

be fixed at any level, without altering the gearing ratio of the firms sector. Thus, financial fragility can increase due to the rising indebtedness of households and firms, without any corresponding increase in investment or in gearing ratios at the level of macroeconomic sectors.

A similar process will take place in the face of a secular rise in house prices[15]: given a restricted supply of housing and rising demand, prices will rise forcing those without housing to take on debt liabilities equivalent to ever greater shares of wage income in order to gain access to the market. A rising share of the wage income of younger workers is thus redistributed, via rising house prices, to fund the consumption of older households. So long as the credit supply remains elastic and the supply of housing inelastic, all that is required to sustain the boom is that the volume of consumption out of capital gains should remain less than the share of wage income flowing into the market. As in the case of equity inflation, such a process is compatible with the net financial balance of the household sector remaining at zero: ΔD and ΔL may be positive and equal, while S_H remains equal to I_H.

In both cases (equity and housing), so long as asset prices continue to rise, the impression given will be that of a robust financial structure: increasing debt liabilities will be offset by holdings of assets which are rising in value. However, the underlying mechanism differs fundamentally from that in which firms use debt-financing to purchase new productive capital assets which generate yields that cover the cost of financing their purchase. Instead, the mechanism described here is one in which debt serves as a mechanism for the redistribution of the shares of (potentially stagnating) incomes within sectors. Although the total increase in debts will be matched by circulating deposits, the redistribution mechanism arising from asset price inflation will mean that these deposits and loans are increasingly unevenly distributed among firms and households. Those who purchased assets early in the boom will have realised capital gains sufficient to repay debt, and will be left holding deposits, while later entrants into the market will face large debts which impose interest payments which must be serviced out of profit or wage income. In this way, instead of financial fragility arising as a result of the increased gearing ratio of the firms' *vis-à-vis* the household sector, fragility arises as a result of the redistribution of increasingly divergent surplus and deficit positions *within* sectors.

---

[15] In Chapter 6 of this volume, Toporowski provides a detailed description of the mechanics and consequences of such a boom.

7. CONCLUSION

It is argued that the Minskian interpretation of financial fragility implies that during an investment boom, the gearing ratio of the firms sector rises, matched by net saving in the household sector. This does not match the empirical evidence on the net financial position of macroeconomic sectors in the United States in the period preceding the financial crisis, in which household net saving was negative while the financial position of firms was close to balance.

Using a simple macroeconomic accounting framework, it is shown that market processes resulting in cyclical debt dynamics can occur without the need for inter-sectoral flows. Instead, financial fragility can arise from a process of debt-financed asset revaluation and redistribution, leading to a divergence between surplus and deficit positions within economic sectors.

REFERENCES

Bellofiore, R., Halevi, J. and Passarella, M. (2010), 'Minsky in the "new" capitalism: the new clothes of the financial instability hypothesis', in D.B. Papadimitriou and L.R. Wray (eds), *The Elgar Companion to Hyman Minsky*, Cheltenham, UK and Northampton, MA, USA: Edward Elgar Publishing, pp. 84–99.

Godley, W. and Cripps, F. (1983), *Macroeconomics*, London: Fontana.

Godley, W. and Lavoie, M. (2007), *Monetary Economics: An Integrated Approach to Credit, Money, Income, Production and Wealth*, London: Palgrave Macmillan.

Hayek, F.A. (1933/2012), 'Monetary theory and the trade cycle', in H. Klausinger (ed.), *The Collected Works of F.A. Hayek, vol. VII: Business Cycles Part I*, Chicago: University of Chicago Press, pp. 168–283.

Hayek, F.A. (1935/2012), 'Prices and production', in H. Klausinger (ed.), *The Collected Works of F.A. Hayek, vol. VII: Business Cycles Part I*, Chicago: University of Chicago Press, pp. 52–167.

Kalecki, M. (1954/1965, revised 2nd edition), *Theory of Economic Dynamics: An Essay on Cyclical and Long-Run Changes in Capitalist Economy*, London: George Allen and Unwin.

Keynes, J.M. (1930/1971), *A Treatise on Money: The Pure Theory of Money*, London and Basingstoke: Macmillan.

Keynes, J.M. (1936), *The General Theory of Money, Interest and Employment*, London and Basingstoke: Macmillan.

Keynes, J.M. (1937), 'The "ex-ante" theory of the rate of interest', *Economic Journal*, **47** (188), 663–69.

Kregel, J. (1989–90), 'Operational and financial leverage, the firm, and the cycle: reflections on Vickers' money capital constraint', *Journal of Post-Keynesian Economics*, **12** (2), 224–36.

Lavoie, M. and Seccareccia, M. (2001), 'Minsky's financial fragility hypothesis: a missing macroeconomic link?', in R. Bellofiore and P. Ferri (eds), *Financial*

Fragility and Investment in the Capitalist Economy: The Economic Legacy of Hyman Minsky, vol. II, Cheltenham, UK and Northampton, MA, USA: Edward Elgar Publishing, pp. 76–96.

Minsky, H.P. (1975/2008), *John Maynard Keynes*, New York and London: McGraw Hill.

Robinson, J. (1969), 'A further note', *Review of Economic Studies*, **36** (2), 260–62.

Schumpeter, J.A. (1938/2008), *The Theory of Economic Development*, New Jersey: Transaction.

Steindl, J. (1952), *Maturity and Stagnation in American Capitalism*, Oxford: Basil Blackwell.

Toporowski, J. (2000), *The End of Finance: The Theory of Capital Market Inflation, Financial Derivatives and Pension Fund Capitalism*, London: Routledge.

Toporowski, J. (2008a), *Excess Capital and Liquidity Management*, Working Paper n. 549, The Levy Institute.

Toporowski, J. (2008b), 'Minsky's "induced investment and business cycles"', *Cambridge Journal of Economics*, **32** (5), 725–37.

Withers, H. (1920), *The Meaning of Money*, New York: E.P. Dutton and Company.

Woodford, M. (2003), *Interest and Prices: Foundations of a Theory of Monetary Policy*, Princeton: Princeton University Press.

8. A structural monetary reform to reduce global imbalances: Keynes's plan revisited to avert international payment deficits

Sergio Rossi

1. INTRODUCTION*

The global financial crisis that broke out in 2007 is the result of a structural disorder that has been increasingly harming the world economy since the full 'demonetization' of gold in international transactions. Under the international gold (-exchange) standard, as a matter of fact, foreign trade imbalances were settled by a transfer of property rights on the equivalent stock of gold between the countries involved. International payments were thus final, as they left surplus countries with no further claims on deficit countries, both defined as the set of their own residents. Since the so-called post-Bretton Woods regime put the US dollar at centre stage in international finance, by way of contrast, international payments have become provisional, as settlements for foreign transactions are carried out using so-called key currencies, which are, in fact, simply promises of payment, as they do not imply the transfer of their object (namely, bank deposits) from the payer to the payee country. To be sure, no unit of US dollar deposits can leave the national banking system when any US importer finally pays an exporter residing in the rest of the world. This is so because of the book-entry nature of bank deposits, and has nothing to do with agents' behaviour. Indeed, the agent who imports any items from the rest of the world, finally pays their exporters when s/he disposes of the required amount of bank deposits. This final payment at the resident level, nevertheless, does not elicit payment finality for the two countries implied by this transaction, since the exporting country still has a claim

* This chapter stems from a lecture that its author was invited to deliver at the University of Bergamo (Italy) on 24 May 2010 by Riccardo Bellofiore. The author is indebted to him as well as to Marco Passarella for their remarks on that occasion. The usual disclaimer applies.

on the importing country when the banking system of the former records a claim on some bank deposits within the latter. Being a final payment for the two agents involved, however, the related promise of payment between their countries has been unnoticed so far in both theory and practice, generally speaking. This is so much so as any conventional economic analyses focus on agents' behaviour, and neglect structural and, indeed, 'systemic' mechanisms, which do not depend on agents' forms of behaviour. Keynes represents a noteworthy exception to this: the proposal he elaborated upon and presented at the Bretton Woods Conference in July 1944 aimed at replicating the structure of the international gold standard system, which was eventually 'a means for trading goods against goods' (Keynes 1980, p. 12). To be sure, as Keynes (1980, p. 18) pointed out in his reform plan, '[any] trading transaction must necessarily find its counterpart in another trading transaction sooner or later', since none, including countries, should be allowed to record a payment deficit, which is different from a trade deficit conceptually as well as empirically. A trade deficit has no negative consequences *per se* (provided that it does not trespass some reasonable limits with respect to national GDP), whilst a payment deficit always has a potentially disruptive outcome, as I will point out in this chapter with respect to the systemic financial crisis elicited by the huge amounts of US dollar deposits resulting from the payment of soaring US trade deficits since the end of the international gold (-exchange) standard. Having to pay interest on these deposits, US banks were led to increase their credits to so-called subprime mortgage borrowers as well as to other banks and non-bank financial institutions, both within and beyond the country's borders, in a framework of increasing financial market deregulation and regulatory arbitrages. This led to the global systemic crisis that burst out in 2007, and to the ensuing negative consequences across a number of Western countries, particularly in Europe.

The next section points out the book-entry nature of money, distinguishing the domestic economy (a monetary production economy) from the international economy, which is a pure exchange economy, as there can be no production in the economic space that exists between countries. In fact, the international economy is a barter trade system, as money is denatured when international transactions are paid using national currencies as if they were 'reserve assets' beyond the issuing country's borders. The third section recalls the characterizing features of the Keynes proposal to reform the international monetary regime, pointing out also some shortcomings of that proposal in light of the workings of modern domestic settlement systems. I will thus argue for the institution of a real-time gross-settlement system between countries, to be run by an international settlement institution issuing supranational currency every time a final payment has to be carried out internationally. The aim of this reform is to make sure that no country in the world will have the 'exorbitant privilege' (Gourinchas and Rey 2007, p. 12) to record any payment deficits (or deficits 'without tears', to use Rueff's (1963, p. 322) famous expression). The fourth section expands on this, explaining the working of the proposed international settlement system with a stylized example, to show that it is in the interest of key-currency countries (notably, the United States) to introduce such an international monetary reform, in order for them to avoid global imbalances in the international economy giving rise to another systemic crisis. Indeed, establishing a new international monetary order will help to rebalance trade between countries, as surplus countries (like China and Germany) will (be led to) spend on imports from any deficit countries (such as the United States) much more than they do in the present 'non-system' for international payments. Today's deflationary hoarding of foreign currency reserves – and the related (problematic) accumulation of sovereign wealth funds within surplus countries – will thereby shrink considerably, if not disappear altogether, to the benefit of both financial stability and economic prosperity across all countries that are finally paid through an international monetary system, respecting the logical distinction between means and objects of payments. The last section concludes, summarizing my main arguments and providing some policy-oriented remarks.

2.   MONEY IN DOMESTIC AND INTERNATIONAL TRANSACTIONS

There is no doubt, at the time of writing, that money is issued by banks rather than falling from the helicopter that Friedman (1969, pp. 4–5) imagined. Further, the fact that banks enter the result of money emissions in their double-entry system of accounts is beyond dispute. If so, conceptual logic leads to the conclusion that money is an 'asset–liability' (Schmitt 1975, p. 13), as it measures both the assets and the liabilities that banks enter in their balance sheets. In this conception, money is thus a numerical instrument, which any economic system needs in order for agents and institutions to measure the object of their transactions in economic (rather than in physical) terms. As such, therefore, money is the means, not the object, of any payment carried out through banks on behalf of the payer. To be sure, the object of any payment has to be provided by the economic system in the form of past, current or future output (that is, as goods, services or assets). In this light, banks do issue money, but the association of money with output stems from both production and banking systems, when these systems interact on the relevant markets for carrying out the corresponding final payments on behalf of the agents involved thereby.

Payment finality is crucial for the orderly working of any payment and settlement systems (see, among others, the reports by the Committee on Payment and Settlement Systems 2008, 2010). It implies a transfer of funds, in the form of bank deposits, from the payer to the payee, which leaves the latter with no further claim on the former (Goodhart 1989, p. 26). This shows that money and bank deposits have to be separated in monetary analysis: money carries out payments, whilst bank deposits finance them. This also implies that money exists within payments only, whilst bank deposits exist also between any two payments (Schmitt 1996, p. 88). Nevertheless, money and bank deposits are intimately related in any payment: 'since it is through payments that money circulates, (. . .) the displacement of bank deposits does not require an interval of time greater than zero, for it occurs at the very moment the account of the payee is credited by the amount transferred by the payer' (Cencini 1988, p. 74).

This monetary circuit is at centre stage of the monetary theory of production that has been developed in continental Europe by both the Schmitt and Graziani schools (for some recent surveys of these schools, see Gnos 2006, Realfonzo 2006 and Rossi 2006). As Graziani (1990, p. 11) points out,

> no one would borrow money from a bank before a payment comes due . . . since there would be no point in borrowing money and paying interest on it while keeping it idle. Money therefore *only comes into existence the moment a payment is made*. At that moment, in one and the same act, money is created, the borrower becomes a debtor to the bank and the agent receiving a payment becomes the creditor of the same bank.

The Graziani school, however, does not go far enough as regards the emission of money, for it does not consider that every unit of money is both created and destroyed within the payment that it carries out between any two agents. Let us show the mechanics of a payment referring to the circular flow depicted by money in Figure 8.1.

Figure 8.1 illustrates the emission of money that a given bank carries out on demand by one of its customers (the payer), in order for the latter to pay some debt obligation to another agent (the payee). The bank carrying out the payment order on behalf of its customer issues a number of (x) money units (m.u.), which it credits ($+x$) and debits ($-x$) to both the payer and the payee. It is indeed impossible, for a bank as for anyone else, to create something (a positive amount of money) out of nothing. What a bank can do, and does indeed, is separate the number zero into a positive number ($+x$) and the same negative number ($-x$) of money units. The sum of a

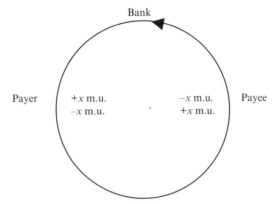

*Figure 8.1   The emission of money as a flow between the three parties
involved*

positive number with the same negative number is obviously zero (respecting the principle of no net creation). Yet, the result of this separation is that the payer can dispose of a number of (x) money units, in order for him to settle an equivalent debt against the payee. The latter is finally paid, in so far as he disposes ($-x$) of the number of money units that the bank carrying out the payment order credits ($+x$) to him. The debit ($-x$) of the payee actually means that this agent disposes of this amount of money to buy a deposit in the relevant bank. Such a deposit, as a matter of fact, is a (liquid) financial asset. Its holder has, thus, a purchasing power equal to x, which the bank records in its own ledger as long as the deposit holder does not dispose of it to finance any payment of his own (Table 8.1).

The bank's book-keeping, in fact, records the result of any payment that the bank carries out on behalf of its customers. The result of a payment is a stock magnitude, that is, a bank deposit, recorded in the name of the payee. The payment itself, by contrast, is an instantaneous circular flow, which cannot be rendered by book-keeping: the latter records only the result of payments, which, being instantaneous circular flows, can only be apprehended by conceptual logic.

Table 8.1   The bank loan and deposit resulting from a domestic payment

Bank			
Assets			Liabilities
Loan to the payer	$+x$ m.u.	Deposit of the payee	$+x$ m.u.

Logically, the purchasing power of a bank deposit cannot but stem from the fact that the payment originating this deposit gives rise to output. If there were no output, all bank deposits would have no purchasing power, as there would be nothing to purchase. It is, therefore, the payment of production costs that provides a purchasing power to the resulting bank deposits, which are thus a stock magnitude that associates the emission of money by a bank with those items that wage-earners produce during the period to which the payment of wages refer. Indeed, as Keynes (1936, pp. 213–14) pointed out, labour is the only true factor of production, as neither land nor capital (the other two so-called factors of production in conventional economics) can create something out of nothing. As a matter of fact, labour is capable of a net creation, although this does not concern the realm of physical items: labour is at the origin of the ('utility') form into which matter and energy are moulded. More precisely, intellectual labour creates the project (the 'design') of any objects, which physical labour fabricates in transforming (literally, changing the form of) matter and energy (see Cencini 2001, Chapter 4 and Rossi 2007b, Chapters 1 and 2 for analytical elaboration on this subject matter).

Now, conceptual logic leads also to the conclusion that the international economic space is an exchange economy: there is no production between countries, as any output is the result of domestic economies, even when (as this occurs frequently) a number of countries participate in the production of any given good, from the first treatment of the raw materials to the finishing and packing of this good with respect to national rules and habits. If so, then international payments ought to vehiculate from the country importing any items (the payer) to the exporting country (the payee) the corresponding purchasing power in the form of a bank deposit. Notice that this payment concerns each country, as defined by the set of its residents: if a country exports some goods, it is the set of agents residing within it that ought to receive something equivalent from the importing country – not simply a claim on an object (such as a bank deposit) that remains within the latter country. Contrary to production, which creates an economic object that did not pre-exist the payment of the relevant production costs, exchange simply moves across space pre-existing objects, transferring them from sellers to buyers independently of their location. In fact, at the time of writing, this principle for an exchange economy does not apply to the international economy: the country exporting a commercial or financial item simply receives in exchange the 'image' of the bank deposit that remains within the importing country's banking system – which thereby does not pay its counterpart finally.

As already noted by Rueff (1963, pp. 323–4), any country subjects its bank deposits to a process of 'duplication', in so far as it pays its imports

Table 8.2   *The result of an international payment in the current 'non-system'*

Banking system of importing country A (BS$_A$)			
Assets			Liabilities
Loan to the payer	$+x$ MA	Deposit of BS$_C$	$+x$ MA

Banking system of exporting country C (BS$_C$)			
Assets			Liabilities
Official reserves ($+x$ MA)	$+y$ MC	Deposit of the payee	$+y$ MC

Note: MA = units of money A; MC = units of money C.

of goods, services and assets from the rest of the world using its local currency. In the current regime for international payments, as pointed out above, country A transfers to country C a mere claim on A's deposits into its banking system, when it pays for its imports from C. The deposits themselves remain actually recorded in A's banking system, within which they have been formed as a result of the working of the monetary production economy of that country. The 'image' of the same bank deposits, however, is recorded also in the banking system of the exporting country, C, which is paid with an amount of money A that it enters, as official foreign-exchange reserves, on the assets side of its own banking system's balance sheet (Table 8.2).

In fact, the claims (notably, a financial capital) recorded as official reserves within the banking system of the exporting country (BS$_C$) circulate erratically on foreign-exchange markets around the world, subjecting exchange rates to erratic fluctuations, which have nothing to do with the alleged flexibility required (by mainstream economists) to make sure that supply and demand equilibrate on the so-called foreign-exchange market.

I, thus, notice two important points for understanding the ultimate origins of the financial crisis. Firstly, within the international economy, national currencies are treated as objects of trade (whose 'price', that is, the exchange rate, fluctuates thereby according to demand and supply conditions), rather than being used in conformity with their nature as means (rather than objects) of payment, as noted above. Secondly, key-currency countries cannot but 'recycle' on their local markets those bank deposits that their national banking systems generate as a result of the payment mechanics explained above. Indeed, elaborating on Table 8.2 allows one to explain that those deposits resulting from the cross-border payments carried out by the banking system of the debtor country (BS$_A$) are available for domestic spending on any kind of markets. In particular, having to pay interest on all deposits, banks in country A are led to find suitable borrowers (so much so that competition among banks leads each of them to implement a variety of predatory lending practices) and, owing to financial deregulation and liberalization, to 'off-load' the more risky of their loans into some sort of structured-investment vehicles. These special vehicles have the purpose of 'securitizing' these credits, to sell them on 'globalized' financial markets – most of the time to unaware institutional 'investors' (like pension funds and insurance companies) – with the marks of complacency given by a handful of American rating agencies. As is shown by the current financial crisis, this chain of events turns into a drama at a global level, as those structured products that result from 'securitization' are sold throughout the globe, affecting (or rather infecting, as they become 'toxic') a number of balance sheets of agents and institutions across the world, so much so that their volume is a multiple of world output – as in the derivatives industry, which is thereby 'several layers removed from any real economic activity of value creation' (Guttmann 2008, p. 9).

3.   THE KEYNES PROPOSAL FOR SUPRANATIONAL MONEY REVISITED

Keynes was aware that a properly functioning international monetary system requires a non-national book-entry money (rather than a commodity like precious metals) to boost foreign trade and avoid payment deficits, which are the structural cause of imbalances in the countries' foreign accounts. His proposal was to let a supranational institution issue its own means of international payment, to be used by participating countries in order to pay for their trade deficits. The Keynes proposal was, notably, to set up an international netting (or clearing) system, where settlements were made in real (barter) terms as long as foreign trade was balanced, while all trade deficits were settled using a supranational bank money – which he called bancor (Keynes 1980, p. 125).

To show how the Keynes system would have worked, suppose that country A has a trade deficit worth z bancor, which must be settled through the International Clearing Bank (ICB) proposed by Keynes (1980, p. 44), to the benefit of country C. When this payment occurs, country A has a debt of z bancor to the ICB, which owes an identical amount of bancor to country C (Table 8.3).

Owing to the principle that bank loans create deposits, the ICB would accept to grant a credit to country A (for the payment of its trade deficit), because the amount of bancor so created is mechanically

Table 8.3   The result of an international payment in Keynes's plan

International Clearing Bank			
Assets			Liabilities
Loan to country A	$+z$ bancor	Deposit of country C	$+z$ bancor

deposited by country C and, as a result, no single bancor can leave the system proposed by Keynes in the early 1940s (see Rossi 2007a for analytical elaboration).

Now, if this international payment system had been put into practice after the 1944 Bretton Woods Conference, it would have given rise to a series of credits that, in the end, net exporting countries would have granted through the ICB to net importing countries. Though expansionary, these international credits would have done very little to curb the inducement to record trade deficits by those countries benefiting from them, at least within the limits proposed by Keynes (1980). Indeed, such a payment system is not essentially different from the 'non-system' for international payments that exists at the time of writing. Today, as a matter of fact, those countries (like China) that record a trade surplus lend willingly or not the amount corresponding to that surplus to countries, such as the United States, whose current account balance is negative (as noted above). It is therefore a matter of form rather than substance to distinguish the current 'balance of financial terror' (Summers 2004) from the situation that would actually exist within the International Clearing Union proposed by Keynes: the 'payments' carried out by deficit countries (like A) would only be possible to the extent that surplus countries (like C) are willing to lend their bancor balances to any net importing country. The vicious circle is thus plain in this regard: as Rueff and Hirsch (1965, p. 2) observed metaphorically, '[i]f I had an agreement with my tailor that whatever money I pay him returns to me the very same day as a loan, I would have no objection at all to ordering more suits from him.'

To avoid this inflating mountain of debt, the Keynes proposal simply needs that a real-time gross-settlement protocol be introduced and run by the ICB, making sure that every time an international payment has to be carried out, the paying country disposes of financial assets (like bonds or securities) rather than merely a number of money units that do not transfer a purchasing power from the payer to the payee in the international space (whose agents are countries and not their residents, let us recall at this juncture).

4. THE NEW INTERNATIONAL MONETARY ORDER: A STYLIZED EXAMPLE

The payment system to put into practice between currency areas has to make sure that supranational money will never spill out of the settlement system required for enabling international payments' finality. If so, then the new international monetary order avoids that a bank deposit labelled in any given currency can give rise to a 'duplicate' in some foreign banking system, whenever an importer disposes of it in payment for commercial or financial imports. In a nutshell, a monetary system for international payments has to make sure that national currencies are used as means of final payment in their monetary space (in conformity with their nature), but are not traded as if they were financial assets that can move beyond the relevant banking system's borders. In practice, the reform of international payments ought to lead to the introduction of a monetary structure between countries pertaining to different currency areas (say, between country A and country C), through which commercial or financial imports are finally paid in local currency by the importer and, symmetrically, all exports are finally paid in local currency in the bank account of the exporter. This requires that in every country there is an institution which acts as a catalyst in any international payments resulting from cross-border transactions on either product or financial markets. This institution can be an external department of the national central bank as proposed by Schmitt (1975), or a national clearing authority as suggested by Schumacher (1943), the important point being that it averts duplication of those bank deposits that residents transform into imported items in the payer country.

Consider a stylized example supposing that the United States of America (country A) has to pay the People's Republic of China (country C) for any given item the former imports from the latter. Let us assume that the amount of this transaction corresponds to z bancor (supposedly equal to x MA and y MC respectively). As proposed by Keynes, a credit of z bancor allows country A to pay country C via an instantaneous circular flow of supranational money issued by the ICB (Figure 8.2).

Similarly to the mechanics for the emission of money within national banking systems, as explained above, the emission of supranational money implies the separation of the number zero into $+z$ and $-z$ bancor within the relevant payment. This amounts to creating and simultaneously destroying z units of bancor in order for the payment between country A and country C to occur. The ICB just measures the object of this transaction numerically.

The result of this international payment is an asset-and-liability record

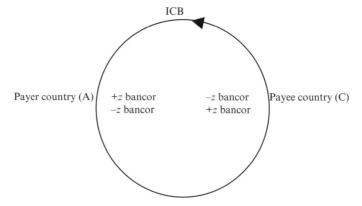

Figure 8.2   *The emission of supranational money as a flow on the*
international market for produced goods and services

in the ICB ledger, as shown in Table 8.3 already. Now, to make sure that
the importing country pays really (that is, finally) its counterpart, two
possibilities exist: either country A transfers to country C a bank deposit
equivalent to its debt obligation, or the former country gives to the latter
country an equivalent purchasing power in the form of financial assets
(such as bonds or securities), which represent the corresponding share
of A's output. The first case can occur if, and only if, the two countries
involved have a single currency (as the euro within Euroland). Being part
of a unified payment system, in that case, there are no monetary borders
impeding the transfer of a bank deposit from country A to country C
(similarly to the transfer of a bank deposit from bank A to bank C within
any domestic payment system as explained by Rossi (2007b, pp. 67–78)).
By contrast, the second case occurs every time when the two countries
involved have each got their own currency. If so, then country A does
not pay finally when it disposes of a property right on a deposit within its
own banking system, as pointed out above. To pay, finally, this country
has indeed to transfer a financial asset, which represents an output (to
be) produced in it. This respects the *do-ut-des* condition clearly noted by
Keynes (1980, p. 18), as '[any] trading transaction must necessarily find its
counterpart in another trading transaction sooner or later' (see above).
   Payment finality at international level requires, therefore, that the payer
country (A) transfers to the payee country (C) an amount of securities corresponding to the value of the traded goods between them. This financial
transaction makes sure that country C is debited of the deposit of z bancor
credited to it in payment of its exports to country A. In that case, the ICB

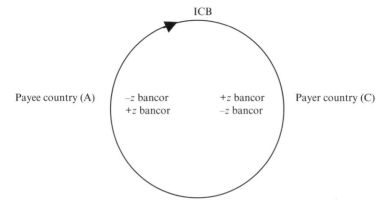

Figure 8.3 The emission of supranational money as a flow on the international market for financial assets

issues $+z$ and $-z$ units of bancor on demand by country C, so as to allow the latter country to pay for the financial assets it buys from country A (Figure 8.3).

Similarly to the international payment for foreign trade (see Figure 8.2), the international payment for the financial assets that country C buys from country A implies that z units of bancor are created and destroyed simultaneously, for both the payer and the payee. In the end, the result of this payment is recorded by the ICB as shown in Table 8.4.

Considered together, the entries in Tables 8.3 and 8.4 show that no country has either a debt or a credit against the other recorded in the ICB, once the net importing country (A) has transferred to the net exporting country (C) a claim on its output in the form of financial assets. Hence, all deposits denominated in bancor within the ICB are destroyed, once the deficit country (A) finally pays for its imported commercial items via a sale of financial assets. This makes sure that countries do not live beyond their income (which they can earn through foreign trade only), as any country that is not in a position to find enough demand for its financial assets on

Table 8.4 The result of an international payment of financial assets

	International Clearing Bank	
Assets		Liabilities
	Deposit of country C	$-z$ bancor
	Deposit of country A	$+z$ bancor

the international market will have to reduce its trade deficits shortly and mechanically, unless it is in a position to export more goods to any surplus countries (see below).

This mechanics of international payments mimics the so-called delivery-versus-payment protocol that regulates the payment traffic within modern securities settlement systems (see, for instance, Committee on Payment and Settlement Systems 2001). This protocol makes sure that delivery of the purchased financial assets occurs if, and only if, the corresponding payment occurs simultaneously. Something analogous ought to occur at international level, that is, properly speaking, between countries, each represented by their national central banks in the international monetary space.

Positive balances with the international settlement institution (ICB) – which will correspond to external surpluses of the creditor country – would thus no longer provide any finance to domestic lending in the debtor country (which would finance excessive consumption within the latter country): reserved for foreign trade only, these balances would finance commercial and financial purchases in the deficit country by the surplus country, as the former country would have incentives to rebalance its trade with the latter country (Rossi 2009). In that framework, for instance, China's trade surplus would no longer correspond to an accumulation of excessive bank deposits within the United States (inducing banks to lend inappropriately), but would give rise to positive balances at the international settlement institution, which China will be induced to spend to pay for imports from deficit countries such as the United States. Indeed, any persistent trade deficit will imply for the relevant country a net sale of financial assets to surplus countries – provided that the latter are willing to buy these assets. Analogously to the international scheme suggested by Keynes in the early 1940s, no interest ought to be paid on creditor country's balances at the ICB, whilst an appropriate rate of interest would be charged on positive balances in excess of a bilaterally agreed limit, as well as on any negative balances with the ICB. This would provide an incentive for both deficit and surplus countries to reduce their imbalances, by stimulating trade between them as a rebalancing mechanism (Piffaretti and Rossi 2010). Also, in order to induce any surplus countries to spend their bancor balances in payment of commercial imports from deficit countries, there should be a 'maintenance period' of 30 days for these balances with the ICB, analogously to what exists for banks' compulsory reserves with their central bank. All bancor balances recorded in a country's account at the ICB beyond this maintenance period will be automatically spent to purchase financial assets sold by deficit countries – as explained above. Hence, either surplus countries spend their bancor balances to buy a financial asset from deficit countries, or the former countries dispose of their deposits at the ICB to pay for imported goods from the latter countries. Both ways, there is a series of international payments that are all final between the countries concerned. This should contribute to rebalance world trade significantly between the two categories of countries involved, although the main contribution of this international monetary reform concerns the mechanical avoidance of excessive bank lending within 'key-currency' countries as argued above.

5. CONCLUSION

Global imbalances do not stem merely from agents' behaviour (that is to say, excessive consumption within deficit countries and excessive saving within surplus countries). In fact, there are structural and 'systemic' reasons to explain these imbalances across the world economy. In this chapter I pointed out that the current regime for international payments does not elicit payment finality between any two countries that have separate currencies. Contrary to widely held beliefs, no deposit can leave the banking system in which it has been formed as a result of the local monetary economy of production. If so, then no bank deposit moves from the importing country to the exporting country, when the local importer pays the foreign exporter finally. The latter country has a claim on the former country whenever the banking system of the exporter records the duplicate of the bank deposit that remains within the importing country. As this is an international issue, it can be settled only by an international monetary reform logically. Provided that one is ready to recognize that countries exist as the set of their own residents, it is a matter of conceptual logic to understand that (1) the international economic space is an exchange economy, and that (2) the economic agents in the international economy are countries as a whole and not their residents. In light of these two characteristics, it should be obvious that Keynes's fundamental proposal at the 1944 Bretton Woods Conference still remains crucial at the time of writing: an international settlement institution ought to be set up as a first step towards making sure that countries pay and are paid finally for any item they exchange between them as a result of their residents' transactions across the borders. As this institution will issue the number of supranational money units required by the payer country in order for the latter to discharge its debt obligations in the international space, it will provide the vehicle through which the payer country has to transfer to the payee country a purchasing power (in the form of either goods or assets), rather than simply a promise of payment void of any substance (as this occurs today with 'key currencies'). This international monetary architecture entails a rebalancing mechanism for countries, as both deficit and surplus countries will have incentives to reduce their net position in the international economic space. Countries whose foreign trade records huge deficits at the time of writing will have to curb them, in so far as surplus countries will not demand enough financial assets from the former group of countries. Further, and more important for curing global imbalances and their negative consequences around the world, surplus countries will be led to spend in foreign trade (hence in imports from deficit countries) the balances they will record at the international settlement institution. These settlement balances will not pay an interest, and, beyond some threshold, the countries owning them will have to pay a fee on them, to be fixed at such a level that induces these countries to dispose of these deposits with the international settlement institution to purchase goods or assets from deficit countries within a short period of time (say, 30 days, analogously to what exists for banks' minimum settlement balances, referred to as the maintenance period in monetary-policy literature).

Although the issue of international payment finality concerns each country around the world, it would be wise and realistic to begin with a bilateral agreement between the two countries that are most exposed to (the negative effects of) global imbalances – that is, China and the United States. A bilateral settlement facility, as proposed by Piffaretti and Rossi (2010), would notably allow both these countries to rebalance their bilateral trade, while allowing for final payments between them that dispose of the vicious circle originating systemic financial crises within the United States – the country issuing the 'key currency' considered as if it were a reserve asset beyond this country's borders. Needless to say, a number of thorny issues will have to be settled at the political level, such as the appropriate initial exchange rate between any national currency involved and the supranational currency to be issued by the international settlement institution. Nevertheless, the benefits of an orderly working international monetary system are so relevant for the global economy (in both deficit and surplus countries) that no political hurdle should hinder the progress towards aligning the nature of money and payments with the practice of trade and finance between any countries involved by globalization, independently of the merits and drawbacks of foreign trade and global markets, which will always exist and therefore divide advocates of global trade and finance from opponents to them. It is a task of the economics profession to explain to both camps that not only money matters, but also that the monetary structure (or architecture) is of the utmost importance to allow for an orderly working of economic activities, both production and exchange within as well as between any countries concerned. As

Rowley and Hamouda (1989, p. 2) pointed out long ago with respect to the current international monetary regime, unfortunately, '[t]he attendant complacency restrains our willingness to accept both novel proposals and the revival of older views, previously rejected for adoption in different situations of the world economy, even though such deviations from fashion might provide important ingredients for solutions to our present difficulties'. Let us hope that the global financial crisis, affecting the world economy at the time of writing, will encourage political leaders to engage with 'old ideas', to get rid of those which ramify into every corner of economists' minds, in order for them to think about international monetary issues anew and afresh, without any ideological argument but inspired by logical thinking. The crisis that broke out in 2007 would thus not be completely in vain, and could in fact represent a turning point in both politics and economics – the two most powerful disciplines when they are right as well as when they are wrong, as Keynes (1936, p. 383) noted cogently.

REFERENCES

Cencini, A. (1988), *Money, Income and Time: A Quantum-Theoretical Approach*, London and New York: Pinter Publishers.

Cencini, A. (2001), *Monetary Macroeconomics: A New Approach*, London and New York: Routledge.

Committee on Payment and Settlement Systems (2001), *Recommendations for Securities Settlement Systems*, Basel: Bank for International Settlements, November.

Committee on Payment and Settlement Systems (2008), *The Interdependencies of Payment and Settlement Systems*, Basel: Bank for International Settlements, June.

Committee on Payment and Settlement Systems (2010), *Market Structure Developments in the Clearing Industry: Implications for Financial Stability*, Basel: Bank for International Settlements, November.

Friedman, M. (1969), *The Optimum Quantity of Money and Other Essays*, Chicago: Aldine Publishing.

Gnos, C. (2006), 'French circuit theory', in P. Arestis and M. Sawyer (eds), *A Handbook of Alternative Monetary Economics*, Cheltenham, UK and Northampton, MA, USA: Edward Elgar Publishing, pp. 87–104.

Goodhart, C.A.E. (1989, second edition), *Money, Information and Uncertainty*, London and Basingstoke: Macmillan.

Gourinchas, P.-O. and H. Rey (2007), 'From world banker to world venture capitalist: US external adjustment and the exorbitant privilege', in R.H. Clarida (ed.), *G7 Current Account Imbalances: Sustainability and Adjustment*, Chicago and London: University of Chicago Press, pp. 11–55.

Graziani, A. (1990), 'The theory of the monetary circuit', *Économies et Sociétés*, **24** (6), 7–36.

Guttmann, R. (2008), 'A primer on finance-led capitalism and its crisis', *Revue*

de la Régulation, no. 3–4, available online at http://regulation.revues.org/
index5843.html.

Keynes, J.M. (1936), *The General Theory of Employment, Interest and Money*,
London: Macmillan.

Keynes, J.M. (1980), *The Collected Writings of John Maynard Keynes, Volume
XXV: Activities 1940–1944. Shaping the Post-War World: The Clearing Union*,
London and Basingstoke: Macmillan.

Piffaretti, N. and S. Rossi (2010), 'An institutional approach to balancing international monetary relations: the case for a US–China settlement facility', *World
Bank Policy Research Working Papers*, n. 5188.

Realfonzo, R. (2006), 'The Italian circuitist approach', in P. Arestis and M. Sawyer
(eds), *A Handbook of Alternative Monetary Economics*, Cheltenham, UK and
Northampton, MA, USA: Edward Elgar Publishing, pp. 105–20.

Rossi, S. (2006), 'The theory of money emissions', in P. Arestis and M. Sawyer
(eds), *A Handbook of Alternative Monetary Economics*, Cheltenham, UK and
Northampton, MA, USA: Edward Elgar Publishing, pp. 121–38.

Rossi, S. (2007a), 'The monetary-policy relevance of an international settlement
institution: the Keynes plan 60 years later', in A. Giacomin and M.C. Marcuzzo
(eds), *Money and Markets: A Doctrinal Approach*, London and New York:
Routledge, pp. 96–114.

Rossi, S. (2007b), *Money and Payments in Theory and Practice*, London and New
York: Routledge.

Rossi, S. (2009), 'International payment finality requires a supranational central-
bank money: reforming the international monetary architecture in the spirit of
Keynes', *China–USA Business Review*, **8** (11), 1–20.

Rowley, R. and O.F. Hamouda (1989), 'Disturbance in the world economy', in
O.F. Hamouda, R. Rowley and B.M. Wolf (eds), *The Future of the International
Monetary System: Change, Coordination or Instability?*, Aldershot, UK and
Armonk, NY, USA: Edward Elgar Publishing and M.E. Sharpe, pp. 1–3.

Rueff, J. (1963), 'Gold exchange standard a danger to the West', in H.G. Grubel
(ed.), *World Monetary Reform: Plans and Issues*, Stanford and London:
Stanford University Press and Oxford University Press, pp. 320–28.

Rueff, J. and F. Hirsch (1965), *The Role and the Rule of Gold: An Argument*,
Princeton: Princeton University Press.

Schmitt, B. (1975), *Théorie Unitaire de la Monnaie, Nationale et Internationale*,
Albeuve: Castella.

Schmitt, B. (1996), 'Unemployment: is there a principal cause?', in A. Cencini
and M. Baranzini (eds), *Inflation and Unemployment: Contributions to a New
Macroeconomic Approach*, London and New York: Routledge, pp. 75–105.

Schumacher, E.F. (1943), 'Multilateral clearing', *Economica*, **10** (38), 150–65.

Summers, L.H. (2004), 'The United States and the global adjustment process',
speech at the Third Annual Stavros S. Niarchos Lecture, Institute for
International Economics, Washington, DC, USA, 23 March, available online at
http://www.iie.com/publications/papers/paper.cfm?researchid=200.

9. The true rules of a good management of public finance. An explanation of the fatal Eurozone crisis[1]

Alain Parguez

1. INTRODUCTION: THE ORIGINAL SINS OF THE EURO-SYSTEM

Contrary to the dictatorial ideology of the new European order in which the Euro is enshrined, running a permanent deficit, even a growing one (and thereby piling up debt), can be the proof that the State is well managed. One should raise the question: what is the existence condition of a well-managed State and thereby of a genuine sound public finance? The answer is straightforward: through its fiscal policy the State must be the anchor of a true long-run growth bestowing a rising welfare on society as a whole. Since true increasing welfare requires true full employment, which means the inexistence of income rationing for the majority of the people, the *sine qua non* of true sound fiscal policy is that it generates permanently that true full employment.

This definition of the normal role of the State contradicts the core postulates of the European Monetary Union ideology, which is rooted in three beliefs:

- the State must behave like any individual private household or corporation. Since all rational private agents strive to balance their account, the State must endeavour to balance its budget;
- contrary to private agents, the State, even acting rationally, can *never* generate growth out of its expenditures. The modern State is always a 'burden' destroying growth;

[1] I have to thank for their comments Riccardo Bellofiore, Joseph Halevi and Mario Seccareccia without implicating them.

- The State deficit is a net destruction of wealth. In the short run, it drains savings from investment and thereby production; in the long run it generates debts that transfer poverty and sacrifice to future generations. Future taxes should permanently rise, which must squeeze future productive private expenditures[2].

2. FIRST PART: THE TRUE RULES OF A GOOD MANAGEMENT OF PUBLIC FINANCE

A lot of converging studies prove that this purely negative vision of the State is just a fantasy: the State is indeed the true long-run anchor of a genuine growth. What hides this vision is just the full dismantling of the State, which must be replaced by the absolute rule of Euro-core (France, Germany mainly) corporations including banking corporations, the so-called financial markets (sic).

The State deficit can be the ultimate foundation of a true stable growth generating genuine full employment. Since State expenditures contribute to the generation of national income while taxes have the inverse impact, it is a pure national accounts identity that the *ex post* State deficit is identical to a *net* creation of income for the private sector as a whole, residents and non-residents. It is tantamount to another pure accounting identity: the State deficit generates an equal surplus or *net savings* for the private sector as a whole (household and corporations, residents and non-residents). Assuming a balanced budget, net new savings of the private sector are *zero*. It is worse if the State decides to run a surplus to pay back its debt: the surplus or net new savings of the private sector becomes *negative*.

With the surplus being shared between residents and non-residents (whose share accounts for the domestic trade deficit) one could argue that it cannot benefit the domestic economy. Again, this is a wrong belief. All empirical accounting data display the proof that the share of the domestic private sector is always strongly positive. This fundamental identity explains the absurdity of the core European countries, especially Germany relative to Greece[3]. Since their sole source of growth is exports, when they

---

[2] These three postulates are of pure Hayekian origin. They were adamantly spelled out in the first blueprint of the European Monetary Union written by the then leading economist Perroux (1943). For a detailed comment, see Parguez and Bliek (2008). On Hayekian economics and political philosophy relying on permanent austerity, see Polanyi-Levitt (2012) and Parguez (2012c).

[3] The distinction is purely *objective*: it is enshrined into the *real* counterpart of the deficits. I do think it reflects the distinction made by Keynes (1936) between the current budget and the capital budget of the States, especially on page 128, note 1.

impose dramatic shock-therapy on Greece, which prevents Greece from running a trade deficit, they squeeze their own exports and hence their growth.

This is the short-run impact of the budget deficit. What about the long-run impact? Answering the question requires a crucial distinction between two kinds of deficits: *Bad* deficits and *Good* deficits. Deficits must be deemed *Bad* when they are not the outcome of a long-run policy targeting the creation of a useful and productive stock of capital, either tangible (all kinds of infrastructure, for instance, and equipment that will *never* be created by the private sector because it is beyond its ability to bet on an unknowable future) or non-tangible (recruiting people working in advanced research, health, teaching: sectors where real capital is labour)[4]. *Bad* deficits may happen in two intertwined scenarios:

- the shock-therapy scenario, the like of which has been imposed on Greece: the collapse of the economy because the cuts in expenditures generate such a fall in tax revenue that deficits appear again and could rise;
- the long-run policies of deflation scenario: whatever the effort to get rid of public employment and cuts in public investment, the government cannot stop the collapse of tax revenue and abolish its deficit.

Bad deficits do not reflect the growth of the stock of social capital. Private agents expect more cuts, more poverty, so they abstain from consuming or investing.

Good Productive deficits reflect a long-run policy of accumulation of social capital. They are *planned*. Their long-run impact is always positive, and they generate accelerating positive expectations for *all* private agents, residents and non-residents. They are the last resort driving force of growth. *Good* deficits are backed by the issue of a public debt that can be self-financing, while being a gift to the future. National income is generated by previous expenditures. Like households and corporations, the State is obliged to spend before getting its tax revenue. Income-generating initial expenditures are to be financed by money creation and pre-existing net savings. These net savings have been created by previous State deficits, as will be explained. Since a State cannot save out of a surplus or net public saving, it is obliged to fund *all* its expenditures out of money creation by the banking system[5].

---

[4] On this crucial question, one must refer to Cesaratto and Stirati (2010–11).

[5] As shown in Parguez (2002), when the State runs a surplus, it destroys a quantity of money. Therefore the State can never recycle a hoard accumulated in previous periods.

State expenditures reflect a credit to the banking system, the counterpart being a liability issued by the State. When the State becomes able to raise taxes, it spends its revenue to cancel or pay back a share of its initial debt. This excess of expenditures relative to tax revenue is a source of wealth for the private sector as a whole; the modern State cannot be obliged to repay its total initial debt – it may run the deficit it wants. The State cannot be dealt with as an ordinary private corporation. In the banking system balance sheet, the counterpart of the deficit on the asset side is the increase of long-run State liabilities; herein lies the cause of the public debt.

Since the State cannot be an ordinary private agent, it must not finance its expenditures by private banks loans, as if it were a mere private corporation. Herein lies the existence condition of the Central Bank as the banking branch of the State. In the Central Bank balance sheet, the counterpart of the deficit on the asset side is the accumulation of State titles of debt earning a rate of interest fixed by the Treasury. In such a case, the public debt is nothing but a debt of the State to itself.

Herein lies the cause of the self-inflicted Euro crisis. Wanting to get rid of the State as the engine of growth, the Euro founders decided to privatize the State to deal with it as any kind of corporation. They created a sovereign Central Bank forbidden to play the normal role of Central Banks. Domestic States were obliged to strive to balance their accounts. The Euro-System cannot survive in its present structure and with its current governance.

Is the public debt a burden in any case? Even if a share of the public debt is acquired by private banks out of sales of bonds by the Central Bank, the answer must be a strong *No* as long as deficits are good ones for three intertwined reasons. First, being the ultimate engine of growth, because of their strong multiplier impact, they automatically generate enough increase in tax revenue in the future to allow the State to meet its commitments. Second, being the counterpart of the provision of socially useful capital accumulation, they provide future generations with an increase in its welfare, inducing more and more dynamic expectations. Herein lies the reason why piling up debt to the Central Bank cannot impose inflation on the economy. Third, public debt titles being perfectly liquid and endowed with a real value (contrary to most private liabilities), they maintain the financial stability of banks that have acquired public titles of debt.

A well-managed State, planning permanent good deficits, can never be bankrupted. Even the European Monetary Union could not, whatever its efforts, create the possibility of a true bankruptcy even for the unhappy Greece. The very possibility of a lack of buyers for Greek bonds was never on the agenda. What was only at stake was to impose more deflation on Greece, especially by slashing labour purchasing power and accelerating the dismantling of the State. The so-called plans of help are just crafted to help foreign banks holding Greek bonds, by sustaining the rise of Greek bond prices. *In times of dark expectations the sacrifice of the people could not be enough!* Finally, the euronomics is a victim of its own self-made strange ideology rooted into its history.

3. SECOND PART: THE BUILT-IN PUBLIC DEBT CRISIS

At the very start of the first Black Plague in 1348, the then Pope summoned an extraordinary council in Avignon. The council decreed special exorcism against the devil and bonfires for its agents: sorcerers, witches, heretics, midwives, etc. Bonfires spread all over christendom; two years later, the plague stopped. Besides burned victims, a third of the population died and it was the start of a first escape from the Malthusian iron heel. Had the holy trinity rating agency judging souls been satisfied by the bonfires, the then austerity policies? What about the new 'black plague', which is destroying not bodies but the balance sheet of the new christendom banks, the Euroland? Overtaken by the panic, banks order rulers of Euroland to impose the new bonfires, harsh programmes of austerity destroying what remains of the real economy. It raises some questions: Could Euroland ever recover from the plague or could it fall into the abyss? Could it be saved by the Euro bonds? Could this innovation be more efficient than the decrees of the Avignon council? What makes sense of this comparison is that the first plague started in a Genoan emporium on the Black Sea, while the second started not very far away in Greece! There is, however, a difference: the panic of the mid 14th Century was not man-made, whereas the panic of this second decade of the 21st Century is purely man-made. What they have in common is folly, the demise of reason and the cruelty of rulers.

From the start, the public debt plague was the outcome of the systematic destruction of the anchor role of the State within the European Monetary Union[6]. Architects (all French) of the Euro-System hoped to have built the most efficient iron straitjacket justifying iron-heel MAP

---

[6] This non-Minskian nature of the crisis has been wonderfully explained in Bellofiore (2011) and in Davanzati (2011), and before by Bellofiore and Halevi (2010–2011). This anchor role of the State was not ignored by Marx as shown by Graziani (2003) in his effort to monetarize Marx's theory of value. Minsky would never have dared to imagine that spiralling financial instability would spark from the public debt because of the destabilizing role of the State. I agree with Bellofiore (2011): *Minsky was a strong supporter of a 'big State'*. He would have been horrified by the Euro-System.

(Modern Austerity Policies)[7]. They could not destroy stage one of State financing whatever their dreams. By abolishing the State sovereignty on its currency, the outcome of a supra-national absolutist set of an oligarchy of Central Banks, the true nature of the mythical European Central Bank (ECB), they destroyed any connexion forever between States, Treasuries and the Central Bank. They went further: Central Banks were forbidden to contribute to State expenditures by buying bonds issued in stage two to back deficits. It was not enough. Increasing limits were imposed on both deficits and the outstanding public debt. Henceforth, the State was dealt with as a private corporation and an unproductive one! What was the secret hope? In stage one banks would ration States, reject conventional credits, which would get rid of the public debt. Laws of economics and greed were still ruling. As the private capitalist sector was more and more reluctant to borrow to spend in the real economy, banks never rationed the States to stay in business. Thereby, whatever the dramatic impact of MAP striving to abolish State investment, in stage two bad deficits never stopped rising, taking care of the unchecked strength of automatic destabilizers and negative multipliers.

I do believe that both stages were stronger and more devastating than in the USA, Canada, even Japan[8]. Henceforth, Treasuries had to auction bonds more and more bereft of any real value and even liquidity. Bonds holders were convinced that they held assets with zero value because States could not repay them in their frenzy to cut public expenditures. Logically, States now being quasi-parasitic corporations, bonds holders asked for continually rising interest rates, which accelerates the total collapse of the system. In a straightforward way, architects of this absurd system denying all economic laws have built, in the ongoing crisis, the public debt black plague they then use to advocate still more destructive policies, achieving the collapse of the real economy. They shrewdly used rating agencies to impose more poverty.

Ultimately, to impose MAP, State rulers apparently enslave themselves to the so-called bonds market, but they enslave bonds holders themselves to an increasingly fragile system. Figure 9.1 explains this race to financial catastrophe, which cannot be deemed 'a Minsky moment' because Minsky had never imagined MAP and the doomed system they encompass. Needless to say, he never dealt with financial crisis in the bonds market

---

[7] I created the concept (Parguez 2012a) to characterize permanent fiscal policies aiming at a systematic reduction of all State productive expenditures (with rising taxation) to get both a strict budget primary surplus and a 'minimal Hayekian State'. They embody a planned dismantling of the State, to impose permanent and rising deflation on the real economy.

[8] On Japan, one must read Koo (2008) to understand how it escaped the collapse thanks to good rising deficits.

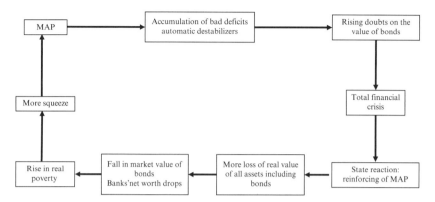

Figure 9.1   The cumulative destabilizing process resulting from European MAP

with fragility being destructive because of State capitulation reinforcing the worst fears of bonds holders.

Especially in the Eurozone, the ongoing economic system resulting from this race to death can be summed up by two relationships, as shown by Figure 9.2. When the curves displayed in Figure 9.2, showing the perfectly inverse relationship between the market value of public and private assets and the real rate of growth, attain the negative real rate of growth of capacity and welfare, it is time sooner or later for the total collapse of the financial system. It reflects what I have deemed the ultimate decadence of the capitalist system. I have proven elsewhere the ongoing mechanism (Parguez 2011)[9]. The accelerating fall in global capacity implies both an accelerating rise in true unemployment, including civil servants, leading to a drop in wage rate, while inflation led by prices fixed by corporations rises unchecked by the rise in labour-productivity. Thereby capitalists are henceforth free to impose the degree of exploitation, the ratio of labour-productivity to the real wage, they want. It is the mirror of the collapse of the share of real labour income in distribution. So the value of stocks is, but only for a while, escaping from the automatic destabilizers. Capitalists are free, or hope to be free, from the constraint of borrowing from accumulation to get real profits. In some way, *the erstwhile Keynesian law of effective demand no more rules*. The proof is final: MAP are ultimately abolishing the dynamic aspect of capitalism, or they accelerate some tendency to the decadence and parasite aspect of the system.

---

[9] On this critical point, one must refer to Bellofiore and Halevi (2010–11), and also Cesaratto and Stirati (2010–11).

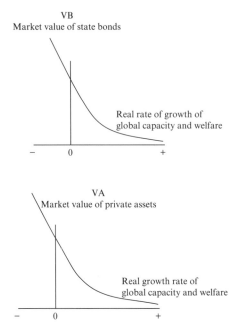

Figure 9.2   The core relationship in a permanently destabilized system like the Euro-System

4.   THIRD PART: THE START OF THE NEW BLACK PLAGUE AND THE TOTAL COLLAPSE OF THE SYSTEM

It is the lethal outcome of the systematic destruction of the anchor role of the State for the sake of imposing the Euro-System enshrining a medieval ignorance of basic economic principles of the dynamic capitalist system, and thereby the substitution of a mix of inquisitorial ideology and folly for sound economic laws. The systematic destruction of the anchor role of the State generated the transmogrification of the public debt into a rats-plague disease. As I proved herein, since the start the supreme purpose of what became the Euro-straitjacket reflected the accelerated decadence of European capitalism towards a pure parasite-feudal rentier system. The metamorphosis started, with no return, with the Mitterrand austerity or destruction plan of 1983. It had nothing to do with either Reaganism or Thatcherism. It was embodied into three core propositions or principles that were the existential conditions of the Euro as the new gold standard.

The major principle was the absolute negation of any positive role for the State, which became dealt with as a mere parasitical or non-productive corporation. It means that, on the one hand, any effort to raise welfare had to be jettisoned; on the other hand, the long-run decline of welfare (including true full employment) and the downwards shift of the global capacity frontier became supreme goals. How to meet the new imposed poverty dogma? By a long-run decline in State planned investment, which should become zero or negative. How to succeed? By imposing a long-run decline in the public expenditures thanks to the prohibition of planned deficits. The impact was indeed a collapse of the real economy. Euro-rulers were not too much worried by the rising effective inflation, a proof that in the modern economy, if the Phillips curve does exist, it is the inverse of the textbook one. As public investment vanished, including investment in human capital, private productive expenditures collapsed, which generated more loss of welfare. Indeed, the outcome was rising *bad* imposed *deficits*, whatever the rise in taxation. Herein lies the true seed of the plague:

- together, the Euro rules imposed an absolute privatization of public finance. Thereby, any connexion with the Central Bank endowed with quasi-imperial power was abolished;
- the State, when it ran a forced deficit, left banks with, on their asset side, an increase in liquidity bearing no interest balanced by accumulation of net savings of the private sector.

Now, being dealt with as a failed private corporation, the State had to strive to convert all its liquid debt to banks into bonds bearing the interest fixed by banks themselves. Again, by the very logic of privatisation, all the objective rules were forgotten or jettisoned.

The hard logic of the system transformed Treasury net transfer into true banks loans. Thereby bonds were transmogrified into a true loan from banks to the State. Since bonds no longer embodied any real creation of value, their value became purely speculative depending on banks' animal spirits. Bankers and their guides, the rating agencies, took care of two major rules:

- the bets on the certainty of being 'reimbursed' for loans they had never truly granted;
- the rate of interest they could hope for when they sell their bonds to other more optimistic and greedy banks or other financial institutions. The more they bet on the demand for their bonds by those new players attracted by the interest forced on the State, the more they valued their bonds. Since bonds could no longer be included

into capital, being deprived of real value and issued by the most dubious 'corporations', the State became obliged to divert a share of their current expenditures, it had otherwise to shrink, to reimburse.

Meanwhile, in the context of the dismantling of the State, all the remaining positive effects of the deficit became forgotten. To understand the Euro-System, one must sadly remember that the fundamental identity explaining the creation of net saving by the State either became forgotten, with all national accounting, or had not even the least positive impact. As I explained, the whole relationships of the dynamic capitalist economy became denied: multipliers became *negative*. At last, the monetary union explictly rejected any economic union. Thereby, the 'market value' of bonds varied strongly between the States leading to two disasters for the future: (i) interest on bonds were more and more divergent; (ii) the all-powerful Central Bank was powerless on interest on bonds. Finally, the emperor was naked, like in the Andersen tale. Fiscal policy and monetary policy are both privatized, banks fix long-run interest rates, the ECB plays no role at all, contrary to what happens in the USA in the Federal Reserve System[10].

The black plague appeared in Greece, the poorest member, in the aftermath of the reversal of expectations of banks on the value of private assets. It revealed the sheer absurdity of the Euro-System and the pure folly, worthy of the Avignon council, of European elites. For reasons I explained, the Greek government was forced to run large deficits, a large share of which being good. The counterpart was an enormous creation of net savings mainly for net exporters: France and essentially Germany in the form of net profits galore. But for the sake of privatization dogma, all those deficits were decreed 'bad' and Greece was forced to absorb banks' tremendous rise in liquidity by auctioning bonds at interest rates decreed by banks, the French and the Germans. Privatization dogma transformed their substitution into a genuine borrowing from private banks, to be reimbursed at will. The sharp reversal of banks' expectations led to panic: so enormous was the debt, so high were interest rates, so strong was the violation of the squeeze of expenditures, that the Greek government would never be able to meet its commitments; henceforth, the market value of its pseudo-debt started to collapse. Thereby, the value of assets became more and more inferior to liabilities, the aggregate net savings. Now, the

---

[10] It could be deemed the useless Central Bank. It is so useless that the new Euro-System drafted by the new treaty imposed by France and Germany relies on 'inflows of capital' from the International Monetary Fund. In some way, for the first time in history, a Central Bank would have to become a net borrower of its own currency and only to finance the postulated bank's losses!

plague ruled – banks holding Greek bonds or pseudo-debt were possessed by the devil of bankruptcy. They could not resist the temptation of imposing outrageous rates on their assets in Greek bonds; henceforth, their stockholders could be awash with dividends as rents.

What spread the plague was the reaction of the French and German governments ruling *de facto* Euroland and the panic or total misunderstanding of the Greek government. Everybody was aware that under the draconian iron heel of the system, Greece could never pay back its pseudo-debt, having lost any sovereignty on the currency. The Greek government had options:

- to stay within the zone and comply with the iron heel without crying for help from the Euro-rulers. It meant that to save its people's welfare it would be obliged to cancel a large share of its pseudo-debt and refuse usury rates. Was this option possible? Could banks close government accounts and thereby leave Greece without a banking system and currency since government had no more account at the Central Bank. Taking care of the folly blinding any reason, banks could have at least drastically rationed the government's ability to spend until capitulation. In any case, Greece would have been excommunicated and expelled from the Euro-System – an option which horrified the government that was an harsh supporter of the iron-heel system;
- to beg for help. Herein lies the seeds of the ultimate plan of salvation not of Greece but of the Euro, the Euro bonds! These only addressing stage two of public finance, the so-called financing of the already realized deficit.

First, no help could be directly provided by the ECB, or rather the ruling couple, the German and French Central Banks. They were adamantly invoking the prohibition of buying State bonds. The 'ECB' dogma is to play no part in State financing. Next, salvation required the intermediation of France and Germany without involving the ECB. Both were only interested in containing the plague to protect the net worth of their banks. Both rejected any kind of solidarity, willing to ignore that Greece's horrendous deficits had led to their exporting corporations being awash with net profits and their banks' stockholders (their major corporations) awash with dividends. They acted like the Avignon council, afraid of doubts over the value of their own pseudo-debt to their banks.

Thereby a weird system, some *Méduse* raft, was imagined in haste: each State issued new bonds, sold to their private banks; proceeds were then borrowed by Greece, which started to meet again its pseudo-debt. Finally, in banks' balance sheets, German and French bonds were substituted for Greek bonds, while in the Greek Treasury, new French and German bonds were substituted for former Greek bonds. But that *Méduse* raft was worthy of the council of the frightened pope and cardinals. The bondfires were horrendous destruction plans of Greek society, which achieved the collapse of the economy, while generating more bad deficits that required more sales of bonds. Now, French and German public debt had been raised. The plague spread all over Europe; doubts on the value of Spanish, Portuguese, Italian and Irish bonds could no more be contained, while French and German bonds themselves became bad assets. New bondfires were decreed in the form of destruction austerity, which destroyed what remained of the real economy and caused more bad deficits, generating more destruction policies. The whole Euro-banking system could die, all logic being ignored[11].

5.   CONCLUSION

Back to Avignon and Malthus, since the dismantling or hate of the State, *its privatization shared by the whole eurodom rulers*, is the cornerstone of Eurodom, what would banks do with what has been robbed from the people? Invest the spoils in private assets never issued for real value generating expenditures? Henceforth, while destroying the real base of the economy and depriving public bonds of any real value, forced 'reimbursement' of what was never borrowed will generate a new wave of hyper-speculation and capital gains, plus dividends to former productive corporations motivating them to abandon, without remorse, the real economy! It is no more the turnpike to slavery, it is the race to death video game transmogrified into real darkness. Finally, the loss of value of private assets, the collapse of the 'financial markets', will be the twilight of the gods of Eurodom Valhalla.

No shrewd financial innovations can save what cannot be saved because it does not want to be saved. Herein lies the final proposition. Thereby I was right in Parguez (1999) to foresee the collapse of the Euro as a false money built to destroy the real economy[12]. Herein lies the crucial point: the Euro

[11] Were it ever imposed, the new Franco-German iron heel would achieve the demise of the State, but also, as dictatorial enforcer of a deflation worse than any other deflation in history, would destroy, once and for all, capitalism as a productive system in the Eurozone. States would be turned into the most feral predators, to rely on the wonderful concept invented by Galbraith (2008).

[12] Finally, relying on the wonderful book of Diamond (2005), Eurozone is a society which freely chose to collapse, without any constraint other than its own fanatical ideology.

was not just a single currency but a new social order which had its own but perverse logic. The most modest proposals of giving to the ECB the right to help the States are to be rejected because they contradict the 'existential nature' of the system. It could be deemed a laboratory experiment of social-engineering, which failed because it was rooted in the wrong economics. Instead of adapting, Euro-rulers reinforced the straitjacket, which explains the 'fiscal consolidation pact' (2012b). Such a choice is unique in modern times (Koo 2008). That fiscally dreadful treaty is not only imposing permanent quasi-zero State deficits out of a permanent decrease in State outlays, but also an accelerated reimbursement of the public debt. To attain these weird goals, States transfer fiscal policy to an independent fiscal authority!

REFERENCES

Bellofiore, R. (2011), 'The ascent and crisis of money manager capitalism', *International Journal of Political Economy*, **40** (3), 3–17.

Bellofiore, R. and J. Halevi (2010–11), 'Could be raining: the European crisis after the Great Recession', *International Journal of Political Economy*, **39** (4), 5–30.

Cesaratto, S. and A. Stirati (2010–11), 'Germany and the European and global crisis', *International Journal of Political Economy*, **39** (4), 57–86.

Davanzati, G. (2011), 'Income distribution and crisis in a Marxian scheme of the monetary circuit', *International Journal of Political Economy*, **40** (3), 33–49.

Diamond, J. (2005, revised edition), *Collapse: How Societies Choose to Fail or Succeed*, London: Penguin.

Galbraith, J. (2008), *The Predator State*, New York: Free Press.

Graziani, A. (2003), *The Monetary Theory of Production*, Cambridge: Cambridge University Press.

Keynes, J.M. (1936), *The General Theory of Employment, Interest and Money*, in *The Collected Writings of John Maynard Keynes* (Vol. VII), London: Macmillan, 1971.

Koo, R. (2008), *The Holy Grail of Macroeconomics: Lessons from Japan's Great Recession*, Singapore: Wiley and Sons.

Parguez, A. (1999), 'The expected failure of the European Monetary Union: a false money against the real economy', *Eastern Economic Journal*, **25** (1), 63–76.

Parguez, A. (2002), 'A monetary theory of public finance', *International Journal of Political Economy*, **32** (3), 80–97.

Parguez, A. (2011), *The True Meaning of the General Theory of the Monetary Circuit: Discovering the Objective Laws of Capitalism to Attain True Full Employment and Welfare*, Paper presented at the conference 'Contemporary Capitalism: the Financial Circuits, its Transformation and Future Projects', University of Ottawa, May 31 (available at: www.neties.com/parguez).

Parguez, A. (2012a), *Modern Austerity Policies (MAP). An Analysis of the Economics of Decadence and Self-destruction*, Paper presented at the Eastern Economic Association Conference, Boston, March, (available on www.neties.com/parguez).

Parguez, A. (2012b), 'The Euro, yes, it was a false money but before dying it destroyed the real economy', forthcoming in H. Bougrine and L-P. Rochon (eds), *The Future of Capitalism*, Cheltenham, UK and Northampton, MA, USA: Edward Elgar Publishing.

Parguez, A. (2012c), 'The fundamental and eternal conflict: Hayek and Keynes on austerity', *International Journal of Political Economy*, **41** (4), 54–68.

Parguez, A. and J.G. Bliek (2008), 'Mitterrand's turn to conservative economics: a revisionist history', *Challenge*, **51** (2), 97–109.

Perroux, F. (1943), 'La monnaie dans une économie organisée', *Revue de l'Economie Contemporaine*, Décembre, 1–20.

Polanyi-Levitt, K. (2012), 'The power of ideas: Keynes, Hayek, and Polanyi', *International Journal of Political Economy*, **41** (4), 5–15.

10. Growth and crises in the Italian economy

Vittorio Valli

1. TWO CRISES

The Italian economy faces a double crisis: a structural long-standing crisis (a relative economic decline) and the economic depression following the 2007–08 financial turmoil originating from the US sub-prime crisis. The two facts – the structural crisis and the recent severe economic and financial difficulties – are intimately inter-related. Thus, a short-term stabilization policy is not adequate to solve the problems, and may even, if badly conceived, worsen them. A crucial change in basic economic trends, a structural break, took place in Italy in 1973, when there was the first great energy crisis and a deepening of the decline of the 'Fordist model of growth' (on this concept, see Valli 2010a).

As Table 10.1 shows, in the 1973–2012 period the rates of growth of population, real GDP, per capita GDP and real investment sharply decreased. Population growth strongly decelerated and the low annual rate of growth of population (+ 0.3) was almost completely due to net immigration. While in the first period (1951–73) Italy had been a net emigration country, in the years 1973–2012 it has become a net-immigration

Table 10.1 *The structural break in the trends of the Italian economy: 1951–2012 (average annual compound percentage rates of change)*

	1951–73	1973–2012
Population	0.7	0.3
Real GDP (in PPPs Geary Khamis)	5.6	1.7
Real per capita GDP (in PPPs Geary Khamis)	4.9	1.4
Real gross investment	6.3	1.2

Sources: Maddison (2007), Conference Board-GGDC (2013, available at http//:www.conference-board.org/data/economydatabase), Istat for investment.

Table 10.2   Italy's economy: the declining trend (1951–2012)

	1951–73	1973–80	1980–90	1990–2000	2000–07	2007–12
Real GDP*	5.6	3.5	2.2	1.6	0.8	−1.4
Real per capita GDP*	4.9	3.1	1.7	1.3	0.7	−1.8
Real gross investment	6.3	2.1	2.2	1.3	1.8	−5.0

Note: * in PPP Geary Khamis.

Sources: Conference Board-GGDC (2013, available at http//:www.conference-board.org/
data/economydatabase), Istat for investment.

country. Moreover, while in the 1951–73 period in Italy real GDP, real per capita GDP and real investment grew faster than in most other industrialized countries, from 1973 onwards they grew much less, and their decline was intensified in the 1990s and the 2000s (Table 10.2).

As Table 10.2 and Table 10A.1 of the appendix show, in Italy the recent crisis has been particularly severe. The fall of real GDP has been worse than in most other industrialized countries, with the exception of Greece and Iceland, while the rate of unemployment has greatly increased, although less than in Spain, Greece and Ireland.

2.   SOME DETERMINANTS OF THE STRUCTURAL BREAK

Why, around 1973, was there a structural break in Italy's economic trends? Firstly, there was a factor common to most other industrialized countries, namely the end of the era of cheap oil. Up to the first great energy crisis, in 1973 oil was bought by Italy and most other industrialized countries at very low prices. In the 1951–73 period the prices of manufactured goods had increased much more than oil prices, notwithstanding the 1956 temporary price hike due to the Suez crisis. Among the major industrialized countries, Italy was the one which most heavily depended on oil and gas imports. Thus, Italy was also the economy which most benefited from the low cost of oil up to 1973, but which was most heavily struck by the following periods of higher cost of oil, natural gas and other raw materials.

Secondly, at the end of the 1960s and at the beginning of the 1970s in Italy there was an almost complete fading of Gerschenkron's advantages of 'relative economic backwardness' (Gerschenkron 1962). In the 1950s and 1960s, Italy had greatly benefited from the possibility of transferring large masses of workers from low productivity sectors, such as agriculture, to higher productivity ones, such as industrial and service sectors, and from poorer Southern regions to the Centre-North. Moreover, Italy's productive system had reduced the productivity and technological gap if compared with the United States and the other most industrialized countries, buying or imitating more advanced technologies. In the 1951–73 period the rate of growth of investment had been higher than in most other industrialized countries, Japan and the four Asian tigers excluded. Hence, Italy could massively import foreign capital goods incorporating advanced technologies. It was, therefore, possible to rapidly increase the level of labour productivity and technology. However, from 1973 onwards, the rate of growth of real investment has dramatically slowed down and has become inferior to the average rate of growth of other major industrialized countries.

Thirdly, at the end of the 1960s and the start of the 1970s there was in Italy, as well as in other industrialized countries, the beginning of a radical crisis of 'Fordism' or of the 'Fordist model of development' (on these two concepts and their differences, see Valli 2010a. On Fordism and the French regulation school, see, for example, Aglietta 1976, Boyer 1990). This crisis was due to many factors, but among them, a brisk decrease of economies of scale and of scope; a slowing down in the growth of demand for important durable consumer goods, such as automobiles and electrical domestic appliances; deep technological and organizational changes; and a great rise in conflicts in industrial relations. This crisis led to a pronounced decrease in the rate of growth of labour productivity and to a rise in the inflation rate, which the 1973 energy crisis and the depreciation of the Italian currency greatly amplified. Moreover, in the 1970s or in the following decades, Italy registered five other basic changes: a strong slowing down in the rate of growth of population, a de-industrialization process, a relative technological decline, a sharp rise in wage and income differentials, and a structural worsening in the balance of current accounts and in public finance.

3. THE DEMOGRAPHIC FACTOR

As with many other industrialized countries, but faster than most of them, Italy has passed from the baby-boom in the post-war period, to a sharply declining trend in birth and mortality rates (Valli and Saccone 2011). From 1974 onwards these trends led to a reduction of the average annual rate of growth of population from 0.7 per cent in 1951–73 to 0.3 in the years 1973–2012, and to a rapid ageing of population. At present Italy has one of the oldest populations in the world, close to Japan, one of the world's lowest fertility rates and one of the highest life expectations at birth.

Excessive ageing determines various negative aspects on economic growth:

- a rising dependency rate (a declining or stagnant active population has to support an increasing number of elderly people and this over-compensates for the consequences of a reduced number of children);
- an economic policy tending to favour older people, given the fact that voters aged over 40 years are more numerous than people aged between 18 and 40;
- less innovative drive and relatively less investment in knowledge;
- declining entrepreneurial dynamism;
- greater caution in consumption and saving decisions and a lower propensity to make risky real investment;
- relatively declining expenditures in new kindergartens, schools, residential buildings, etc.;
- growing expenditure in pensions, health care, personal assistance to elderly people, with negative consequences on public budget and public debt, etc.

4.   DE-INDUSTRIALIZATION AND THE BALANCE OF PAYMENTS

With a considerable delay compared to early industrializing countries such as the United Kingdom and the United States, Italy – a late-comer country – began its de-industrialization process during the 1970s. The share of industry in total GDP began to gradually fall after 1974, while the total number of people employed in industrial activities began to decline in the 1980s. As Table 10.3 shows, this de-industrialization trend has also continued in recent years. Employment in industry as a percentage of total employment has diminished from 30.7 per cent in 2004 to 27.7 per cent in 2012.

Being strongly dependent on imports of raw materials (oil, natural gas, coal, iron ore, copper, etc.) and having registered also, since the late 1950s, a considerable deficit in agriculture and the food industry, Italy was obliged to focus its productive system on the production and export of manufactured goods in order to try reaching a difficult equilibrium in the balance of current accounts. As regards exportable services, the traditional positive balance in tourism has gradually diminished, while for other services such as software, consultancy to firms, insurance, flights, etc., the deficit has risen. The de-industrialization process has reduced

Table 10.3   Employment in the Italian economy by sector (per cent)

Sectors	2004	2012
Agriculture, forestry, fisheries	4.4	3.7
Industry excluding construction	22.5	20.1
Construction	8.2	7.6
Total Industry	30.7	27.7
Services	64.9	68.6
Total	100.0	100.0

Source: Bank of Italy (2013, p.72).

the share of exportable goods and services in total GDP or employment, also because a large part of services are not exportable: they must be used within the country. Ageing of the population worsened the situation, because it greatly increased the needs of elderly people for health care and personal assistance, partly provided by foreign workers.

De-industrialization is one of the explanations for the structural difficulties in the balance of current account that occurred in Italy and in several industrialized countries (with the notable exception of Germany and Japan) which have struggled to maintain a large industrial basis. Italy too has tried to maintain a large industrial basis, but with much less success, especially with its growing weakness in medium and high technology industry (see next paragraph). In 2010, after nine consecutive years of deficits in the current account of the balance of payments, Italy's deficit had risen to 54.5 billion euros, 3.6 per cent of GDP. In 2011, and especially in 2012, the deficit has decreased mainly because of the decline in imports of goods and services due to the heavy fall in consumption and investment. There was also some recovery in exports, and notably in the food and wine industry, so that the deficit in the current account diminished to 8.4 billion euros in 2012.

In the 1973–96 period, Italy's productive system had been able to maintain in the mid-term the equilibrium in the overall balance of payments only by means of repeated devaluations of the Italian lira[1] or an increased recourse to external debt. However, from 1996 onwards, because of the attempt to enter the euro-zone, Italy could no longer make recourse to the devaluation of the lira, and naturally that policy has not been possible

---

[1] The accumulation of heavy deficits in the current account of the balance of payments determined a severe currency crisis in September 1992, which led to a strong and prolonged devaluation of the Italian lira and the consequent return to a small surplus in the current account in the years 1993–99.

since the introduction of the euro in 1999. The 23 per cent appreciation of the euro relative to the US dollar from 1999 up to mid-2013 has contributed to the reduction of Italy's exports growth to the United States and to the countries with a rate of exchange more or less linked to the dollar, but has helped to contain inflationary pressures.

It must be noticed that since 1973, Italy has become a net-immigration country. Thus, the net positive balance between the inflows of remittances from Italians working abroad and the outflows from foreign immigrants working in Italy has diminished. Moreover, while Italy had traditionally registered a positive surplus in the services section of the balance of payments, mainly due to tourism, from 2002 onwards the services balance has become structurally negative. The positive balance on tourism has diminished over time and other branches of services, such as transport, insurance, communication and services to the firms, have registered a structurally growing deficit, while the interest payments to foreign holders of Italian bonds have continued to grow. In these conditions – scarce ability to enter new high-tech sectors both in industry and in services; reduced growth of labour productivity, partly due to the semi-stagnation in real investment and in R&D activities; no possibility to use currency devaluation – the Italian productive system has registered heavy deficits in the balance of current account in the 2000s, therefore accumulating a growing stock of net external debt, which has risen to 54.2 per cent of GDP in the third quarter of 2012 (Eurostat 2013a).

5.   RELATIVE TECHNOLOGICAL DECLINE

Since 1973 Italy's rate of growth in real investment has strongly decreased, becoming lower than the rate of growth of major industrialized and emerging countries. This has severely reduced the access to incorporated technological progress, which had been very important in the 1951–73 period. Thus, to avoid a relative technological decline, a great change in economic policy, based on an extremely rapid rise in human capital and knowledge, would have been necessary (on Italy's fragile policy on knowledge, see, for example, Visco 2009. On university policy see Geuna and Rossi 2013).

This change did not occur, because of the myopic choices of politicians and entrepreneurs. Expenditure in R&D activities has remained very low, around 1.1–1.2 per cent of GDP, while most major industrialized countries had a ratio of between 2.5 and 3.7 per cent. Expenditures in the university system and the number of university graduates as a percentage of the population, though gradually rising up to 2007, have remained much lower than in other major industrialized countries. Moreover, after the 2008–09 financial crisis, substantial cuts in public funding of schools, universities and R&D, and the scarce importance given to quality improvement in the education system, contributed to further worsen Italy's relative position for human capital and to accelerate Italy's brain drain towards other countries.

Finally, the Italian productive system is mainly based on small and medium-sized enterprises concentrated in traditional sectors. Because of their nature, and the myopic choices of their owners or managers, Italian firms have continued to spend very little on R&D. Moreover, Italy has been unable to improve, or conserve, its relative position in medium and high technology sectors (information and communications technology (ICT), chemicals, pharmaceuticals, etc.) and to attract a substantial amount of foreign direct investment (FDI) in technologically advanced sectors. Some important exceptions come from the production of specialized machines and from helicopters and aircraft components, in which Italy has maintained a good competitiveness in the world markets, from the wide international presence of ENI and ENEL in oil and energy industries, from the acquisition of Chrysler by the Fiat group and from the large presence of Generali (insurance), Intesa-S.Paolo and Unicredit (banking) in Eastern European countries.

However, Italy has been unable to continue producing, after Olivetti's deep crisis, significant volumes of PCs, faxes, printers and tablets. Moreover, it has been unable to enter the market of mobile phones, although the Italian–French corporation, ST microelectronics, has maintained a good presence in the production of specialized chips, including the ones utilized in mobile phones. After the collapse of its main chemical corporations, Montedison and Enichem, and the passage to foreign capital of its major pharmaceutical groups, Lepetit and Farmitalia-Carlo Erba, Italy has also registered a large increase in the foreign dependence for chemical and pharmaceutical products. Thanks mainly to the effort of several medium and small-sized firms, Italy has remained the third major chemical producer in the European Union, at a distance from Germany and France, but it has a negative sectorial trade balance and has been surpassed in output by emerging giants like China and Brazil and by South Korea, a smaller, but more dynamic country.

Finally, Italy is also a large net importer of products and services relating to green technologies, owing to the uncertainties and delays of its policy in this field. Weakness in medium and high technology leads to a reduced possibility of product innovation and of entering the most dynamic markets, where demand, productivity, wages and profits grow more rapidly. Moreover, in Italy there are relatively weak processes of

Table 10.4   Employment, wages, productivity and unemployment rates in
Italy

	1951–73	1973–2012
Total employment*	−0.1	0.5
Real wages*	4.8	1.0
Real labour productivity (real GDP per person employed)*	5.5	1.2
	1973	2013 Q1
Unemployment rate (%)	6.4	12.8
Youth unemployment rate (15–24 years)		41.9

Note: * annual average rates of change.

Sources: Conference Board-GGDC (2013, available at http//:www.conference-board.org/data/economydatabase), Istat, Bank of Italy (2013) for wages and the unemployment rates.

learning-by-doing in advanced sectors for the labour force, and in particular for younger workers, and this contributes to the long-run decline in productivity growth (Table 10.4). Lower profits and the slowing down in aggregate demand reduced the rate of growth in investment. The industrial firms have concentrated their effort mainly in intensive investment and process innovations, reducing extensive investment and product innovation (Valli 1999), thus diminishing the growth of output and employment in manufacturing. Employment grew principally in services activities, some of them characterized by relatively low wages, precarious jobs and the large recourse to irregular labour, mainly provided by immigrants or indigenous young people. There has also been an exceedingly slow penetration into modern services, where demand, profits, productivity and wages grow more rapidly than in traditional services.

There is a sort of vicious circle: low rates of growth of real investment and low expenditure in knowledge lead to a relative technological decline, to a declining trend in productivity, wages and aggregate demand and thus to declining investment rates and fewer public and private resources to be employed for the growth of knowledge. However, Italy's fall into this vicious circle is largely due to wrong development policies. Countries such as South Korea, which in 1973 was much poorer than Italy, made very different strategic choices, rapidly improving basic education, university and R&D activities and obtaining, in the long run, much better economic results (Valli 2010b).

6. GLOBALIZATION AND THE RISE IN INEQUALITIES

From the 1970s onwards, Italy has registered a deep globalization process and, after some years of delay, a relevant increase in wages, income and wealth inequalities. Table 10.5 shows some important aspects of the globalization process. In Italy the degree of openness[2] has increased from 18.4 per cent in 1973 to 29.7 per cent in 2012. The inward stock of FDI as a percentage of GDP has increased to 17.7 per cent in 2012, while the outward stock went up to 28.1 per cent. In the 1973–2012 years, Italy has thus greatly increased its commercial openness and its productive interconnection with other economies, although it has been unable to attract large amounts of FDI. Italy has also considerably reduced the level of its tariff and non-tariff barriers. Moreover, it has enormously increased capital movements, especially after the almost total liberalization of capital flows decided in the 1980s and the banking and insurance liberalization taking place in the European Union after the great unified market of 1992. Economic globalization and financial globalization have moved together in the last decades, with important consequences both on the productive system and on Italy's financial system.

In the 1990s and 2000s, economic globalization has powerfully contributed to the diminishing of inflationary pressure, thanks to the growing imports of cheaper goods and services coming from China, India and other emerging countries, and the increased competition in the world market for many goods and services. However, in several industrialized countries, economic globalization has also contributed to a rapid de-industrialization and de-localization process and, together with financial globalization,

Table 10.5   Globalization and the Italian economy: some indicators

	1973	2012
Degree of openness	18.4	29.7
Stock of outwards FDI (% of GDP)		28.1
Stock of inward FDI (% of GDP)		17.7
Stock of outward portfolio investment (% of GDP)		50.6
Stock of inward portfolio investment (% of GDP), 2008		73.2

Source: Eurostat first row, Bank of Italy (2013, pp.44, 99), UNCTAD (2013).

---

[2] The degree of openness is measured by the sum of exports and imports divided by two, as a percentage of GDP.

to enlarged wage and income differentials. In fact, various forms of de-localization or of 'fragmentation of production' in multinational corporations have led to the concentration of a great part of top management and some important functions (R&D, product design, finance and central administration, marketing, etc.) in headquarters, while distributing growing sections of the productive process to different countries. This has contributed to the maintaining of large profits and generous compensations and stock-options to the top managers of multinational corporations, along with growing wages to the upper part of the white-collar workers working in the headquarters. However, blue-collar workers have often registered stagnation in their real wages, due to the pressure coming from the competition of migrant workers or from the managers' menace of closing plants and transferring production to low-wage countries. Moreover, because of the sweeping liberalization of capital movements, investors now had three options: make real investment in their firms, buy real estate or buy financial assets in the world markets. Often, especially in periods of real crisis in a country, the third option resulted, being more convenient than the first one, thus, strongly reducing the propensity to make inland productive investment. While in Keynes's time low interest rates generally led to higher domestic investment, now they often lead to more de-localization or more speculation in financial assets.

Globalization has led to more uncertainty and instability in firms' decisions, and thus to a rise in the need for greater flexibility in the labour force. In Italy this has induced the Parliament to pass two laws[3], which have increased labour flexibility and employment, but have contributed to the reduction of investment in human capital by the firms and to the decline of the rate of productivity growth (Damiani and Pompei 2010) and have created a large mass of precarious and low-paid jobs, especially among young people. Financial globalization has further increased wage inequalities, enriching in the expansive phases top managers and main operators of financial institutions, but damaging in the succeeding crises hundreds of millions of people in a large part of the world, millions of enterprises and entire countries. There has been an increase in economic instability in the world economy through a series of financial crises, which have contributed to the generation of real crises. These crises have slowed down development and worsened public finance, reducing the resources available for social interventions and development policies. Finally, in the 1980–2013 period, in several industrialized countries, Italy included, real interest rates were positive and in some years strongly positive and higher than the rate of growth of real GDP. In this case the growth of financial rents tended to exceed

---

[3]   Treu's law in 1997 and Biagi's law in 2003.

Table 10.6   Gini index of income inequality in selected countries

Countries	mid-80s	mid-90s	mid-2000s	Late 2000s (a)
Austria	0.24	0.24	0.27	0.26
Denmark	0.22	0.21	0.23	0.25
Finland	0.21	0.23	0.27	0.26
France	0.30	0.28	0.29	0.29
Germany	0.25	0.27	0.29	0.30
Italy	0.31	0.35	0.35	0.34
Netherlands	0.27	0.30	0.28	0.29
Spain	0.37	0.34	0.32	0.32
Sweden	0.20	0.21	0.23	0.26
United Kingdom	0.29	0.31	0.33	0.35
United States	0.34	0.36	0.38	0.38

Note: (a) Year 2008.

Source: OECD (2011).

the rate of growth of the economy, and this contributed to the increase of inequalities, because rich people generally have higher volumes of financial assets than the middle class and poor people (Atkinson *et al.* 2011).

For all these reasons there has been in Italy a sharp increase in inequalities, both among households and among regions, in the last three decades. OECD's statistics show that Italy's Gini coefficient on income distribution after taxes and transfers has risen from 0.31 in the mid-1980s to 0.34 in 2008, reaching one of the highest levels in Western Europe (Table 10.6).

In the same period there has been in Italy, as well as in most other industrialized countries, a rise in wage inequalities, especially in favour of top managers, entrepreneurs, high-level lawyers, firm consultants and top public servants, while many blue-collar workers and young workers had to accept low wages and often precarious jobs. Wealth inequalities in Italy, as in most other major countries, are higher than income inequalities and have risen in the last three decades. Regional economic differences, which at the beginning of the 1950s were, in Italy, particularly wide, have remained very large, though moving over time in alternate directions.

7.   PUBLIC DEBT AND EXTERNAL DEBT

In 1973 public finance was in relatively good shape in Italy. Public deficit as a percentage of GDP was relatively low and public debt as a percentage of

GDP was 50.6 per cent, lower than the 60 per cent threshold that would be established as a Maastricht parameter in 1992. However, policy decisions and structural factors contributed to rapidly rising public expenditure. In 1978 it was decided to create a comprehensive public health service, which was very important for society, but more costly than the previous limited health system. The public pension system was strengthened and began to distribute increasingly over-generous allowances, due to the fact that in the 1970s there was a distributive mechanism, a large number of young workers and a limited number of retiring people. The school and university system registered a rapid rise in the number of students, due to the delayed effect of the baby-boom of the 1960s, the rise in the length of schooling and the liberalization of university access decided in 1969. So, public expenditure in schools and universities rose rapidly, though starting from relatively low levels. However, in the 1973–81 period, the rapid rise in public expenditure was almost wholly compensated for by a rapid rise in fiscal revenues, partly due to the large 'fiscal drag' made possible by the high rate of inflation. Moreover, in a great part of the 1970s, real interest rates were negative. Thus, in 1981 the public debt/GDP ratio increased only to 58.5 per cent (Table 10.7).

The real catastrophic rise in public debt took place in the 1982–94 period, when the public debt/GDP ratio went up rapidly to 121.8 per cent. In the 1982–92 years, the government introduced a truly devastating economic policy allowing fiscal revenues to increase much less than public expenditures, thus amplifying public deficit and public debt. After Italy's acute currency crisis in September 1992, the government adopted a severe restrictive economic policy, but the expanding mass of interest paid on the huge stock of public debt continued to determine a rise in the debt/ GDP ratio up to 1994. The massive deterioration in public finance of the 1982–92 years had been largely due to government's laxity. A compromise between the ruling Christian-Democratic and Socialist parties temporarily increased the rate of growth of the economy by rapidly increasing public expenditure without levying adequate taxes, but this contributed heavily to a rapid rise of inflation, public deficit and public debt. Moreover, the rapid rise of real interest rates in international financial markets, due to Reagan's economic policy in the first half of the 1980s, determined the passage, in many countries, from negative to positive real interest rates, and this contributed to the increase in interest payments on Italy's public bonds.

Finally, the ageing of population led to a rapid rise in expenditures for pensions and health services. In the 1990s and 2000s this obliged the government to introduce a series of reforms in the pension system (with a gradual passage from the distributive mechanism to the one based on the accumulation of contributions and the rise of pension age), which tried to reduce the rate of growth of pension disbursements.

Meanwhile, Italy has not succeeded in reducing the two great structural weaknesses of its fiscal system, namely the large size of its irregular or submerged economy and the high rate of tax evasion. The submerged economy is at present estimated at around 17 per cent of total GDP, while annual total tax evasion amounts to about 120 billion euros, and in the 1980s and 1990s the relative importance of these two phenomena was not far from these levels. While, because of tax evasion, many people and many firms paid much lower taxes and social contributions than the majority of taxpayers, the latter had to pay very high tax rates. Therefore, any further increase of taxation or social contributions was scarcely popular. The centre-left governments tried to reduce tax evasion, while Berlusconi's centre-right governments were at first rather lax against tax evasion and tried to reduce both public expenditure and the tax burden. However, when in 2010–11 the crisis of public finance had become extremely dangerous, Berlusconi's government also had to increase taxation and try reducing evasion, and the succeeding Monti's government continued to raise taxation, mainly through a local tax on buildings (IMU) and an increase in the rate of VAT and the tax on oil products.

As Table 10.7 shows, the public debt /GDP ratio, after a period of rapid increase up to the level of 121.8 per cent in 1994, had a gradually declining trend to 103.3 per cent in 2007, due to several periods of restrictive monetary and fiscal policies. However, in the recent crisis, the ratio went up again to 127.0 per cent in 2012, largely because of the fall in GDP. It

Table 10.7   Public debt in percentage of GDP in Italy: 1980–2012

Years	%	Years	%	Years	%
1980	56.1	1991	98.6	2002	105.7
1981	58.5	1992	105.5	2003	104.1
1982	63.1	1993	115.7	2004	103.7
1983	69.4	1994	121.8	2005	105.7
1984	74.9	1995	121.5	2006	106.3
1985	80.9	1996	120.9	2007	103.3
1986	85.1	1997	118.1	2008	106.1
1987	89.1	1998	114.9	2009	116.4
1988	90.8	1999	113.7	2010	119.3
1989	93.3	2000	109.2	2011	120.8
1990	95.2	2001	108.8	2012	127.0

Sources: Francese and Pace (2008), Bank of Italy (2013, p.154).

must be noticed that the ratio has remained in any case well above the Maastricht parameter of 60 per cent, and that the share of public debt owned by foreign residents or institutions has gradually risen to over 35 per cent (Bank of Italy 2013).

Though the public debt/GDP ratio is considered an important indicator, and has been extensively used by the European Union and by major rating agencies for the assessment of the financial solidity of a country, its rationale is rather weak. Firstly, it is a ratio based on a stock value as the numerator and a flow value as the denominator, while it would be much better to use two stock values (for example, the ratio of public debt to wealth). Secondly, it considers only public debt, overlooking private debt, whose situation considerably differs among countries and in Italy is better than in several other industrialized countries. Thirdly, it is a ratio and, therefore, when in an economic crisis and GDP falls, the ratio increases, and this can induce the government into making severe macro-economic restrictive policies, which can further reduce real GDP, amplifying and prolonging the recession. This will reduce tax revenues, and thus increase public deficit, and so on, in a vicious circle very difficult to break. The recession in a country can, moreover, decrease its imports and so the exports and the aggregate demand of other countries, diminishing both their GDP and their tax revenues and thus increasing their debt/GDP ratio. Restrictive policies pursued in the same years in several EU countries can have cumulative negative effects, due to the high economic interconnections existing between those countries.

Finally, it must be stressed that the same level of public debt/GDP ratio may apply to very different financial situations, depending on what proportion of the public debt is owned by foreign or national residents and on the situation regarding private wealth, private net debt and the balance of current account. In fact, a country like Japan, which in 2012 had the highest level of public debt/GDP ratio in the world (214 per cent), is not considered to be in financial trouble by the world financial markets for four main reasons: Japan has almost all its public debt in the possession of national residents (Japanese households or institutions); it maintains a structural surplus in the balance of current accounts; it is the top net creditor country in the world financial market; and it has a huge net private wealth. On the contrary, Greece has a lower debt/GDP ratio than Japan, but it has public bonds mainly in the hands of foreign residents, a balance of current accounts in structural deficit, a net debtor position and a private wealth concentrated in relatively few families. Thus, Greece is considered to be in a much weaker situation than Japan and has been exposed to huge speculative pressures since 2010. Italy is in an intermediate position: it has a large public debt/GDP ratio, around 127 per cent in 2012, but lower than in Japan and Greece; a relatively small public deficit, at about 3 per cent of GDP in 2012; a structural deficit in the balance of current accounts; and a consistent net debtor position as a percentage of GDP. But all these indicators are much better than those of Greece and there is a large private wealth and a relatively low private debt for households.

8. FROM FINANCIAL CRISIS TO A REAL CRISIS

In 2007, in the United States there was the great sub-prime crisis and the beginnings of a devastating financial crisis, which in 2008 rapidly spread to the EU and to other industrialized countries (on the main determinants of the financial crisis see, for example, Attali 2008, Valli 2010a, Chapter 8, and Stiglitz 2010). The crisis had a less negative impact on major emerging countries (China, India, Brazil, etc.), which had relatively fewer financial interconnections with the United States, although China had become the most important foreign holder of US public bonds. In 2008–2009, in the United States and in Europe the financial crisis worsened after the bankruptcy of Lehman Brothers on September 15, 2008. The indexes in major stock exchanges collapsed and there were severe liquidity problems for all banks, but especially for the banks more exposed to 'toxic' assets and risky derivatives. Massive public interventions in the United States, in Europe and in China reduced the scope and intensity of the financial crisis, but badly worsened the conditions of public finance in several industrialized countries, because of the enormous costs of intervention.

In 2008–09 the great financial crisis led to a severe recession in the real variables of the economy (real GDP, investment, consumption, exports, employment, etc.). Many mechanisms cooperated in transforming the financial crisis into a real crisis. The core of this process was the *relation between stocks and flows*. This relation is largely overlooked in economic literature, although it has been at the basis of other great financial and real crises, as for example in Japan at the end of the 1980s and in the 1990s. If, on the medium to long run, there is the gradual creation of a *structural bubble* both in the real estate market and in the stock exchange market, it is sufficient for a 20–30 per cent fall in the price of houses and shares to determine explosive negative wealth effects, which may have dramatic consequences on consumption, investment, bank accounts, GDP and employment. There is a painful negative feedback. The reduction of wealth, a stock concept, generates a reduction of flows, such as GDP, consumption and investment, and this leads to a further reduction of wealth, and so on.

When in the summer and autumn of 2008, as a result of the US financial crisis, most European banks began to feel a large lack of liquidity (a 'liquidity crunch'), they tried to reduce loans or increase their price. At the same time the value of the 'collaterals' given to the banks as a guarantee for loans was rapidly decreasing. Prices of housing had fallen badly, not only in the United States, but also in Spain, Ireland, the United Kingdom and other countries where there had previously been a huge structural bubble. Shares and many financial assets had lost a large part of their market value. Banks were no more covered by the value of collaterals. So they reduced credit and this led to a severe fall in real investment and aggregate demand. This contributed to feeding the recession and, therefore, to increased failures and non-performing loans, further worsening the banks' situation and reducing their propensity to make credits to firms.

There was a large negative 'wealth effect'. The fall in the prices of houses and financial assets decreased the value of wealth. There was, therefore, the tendency to reduce consumption and aggregate demand. The simultaneous crisis of other industrialized countries reduced exports and aggregate demand. The sharp reduction in aggregate demand caused by the fall in investment, consumption and net exports, badly worsened the expectations of entrepreneurs, further reducing investment. Following some delay after the decline of production, there was, in most industrialized countries, also a sharp reduction in employment and often in real wages. This decreased total wages and, therefore, diminished consumption. The fall in real GDP led to a fall in tax revenues, while the rise in unemployment compensations or other social measures increased public expenditures. This raised public deficit and public debt, later inducing governments to raise taxes or cut other sections of public expenditure, with negative consequences on total wages, employment, consumption, investment and real GDP.

In years of deep recession such as 2009, there has been an increase in public deficit and public debt and a fall in GDP, and this has rapidly increased the public deficit/GDP and the public debt/GDP ratios in several countries, including Italy, because the numerator of the ratios had risen and the denominator had decreased. In several countries the government had to lavishly finance banking and insurance companies in order to avoid the collapse of the system. This worsened public finance, badly deteriorating the international public financial situation and reducing the possibility for most governments to make other massive interventions in the future. In Italy the recourse of banks to government's aid was limited, since major banks, with the partial exception of Monte Paschi di Siena, were relatively solid and less exposed to toxic assets and risky derivatives. However, there was a rapid increase in public debt, essentially due to the sharp reduction in real GDP. The rise in the debt/GDP ratio exposed governments bonds to a decline in rating. Italian banks too, which had a consistent and growing proportion of their assets invested in Italy's public bonds, registered a decline in rating and needed to further re-capitalize in order to reduce the risk of default.

The combination of all these factors led to a severe economic crisis in the real variables of the economy (investment, consumption, public expenditure, employment, etc.). The recession was harsher in the countries where the pre-2007 structural bubble in finance or in housing had been greater, as in Iceland, Ireland and Spain, and where public finance or the current account of the balance of payments were worse, as in Greece, Portugal, Italy and some Eastern European countries. In all these countries, it was particularly difficult to introduce anti-cyclical expansionary policies to attenuate the consequences of the fall in aggregate demand. Moreover, anti-Keynesian neoclassical views were prevailing in most countries and were imbedded in the incongruous and rigid Maastricht parameters and ECB statute. The United States, whose financial system was primarily responsible for the global crisis, could react better than most EU countries, thanks to the privileged role of the dollar as the key currency in the international monetary system and its more expansionary monetary and fiscal policies. However, the massive financial public aid given to banks, insurance companies and some industrial groups (such as GM and Chrysler) has badly worsened the US public deficit and public debt.

In the years 2010–13, several industrialized countries began to recover, but other countries, which had a less solid public finance situation, continued their slump and were exposed to increasing pressures from the financial markets. Greece was the first EU country that could not recover in 2010–11 to suffer from massive adverse speculation. The weakness of Greece was due to various factors: a) its statistical data had been repeatedly falsified in order to enter the euro-zone and to show a better economic performance; b) Greece has a low-productivity agriculture and a relatively small industrial sector, with a large service sector, mainly based on public administration, tourism and the earnings of the shipping industry; c) Greece has registered a structural deficit in the current account of the balance of payments since the 1980s and, consequently, a large and growing external debt; d) the great majority of its public bonds had been in the possession of foreign banks and other foreign investors.

When the 2008–09 global crisis hit Greece, real investment collapsed, tourism and transport revenues shrank badly, real GDP and employment fell and unemployment rose rapidly. The public deficit/GDP ratio almost doubled, passing from −5.4 per cent in 2007 to −10.5 per cent in 2010 and −10 per cent in 2012. The public debt/ GDP per ratio rose briskly from 105.4 per cent in 2007 to 156.9 per cent in 2012. In 2010 the confidence in

Greek public bonds had collapsed, so that new issues of bonds were made at high and dramatically growing interest rates. The Greek government desperately tried to cut public expenditure and wages and begin a vast privatization programme, but the brutal cuts in public expenditure and the rapid rise in unemployment, and in particular in youth unemployment, led to severe political tensions and a growing social unrest. The answer of EU authorities and the ECB to the deep crisis of Greece, a member of the euro-zone, was very slow and hesitant. While the speculative attacks on Greece had been evident since the end of 2009, internal political worries induced the German Prime Minister, Angela Merkel, to procrastinate from taking action for several crucial months. The long inactivity of the EU on the Greek crisis led to a heavy fall in the value of the euro. From November 2009 to June 2010 the exchange rate of a euro to a US dollar rose from 0.670 to 0.819, later fluctuating around 0.720–0.770. However, in a closer analysis we can find that in 2012 the rate of exchange had merely returned in proximity to the 2007 average level, and it was close to the ratio of euro-zone–US purchasing power parity (PPP). Since the crisis struck the United States first and then the euro-zone, in 2008 the US dollar was indeed too weak and the euro was thus strongly overvalued, while from autumn 2010 onwards the euro has returned to a lower and more sustainable level.

At last, on May 9, 2010, the EU decided to create a badly needed financial special vehicle (the *European Financial Stability Facility*, EFSF), finally ratified on October 13, 2011, which conceded to Greece some loans, subject to very severe constraints: strong restrictive fiscal policy, massive privatizations, etc. However, the harsh restrictive measures contributed to the further reduction of real investment, consumption and GDP, sharply increasing unemployment, creating social unrest and prolonging the fall of the economy in the years 2010–13. In the meantime, the European Central Bank (ECB) had indirectly sustained Greece, buying Greek public bonds on the secondary market and supporting foreign banks (mainly French and German ones) holding large quantities of Greek bonds.

However, the delays and hesitation of the EU on the Greek case had led to a contagion effect, favouring massive speculative attacks on other financially weak members of the euro-zone: Ireland, Portugal, Spain and Italy. Credit default swaps (CDS) on their sovereign debt became more expensive and there was a marked rise in the spread of interest rates of the public bonds of these countries if compared with German bonds. This induced the EFSF to also intervene in support of Ireland, Portugal and the Spanish banking system, while Spain's and Italy's problems obliged the increase of the guarantees and the lending capacity of the EFSF. The ECB provided massive liquidity to EU banks, which could buy a great bulk of national public bonds, thus reducing the spreads. However, this contributed to weakening the confidence of international financial markets in some of the major banks of financially weaker countries.

9.   ITALY AND THE CRISIS

The Italian economy entered the 2008–09 crisis under the heavy burden of its structural imbalances. Unfortunately, its centre-right government seemed not to be fully aware of the danger of a collision between these long-standing problems and the dire consequences of the global financial crisis. In the second half of 2008 and in 2009 there was an overly optimistic approach, which tried to conceal the worse aspects of the crisis, hoping for a rapid recovery. In 2009–11 the Economy Minister, Giulio Tremonti, tried to avoid an excessive increase of public deficit with cuts in public expenditures and increases in taxation, which contributed to the depression of aggregate demand and real GDP. Very little was done to sustain economic growth or to face the structural problems of the country. Heavy cuts in school, university and research funds even worsened the mid-term perspectives for the future. As Table 10A.1 shows, in Italy there was a deep recession in 2008–09 and a very weak and partial recovery in 2010 and in the first part of 2011, while from the second half of 2011 through to 2013 the financial difficulties and the more restrictive fiscal policies led the economy into a new economic depression.

In mid-2011 the depth of the crisis and the difficulties in the recovery could not be denied any longer. There were some hasty attempts to introduce measures in order to reduce the public deficit/GDP ratio and the debt/GDP ratio. The objective of reaching structural equilibrium in the public budget was anticipated to happen in 2013, instead of 2014, so that large taxation rises (an increase of VAT from 20 per cent to 21 per cent; the introduction of IMU, a local tax on housing; etc.) and further public expenditure cuts were announced. However, the worsening of GDP expectations due to macro-economic restrictive policies and the rise of interest rates due to growing financial tensions contributed to strongly reducing the positive effects on Italy's deficit/GDP ratio, while the debt/GDP ratio continued to rise. The confidence in Italy's sovereign debt declined, Italy's public bonds ratings were reduced and the spread of Italy's interest rates of ten-years public bonds (BTP), if compared with similar German bonds, rose to a maximum of 532 basis points on November 9, 2011. The fading political confidence in Berlusconi's centre-right government, the rising spread and the worsening public finance led to the passage to a new, predominantly 'technical' government, headed by Mario Monti, and sustained by a hybrid coalition of a centre-right party (PDL) and centre-left ones (mainly PD and UDC). Monti's government lasted from November 16, 2011, to April 27, 2013, but was politically effective only up to December 2012, when PDL announced the intention to retire its political support. In 2011–12 Monti's administration took harsh measures in order to reduce public deficit and restore the confidence of the international financial markets. It introduced a new pension reform, extending both the contribution system and the retirement age and suspending the price indexation of higher pensions. This reform ensured remarkable savings in pension disbursements, but led to social unrest, especially because it did not give enough coverage to a large part of so-called *esodati*, namely people who had just left work expecting to immediately receive a pension and had instead to wait for pension payments for some years because of the sharp increase in retirement age. The pension reform, heavy tax rises (the already announced 1 per cent increase in VAT tax rate, a large rise in taxation on oil and natural gas and the introduction of IMU instead of ICI), together with further cuts in public expenditure, contributed to re-establishing the confidence of international markets and reducing both public deficit and the spread. However, these measures, not accompanied by a sufficient stimulus to growth, contributed to further depressing the economy, to a reduction of real GDP and to an increase of the public debt/GDP ratio.

A controversial, albeit timid, labour reform did not solve the problems of the excessive recourse of the firms to precarious jobs. The imposition of more rigid legal constraints and higher social contributions reduced the convenience of hiring young people on a temporary basis, but the severe economic crisis led to a reduction both of temporary and stable jobs. Also, the improvement in the apprenticeship regulations did not display an important effect because of the depth of the crisis.

The elections held in April 2013 led to a confused political situation. The two main political parties, PD (centre-left) and PDL (centre-right), and the new political movement (M5S), had almost the same results, so two of them had to make an alliance to give some stability to a new government. At last, on April 28, 2013, PD and PDL formed a coalition government, headed by the PD exponent Enrico Letta, who tried to painstakingly mediate between different approaches to economic policy. Up to the end of 2013, the result has been a weak and hesitant policy, unable to tackle the vast structural and short-term problems of the Italian economy.

10. AN ALTERNATIVE STRATEGY

A more far-sighted expansionary EU policy is necessary to avoid aggra-
vating the economic depression and defaults of the sovereign debts of
Greece, Ireland, Portugal, Spain and Italy, as well as the consequent difficulties of French, German and British banks possessing huge amounts of
those countries' bonds. However, in the case of Italy, much depends also
on the Italian economic policy. A complex mix of short-term and long-
term policies would be necessary, but it must be radically different from
monetarist anti-Keynesian views, which have prevailed within the Italian
government, many EU authorities and financial circles.

In the short run it would be appropriate to gradually reduce the debt-
exposure to foreign creditors. A progressive tax on wealth ought to be introduced and at least half of its annual revenues ought to be used to buy back
some public bonds, gradually reducing public debt. The remaining revenues
may be used to promote growth. Since the worst structural problems of the
Italian economy are ageing, low investment, relative technological decline,
de-industrialization, unemployment or job precariousness of many young
workers, tax evasion and the weakness of the balance of current accounts,
the medium to long-run economic policies must principally face these
problems. It would be necessary to promote policies that favour a drastic
reduction of job precariousness. An improvement in public assistance for
childcare, housing and the support of households, following, for example,
the French experience, would also be of great importance. Moreover, it
would be essential to reduce tax evasion and increase investment in productive activities and competitiveness through a gradual elimination of IRAP
(an Italian regional production tax) and the gradual reduction of taxes on
profits and social contribution rates to the EU average. A gradual rise in
expenditure on education, universities and R&D to the level of Northern
Europe, the United States, South Korea and Japan would be necessary in
order to be competitive in the most dynamic economic sectors.

Deep fiscal and pension reforms would be necessary. As regards pensions, it would be important to accelerate the passage of all workers to the
method based on the accumulation of contributions, which now includes
only the workers of the latest generations. Moreover, it would be appropriate to allow some freedom of choice on the retirement age, giving, for
example, the possibility of retiring between 62 and 70 years, with some
exceptions conceded only for very hard physical jobs. Most workers would
choose to prolong their activity in order to obtain a higher pension, while
people with bad health conditions or heavy family problems might choose
to leave work at about 62–5 years. As regards the fiscal system, it would
be essential to reduce evasion through further reductions of the limits for

the use of cash and a more simplified and efficient fiscal system. A part of the extra revenues might be used to reduce public debt, and a part to diminish taxes on lower incomes and to increase education and research expenditures. The introduction of a progressive tax on wealth, including both real and financial assets, a local tax on consumption, a Tobin tax, a European carbon tax, and the severe reduction of discretional incentives to firms, might furnish the means to finance other growth programmes, and, in particular, to abolish, in the long-run, IRAP and to reduce taxes on profits and social contributions, both on the part paid by firms and the part paid by workers. So firms would have lower labour costs and an improved international competiveness and workers would have higher net incomes. All this might contribute to raising both investment and consumption, reducing the deficit on current accounts, encouraging economic growth and employment and lowering, at the same time, tax evasion and economic inequalities. The intervention on public expenditure ought to be concentrated on the reduction in the costs associated with the service of public debt, on the cutback of the direct and indirect costs of political institutions, and on the rationalization of public current expenditures. However, Italy badly needs the support of public expenditures in order to restore hope for the future. School, university R&D activities, cultural goods and services and start-up firms must be sustained in order to design a better future for our children and grandchildren.

REFERENCES

Aglietta M. (1976), *A Theory of Capitalist Regulation: The US Experience*, London: Brookings, Verso Books.

Atkinson A.B., T. Piketty and E. Saez (2011), 'Top incomes in the long run of history', *Journal of Economic Literature*, **49** (1), 3–71.

Attali J. (2008), *La Crise, et Après?* Paris: Fayard.

Bank of Italy (2013), *Relazione Annuale*, Rome.

Boyer R. (1990), *The Regulation School: A Critical Introduction*, New York: Columbia University Press.

Damiani M. and F. Pompei (2010), 'Labour protection and productivity in EU economies: 1995–2005', *European Journal of Comparative Economics*, **7** (2), 373–411.

Eurostat (2013), http://epp.eurostat.ec.europa.eu/tgm/table.do?tab=table&init=1&language=en&pcode=tipsii30&plugin=0.

Francese M. and A. Pace (2008), *Il Debito Pubblico Italiano dall'Unità ad Oggi: Una Ricostruzione Della Serie Storica*, Occasional paper, n.31, Rome: Banca d'Italia.

Gerschenkron A. (1962), *Economic Backwardness in Historical Perspective*, Cambridge, MA: Harvard University Press.

Geuna A. and F. Rossi (2013), *L'Università e il Sistema Economico*, Bologna: Il Mulino.

Istat (2013), http://dati.istat.it/Index.aspx?DataSetCode=DCCN_AGGRPIL.

Maddison A. (2007), *Contours of the World Economy. 1–2030 AD*, Oxford: Oxford University Press.

OECD (2011), *Factbook 2011: Economic, Environmental and Social Statistics. Income Inequalities*, Paris: OECD.

Stiglitz J.E. (2010), *Free Fall: Free Markets and the Sinking of the World Economy*, London and New York: W.W. Norton & Co.

UNCTAD (2013), *World Investment Report*, Genève: UNCTAD.

Valli V. (1999), 'Intensive and extensive investment, employment and working time in the European Union', in R. Bellofiore (ed.), *Global Money, Capital Restructuring and the Changing Patterns of Labour*, Cheltenham, UK and Northampton, MA, USA: Edward Elgar Publishing, pp. 162–74.

Valli V. (2010a), *L'economia Americana da Roosevelt a Obama*, Roma: Carocci.

Valli V. (2010b), *The Economic Ascent of a Technological Power: South Korea*, Department of Economics Working Paper QR. 10, N. 14, University of Turin.

Valli V. and D. Saccone (2011), *Economic Development and Population Growth: An Inverted U-shaped Curve*, Department of Economics Working Paper QR. 11, N. 5, University of Turin.

Visco I. (2009), *Investire in Conoscenza. Per la Crescita Economica*, Bologna: Il Mulino.

APPENDIX

Table 10A.1 Rates of change of real GDP and the rate of unemployment in selected countries

	Rate of change of real GDP						Unemployment rate					
	2007	2008	2009	2010	2011	2012	2007	2008	2009	2010	2011	2012
China	14.2	9.6	9.2	10.4	9.3	7.8	4.0	4.2	4.3	4.1	4.0	4.1
France	2.3	−0.1	−3.1	1.7	2.0	0.0	8.0	7.4	9.1	9.7	9.6	10.3
Germany	3.3	1.1	−5.1	4.2	3.0	0.7	8.4	7.3	7.4	7.1	6.0	5.5
Greece (p)	3.5	−0.2	−3.1	−4.9	−7.1	−6.4	8.3	7.7	9.5	12.6	17.7	24.4
Ireland	5.4	−2.1	−5.5	−0.8	1.4	0.9	4.6	6.0	11.7	13.9	14.7	14.7
Italy	1.7	−1.2	−5.5	1.7	0.4	−2.4	6.1	6.8	7.8	8.4	8.4	10.7
Japan	2.2	−1.0	−5.5	4.7	−0.6	1.9	3.9	4.0	5.1	5.1	4.6	4.4
Portugal	2.4	0.0	−2.9	1.9	−1.8	−3.2	8.0	7.6	9.5	11.0	12.9	15.9
South Korea	5.1	2.3	0.3	6.3	3.7	2.0	3.2	3.2	3.6	3.7	3.4	3.2
Spain	3.5	0.9	−3.7	−0.3	0.4	−1.4	8.3	11.3	18.0	20.1	21.6	25.1
UK	3.4	−0.8	−5.2	1.7	1.1	0.2	5.3	5.6	7.6	7.8	8.0	7.9
US	1.9	−0.3	−3.1	2.4	1.8	2.2	4.6	5.8	9.3	9.6	9.0	8.1

Note: (p) preliminary estimates (2008–12).

Sources: For real GDP data, OECD for China and South Korea; Eurostat for the remaining countries. OECD for unemployment data. For China the data regard only the urban registered labour force and probably they underestimate unemployment.

11. What's gender got to do with the Great Recession? The Italian case

Giovanna Vertova

1. INTRODUCTION

What began as a subprime mortgage debacle in the US has become the worst global crisis since the Great Depression, resulting in a widespread destruction of livelihoods and jobs. So a great deal of attention has been focused on understanding the causes of the unfolding crisis, in order to implement policy measures and recovery plans. Many different explanations have been offered by various schools of economic thought (some also in this volume). Most mainstream explanations tend to concentrate on the imperfections of the financial markets (Schiller 2008); on the mistakes of the monetary policy (Taylor 2009); and on the phenomenon of the global saving glut (Bernanke 2013). Heterodox explanations share the view that the crisis is due not only to financial market imperfections, mistakes in monetary policy or exogenous shocks, but also, and more importantly, to the endogenous dynamic of this new phase of capitalist accumulation. Post-Keynesian accounts range from Minsky's financial instability hypothesis (Wray 2009) to insufficient aggregate demand (Fitoussi and Stiglitz 2009; Barba and Pivetti 2009). Under-consumption is the basis of the Sraffian arguments (Brancaccio and Fontana 2011). Marxists' explanations span from the tendency of the rate of profit to fall (Kliman 2011) to the limits of monopoly capital (Magdoff and Foster 2009). More eclectic explanations are based on capital asset inflation (Toporowski, Chapter 6 in this volume) or on the novelty of the structure of production and finance in this 'new' capitalism (Bellofiore 2013 and Chapter 1 in this volume).

It is not an aim of this chapter to review this literature. Yet, it is important to recall it in order to show that, despite the growing debate about the causes of the crisis, less attention is given to its gender dimension. There is very little discussion about the gender implications of the crisis, despite the fact that *feminist* and *gender economics* have assessed that every economic phenomenon affects men and women differently because of gender-specific inequalities in the capitalistic society (Farber and Nelson 1993; Picchio 2003).

Early attention to gender considerations was given by international organizations. The 53rd session of the Commission on the Status of Women of the United Nations was entirely dedicated to *The Gender Perspectives of the Financial Crisis* (UN 2009). Also the International Labour Organization (ILO) grew immediately concerned about the impact of the crisis on the labour market (Otobe 2011). These works tend to be focused on women's situations in developing countries, remarking that those women might be more affected by the crisis for a number of reasons. Firstly, the financial crisis has had a huge impact on the real economy. Export-oriented countries, both industrialized and developing, have experienced substantial declines in export levels due to a drastic reduction in world demand. Manufacturing production levels have been impacted not only by the reduction of liquidity in the financial market, but also by the reduction of consumer demand, both domestic and external. Developing countries with mono-production/ exports, in particular in labour-intensive manufacturing such as textiles and clothing, have been particularly negatively affected by the downturn in international trade. Women and men have been affected differently from country to country, depending on the gender composition of the labour force in the most affected sectors. Where labour-intensive export industrial sectors have been negatively affected, women have tended to be more disproportionately affected, given the higher concentration of female workforce in those sectors. Secondly, the crisis has had an impact on migrant workers and remittances. Migrants working in such sectors as manufacturing and construction are the first to be retrenched. For the sending countries, this would mean a decline in remittances and overall national income, as well as loss of jobs for those migrant workers who are being sent back home. At the household level, this would mean reduced/loss of income for the families back home. About half of the world's migrants are women, and how women and men migrants have been affected depends also on the gender division of labour. Thirdly, the fiscal space for governments' policies has been narrowing. Developing countries' already narrower fiscal space has been further constrained in the global economic crisis. As a general trend, both public investments and social expenditures have been reduced, thus leading to disproportionate negative impacts on women who rely on common public goods and services. Fourthly, the social and poverty impacts are very gendered. Given that women workers form the bottom rung of the world's working poor, the global economic crisis has a long-lasting negative socioeconomic impact on the most vulnerable part of the population, the female one. Finally, the crisis has impacted girls' and women's well-being. As past financial and economic crises show, even when women may not be directly affected by the reduction in employment and income opportunities as workers, they tend to increase their hours of both productive and reproductive work, as a household-level coping mechanism. Those women who had not been previously engaged in paid work would try to seek income and job opportunities outside the household in order to compensate for the loss/reduction of overall household income when their male family members lose jobs or reduce their working hours. This is called the 'additional workers' effect. Furthermore, because mothers have to increase their hours of paid work, female children are likely to face a high risk of being withdrawn from schools, in order to replace the mother's role in the household. The reduction of income in the households could cause excessive hours of both paid and unpaid work, having a negative impact on the well-being of poor working women and girls. This could also be exacerbated by the cuts in the public expenditures for public services and investments in infrastructure.

Fewer works analyse the situation in developed countries (Dütting 2009; Peterson 2012; Ruggeri 2010). At the beginning of the crisis, the main problem was to discover whether the crisis would hit more men or more women. For example, in the US and the UK the crisis was a 'male' one because job losses were mainly concentrated in the manufacturing sectors (mainly automobile and construction), which are more male-dominated. With the unfolding of the crisis and the implementation of fiscal stimulus packages, the concerns were related to the presence (or absence) of gender considerations in the anti-crisis policies.

Due to the small number of works with gender perspective, this chapter attempts to fill this gap with a twofold goal. On the one hand, it proposes a theoretical framework which enables gender considerations to be taken into account; on the other hand, it empirically applies this framework to the Italian case. The framework presented is intentionally created only for developed countries. I am well aware of the fact that the crisis hits developing as well as developed countries, but I believe that a unified framework of analysis is impossible due to the strong differences among them.

The chapter is organized as follows. The next section presents the theoretical framework in order to put women in the analysis. Section 3 applies the theoretical framework to the Italian case. Section 4 closes the chapter with some conclusions.

2. PUTTING WOMEN IN THE ANALYSIS: A THEORETICAL FRAMEWORK

In order to analyse the crisis with a gender perspective, I propose a theoretical framework which puts together gender and class dimensions. The need to intertwine these two dimensions arises from the fact that working women are likely to be affected in different ways by the crisis than working men. This intersection is necessary because the neglect of either dimension gives rise to very partial and bizarre explanations.

A 'gender-without-class' type of explanation leads to the awkward idea that this is a 'macho' crisis: if Lehman Brothers had been Lehman Sisters, run by women instead of men, the credit crunch might not have happened (or it might have been lighter). In February 2009, the *World Economic Forum* was animated by the discussion around masculinity as a source of the crisis. The debate was immediately taken up by both international media and academic literature speculating about the more prudent investment style of women (for a very good review of this debate, see Prügl 2012). The main argument was that, since the financial and banking sectors are dominated by men, with women occupying a small portion of top positions, and since men have a greater risk-taker behaviour when speculation is concerned, more women in leading roles might have lessened or even avoided the crisis. This discourse tends to create and enforce a mythological idea of both sexes: 'macho Wall Street bankers brought to their knees and the feminine phoenix rising from the ashes of casino capitalism' (Prügl 2012, p. 26). Moreover, most of these studies tend to offer explanations based on biological determinations: 'boys will always be boys' (Barber and Odean 2001), testosterone (Apicella *et al.* 2008; Sapienza *et al.* 2009), and the 'chromosome Y factor' in general. By contrast, women and their 'natural' prudent behaviour are shown to be good for business and, consequently, for capitalism. The gender-diversity management literature offers the scientific support: firms with more women in top positions show better economic results (Luckerath-Rovers 2013; McKinsey & Company 2007). This kind of explanation has two main flaws. Firstly, it easily forgets the feminist philosophical debate on the difference between 'sex' and 'gender' (Scott 1986), thus reaffirming the idea that differences in men's and women's behaviour is due to 'nature' instead of social constructions. Secondly, it gives an explanation of the crisis based on individual behaviours of a certain social group – male bankers and financial CEOs – thus diverting the attention from the capitalism system as a whole, as if the law of motion of capital depends upon the sex ruling it. It is a crisis of 'the system': the capitalism system which came to life after the Golden Age, especially since the 1990s, with its new features like the return of monetarism, supply-side economics, the financialization of the economy, just to cite a few.

By contrast, a 'class-without-gender' type of explanation hides the impacts of the crisis on the social reproduction system. Despite different approaches, the 1970s feminist debate over domestic labour had the merit of drawing attention to two important, and today taken-for-granted, insights: (i) capitalist production is not self-sufficient but depends on domestic labour that goes outside capitalist relations; (ii) men and women participate in the labour market in different ways due to their unequal domestic responsibilities (Dalla Costa and James 1972; Coulson *et al.* 1975; Himmelweit and Mohun 1977; Benería 1979; Molyneux 1979). More recently, a number of feminist economists have extended the classical political macroeconomic approach in order to include the social reproduction system (Benería *et al.* 2011; Picchio 2003). This approach conceives well-being not in terms of individual choices, but as a part of a structural framework that includes the material process of production, distribution and exchange of wealth together with the process of social reproduction of the working class. Placing the unpaid work within the macroeconomic circular flows makes it possible to address the question of the quality and adequacy of living conditions and well-being of the working class, not as women's responsibility but as a central and general problem of the capitalist system, thus redefining the traditional view in which the functioning of the system is reduced to monetary transactions. The point is not to reduce the work of social reproduction to an economic variable, but to find an approach that does not relegate it to the margin of the analysis of the system and its dynamics. Therefore, domestic labour performed for social reproduction needs to become a central category for a feminist study of the capitalist system and its crises.

That is the reason why an exhaustive look at the impact of the crisis must keep these two dimensions – class and gender – together, thus unveiling the general and orthodox assumption that the capitalist system is class as well as gender neutral. In order to do that, I create a framework for the analysis, taking the basic idea from Elson (2010). The theoretical framework is shown in Table 11.1, where the rows represent the economic spheres to look at and the columns the evolving time.

The rows represent the sphere of the economy, when gender considerations are taken into account. The first row stands for the *production system* (PS), providing goods and services throughout market transactions, grounded on wage labour commanded by capital, and productive of value. The focus here is on the gender division of the labour market. The second row represents the *public social reproduction system* (public SRS), based on the paid (but non-market) work in public services. This system has a twofold dimension. On the one hand, it provides social public goods/services throughout the welfare system. Some of them are strictly related to the reproduction of the working class (i.e. healthcare, pensions systems, etc.); while others are ways to help families to reconcile paid work and family responsibilities (i.e. nursery school, etc.). On the other hand, it

Table 11.1   The theoretical framework

	Pre-crisis situation	Impact of the crisis	Today's situation
PS	Lower female labour market participation than male one Occupational segregation Contractual inequality Gender pay gap Pension inequality	Which sectors are hit most? Which gender division of labour in those sectors?	Which 'new' gender division of labour?
'Public' SRS	Privatization and 'commodification' of social public goods/ services Public expenditure cuts in social public goods/ services	Any gender considerations in the stimulus fiscal packages?	Any gender consideration in the fiscal austerity policy?
'Familiar' SRS	Gender inequality (with strong differences among countries due to different gender norms)	Visible in the long-run	Which 'new' gender division of the domestic/ care work?
Gender norms	Strong national differences according to cultural beliefs and values, social traditions and habits	High risk to bring back the male breadwinner family model	

is a source of female employment, because in general, women are more employed in public sectors. The third row represents what I called the *familiar social reproduction system* (familiar SRS), given by the domestic, unpaid and voluntary work carried out within the households by family members. According to countries' social, cultural and traditional beliefs, which can be often supported by public policy, this 'system' can be very gendered.

Splitting the SRS into two parts (the public and the familiar one) enables attention to be drawn to their negative relationship: the burden of unpaid labour increases when the supply of social public goods/services declines, with the 'familiar' welfare becoming a substitute for the lack of the 'public' one. Yet, while the reduction of social public goods/services is visible, recorded and accountable in a country's public budget, the increase in the unpaid labour is invisible, not registered in any national accounts. It is just an increase in the unpaid labour time. For example, a reduction of hospital stay, politically implemented in order to reduce the public expenditure of the national health service, immediately becomes more care work for the person who, within the family, takes care of the sick person. So, the 'public' and the 'family' part of the SRS are both affected by the government fiscal and budgetary policy, directly the former and indirectly the latter. This is the reason why the fiscal policy becomes an important variable within a gender analysis of the crisis.

The last row takes into account some kinds of *patriarchal dimensions*. I borrow Elson's (2010, p. 203) concept of 'gender norms' and her definition as 'social norms that constrain the choices of men and women, and their associated social sanctions, encouraging forms of behaviour that conform to the norms, and discouraging behaviour that does not'. Gender norms are based on gender stereotypes, social and cultural beliefs, and can have strong influences on male and female behaviour. They can also affect economic outcomes (Badgett and Folbre 1999). Examples of gender norms can be found in the education sphere (i.e. high professional qualification is considered to be important only for men), in the profession one (i.e. the workplace is not considered to be the primary area for women, therefore career and professional advancement is deemed unimportant for them), in the housework (i.e. housekeeping and childcare are considered to be the primary functions of women) and in the decision-making process (i.e. in case of conflicts, men have the last say, for example in the choice of the place to live, the school for children, the buying decisions). Therefore, gender norms can contribute to increase or decrease gender inequality. In periods of crisis, gender norms can work as backlash mechanisms. For example, when jobs are scarce it becomes socially and culturally acceptable that men have more right to keep theirs, because they have a family to support. This belief tends to bring back the traditional *male breadwinner family model*. So, changes in gender norms must be taken into consideration in order to see whether new ones come about because of the crisis and how they can influence the long and difficult road towards gender equality.

The framework presented here is suitable for advanced countries only, because I believe that a unified framework for developed and developing countries is not possible, due to their differences. Moreover, the analysis is based on some stylized facts about the current phase of capitalist accumulation common to all advanced countries. Yet, those facts must be taken *cum grano salis* because they are great generalizations and cannot account too much for different national specificities. Finally, it must be kept in mind that the form the crisis has taken and the government responses can vary widely between different countries. The next section deals with the application of this theoretical framework to the Italian situation.

3. THE EMPIRICAL ANALYSIS: THE ITALIAN CASE

The theoretical framework presented earlier is here applied to the Italian situation.

3.1. The Pre-crisis Situation

As far as the PS is concerned, the labour market of all advanced countries is still characterized by strong gender inequality, despite the feminist movements of the 1970s and the process of feminization of work. To start with, total employment is still male-dominated (Table 11.2).

Furthermore, strong qualitative differences exist. The most significant are: (i) occupational segregation; (ii) contractual inequality; (iii) gender pay gap. Vertical (the so-called glass ceiling phenomenon) and horizontal segregations[1] are still common features among advanced countries (Charles and Grusky 2004). Contractual inequality refers to the fact that men and women are employed with different types of contracts: women have more vulnerable, less secured, informal, flexible and part-time jobs. The neoliberal political agenda with its pressure on labour has pushed towards more flexibility in the labour market. In the advanced countries, there was a general tendency towards a declining of 'secure' jobs, which give welfare protection and social security, and an increase of temporary

Table 11.2   Total employment ('000), 2007

	M	F	Total	Feminization rate F/(M+F)
Italy	14,057	9,165	23,222	39.4%
Euro-zone	78,314	61,400	139,714	43.9%
EU27	121,463	97,607	219,070	44.5%
USA	78,254	67,792	146,046	46.4%
Japan	37,530	26,590	64,120	41.4%

Sources: Eurostat (for Italy, the Euro-zone and the EU27); ILO (for USA and Japan).

---

[1] Vertical segregation is the unseen, yet unbreakable barrier that keeps women from reaching top positions in both traditionally male and traditionally female occupations. Horizontal segregation (the 'sex-typing' phenomenon) occurs when women are relegated only in some jobs and activities. Both these phenomena are the results of social and cultural stereotypes. In the former case, women are never considered to be as good as men for top positions, despite their qualifications. In the latter case, there is the idea that some jobs are just for women (i.e. the secretary).

positions, characterized by uncertainty, irregularity and interruption, and very little, if any, security. The rise of these temporary positions affected all workers, but their diffusion coincides with the feminization of the labour market (Standing 1999). The gender pay gap is the obvious outcome of the previous inequalities (ILO 2013). Women are prevented from reaching top positions, are stuck in 'typical' female jobs, which are generally low paid, and have more fixed-term and part-time contracts. The result cannot but be less income. Last but not least, in those countries, like Italy, having a public pension system, at the end of their working life women will have lower pensions due to their uneven participation in the labour market (European Commission 2013).

As previously mentioned, the burden of the care and domestic work is strictly related to the welfare system (the 'public' SRS, in my analysis). A common trend of the neoliberal agenda of the advanced countries has been privatization, liberalization and deregulation of many state-owned enterprises, together with the idea of reducing the welfare state. Privatization began in the 1980s in the US and the UK with the neoliberal turn of Reagan and Thatcher. Afterwards it became the inspiration of the European integration, the Maastricht Treaty and its parameters[2]. On the one hand, privatization was promoted with the idea that it would substitute inefficient state industries, and it became one of the ten ingredients of the Washington consensus (Williamson 2004–05). On the other hand, for some of the European countries wishing to enter the Economic and Monetary Union (EMU), privatization became a tool for monetary convergence, used to tackle budget deficits and meet the stringent criteria for monetary integration. Furthermore, privatization programmes went hand in hand with the reduction of the welfare state ('we cannot afford a welfare system anymore' used to be the general refrain). This common trend was even stronger in the countries of the Euro-zone. The strong preoccupation with public deficit and debt has pushed towards a reduction in public expenditure, which has generally hit social expenditures. The shrinking of the welfare system has been translated into an increased burden of unpaid work, mostly done by women. Nevertheless, economic policy-makers paid very little attention to this problem, thus hiding a withdrawal of firms and state from their social responsibility towards the quality of life.

Privatization programmes, together with the reduction of the welfare state, led to an increased 'commodification' of social public goods/services. More expensive, or even inaccessible, public goods/services means more unpaid work for domestic and care responsibilities. Moreover, since the public sector is generally a source for female employment in all

---

[2] For a critic of the 3 per cent deficit/GDP Maastricht parameter see Pasinetti (1998).

advanced countries, privatization and reduction of public goods/services meant the lay-off of female public workers. In Italy the situation is even worse, because Italy never had a well-functioning welfare system, even during the Golden Age (Boeri 2000; Del Boca 2009). Moreover, Italy has chosen a welfare in money instead of a welfare in kind, thus reducing its impact on the citizens' well-being.

As far as the 'familiar' SRS is concerned, it is possible to use *Time Use Surveys* to measure unpaid work, although they must be handled with caution (Fleming and Spellerberg 1999; Budlender 2007). At any rate, they are helpful in making the unpaid work carried out within families visible. The 'familiar' SRS is as much gendered as the productive system, despite strong national disparities. Italian women carried out the most part of it (Table 11.3). Yet, the contribution of migrant women, whose work is often informal, flexible and low paid, must also be acknowledged.

Finally, there are also strong national specificities in gender norms, since they are the results of national cultural beliefs and values, acceptable social traditions and habits.

Table 11.3   Time use of a person aged 20–74 (hours and minutes)

	M		F	
	Paid work*	Unpaid work	Paid work*	Unpaid work
Italy	4:26	1:35	2:06	5:20
Estonia	3:40	2:48	2:33	5:02
Hungary	3:46	2:39	2:32	4:48
Slovenia	4:07	2:40	2:59	4:58
Spain	4:39	1:37	2:26	4:55
Poland	4:15	2:22	2:29	4:45
Belgium	3:30	2:38	2:07	4:32
France	4:03	2:22	2:31	4:30
Lithuania	4:55	2:09	3:41	4:29
UK	4:18	2:18	2:33	4:15
Germany	3:35	2:21	2:05	4:11
Finland	4:01	2:16	2:49	3:56
Latvia	5:09	1:50	3:41	3:56
Norway	4:16	2:22	2:53	3:47
Sweden	4:25	2:29	3:12	3:42

Note: * paid work includes time dedicated to study.

Source: Istat (2008, pp. 21–2).

3.2.   The Impact of the Crisis

To understand the gender transmission of the crisis in the PS it is necessary to see the gender composition of employment in those sectors which were hit most. It becomes, therefore, fundamental to have disaggregated data by gender. Yet, unemployment statistics might not be good indicators because of the 'discouraged worker' phenomenon, which is more typical for women than men. The decrease of female unemployment can be just a statistical illusion. Women who lose their jobs may disappear altogether from the labour force statistics because they give up looking for one (thus, they are not counted among the unemployed), or because they increasingly experience difficulty in reconciling work and family commitments. For this reason, I prefer to use employment data.

In advanced countries, the crisis has hit industrial sectors more heavily. For example, in the US and in the UK the crisis struck particularly the automobile and the construction industries, which are typically male-dominated sectors as far as employment is concerned (Hartmann *et al.* 2010). In those countries, women lost fewer jobs because they are employed mainly in retailing and services sectors. Something similar occurred in Italy as well. The Italian labour market started experiencing the effects of the crisis in 2009. Since then, men have lost more jobs than women because the crisis hit heavily the industrial sector as a whole (Table 11.4). It seems that occupational segregation – the fact the more women are employed in the services sectors – has prevented women from being stricken by the crisis. Moreover, the service sectors are those where there seems to be a substitution effect: men are fired while women are gaining jobs.

Yet, the good performance of the services sectors for female employment must be investigated in more detail. The increase in female occupation in

Table 11.4   Absolute variation of Italian total employment ('000), 2009–2012

	M	F	Total
TOTAL	−623	117	−506
Agriculture	2	−21	−19
Industry, total			
– industry (construction excluded)	−216	−176	−392
– construction	−235	2	−233
Services	−174	312	138

Source: Istat.

the services sectors is due to the increase in clerks, sellers and unskilled professions.

In the 'public' SRS the effect of the crisis is related to the kind of fiscal policy adopted. In order to reduce the severity of the downturn, most advanced countries included a fiscal boost as part of their policy to respond to the crisis. As a general trend, many European countries used 'automatic stabilisers'; while in the US such expenditure is treated as discretionary to a greater extent. The fiscal stimulus packages of advanced countries were very different in quantity (Figure 11.1) and in the kinds of measures they adopted.

Yet, they did share a common feature: none of them showed any gender consideration (European Commission 2009). A gender audit and budget analysis of these packages concludes that male-dominated industries benefit most. For example, Scheele (2009) points to the gender imbalance of the stimulus packages of the US, the UK and Germany, thus reflecting the underlying gender-political conservatism still orientated to the idea of the *male breadwinner family model*. In those cases analysed by Scheele, the main beneficiaries of the expansionary fiscal policy were male-dominated industries (i.e. the automotive industries and its suppliers, engineering and the construction and transport industries). Scheele looks more closely at the German case. At first glance, it was assumed that the funds for education might have meant new teachers and nurses, thus supporting predominately female sectors. But, in fact, the money was used for physical infrastructures (i.e. the physical restoration of their buildings), thus boosting the male-dominated construction industry. The European Economic Recovery Plan (EERP) and the G20 Global Plan for Recovery and Reform are other examples along the same lines. They both promote forms of employment but they do not include any kind of gender considerations. As far as Italy is concerned, the case was much simpler to audit because the fiscal packages were practically non-existent (Figure 11.1). Therefore, there was nothing to audit.

Contrary to what has been done, fiscal stimulus packages should have been designed with the goal of achieving gender equality. The support for physical infrastructures should have been accompanied with support for social infrastructures and services. Moreover, since the public sector is an important source of female employment, governments should have avoided budget cuts. Unfortunately, none of this happened. Walby (2009) is very clear: those stimulus packages do not mention any gender-specific impact of the crisis; nor do they include gender-awareness.

The effects of the crisis on the 'familiar' SRS, as well as on gender norms, can be seen only in the long run. Yet, as far as gender norms

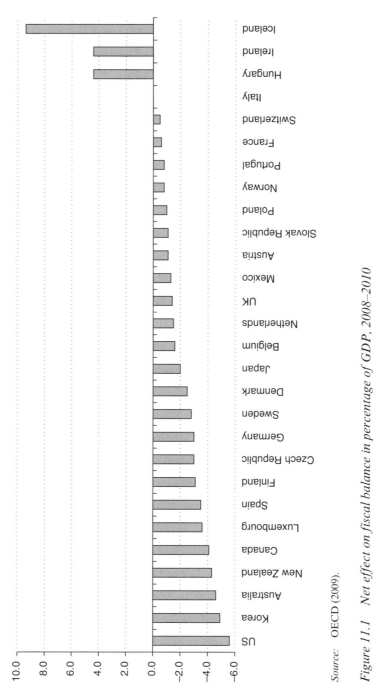

Source: OECD (2009).

Figure 11.1 Net effect on fiscal balance in percentage of GDP, 2008–2010

are concerned, what happened in Italy during the summer of 2011 can be taken as an example of the way they work. Ma-Vib, a family-owned engineering firm based in Inzago, near Milan, responded to a downturn in sales by cutting half its workforce and selecting only women for redundancy. FIOM[3] was not only shocked by that decision but, even more, by the reasons given. 'We are firing only women so they can stay at home and look after the children. In any case, what they bring in is a second income', said the company (Hooper 2011). But, what was even worse was that when the union called a strike to protest against the move, only one of the men whose jobs had been saved at the women's expense heeded the strike call. This example shows that the prevalence of 'male breadwinner norms' led the employer and even the male workers to think that men have more right to retain their jobs.

Unfortunately, this belief is quite widespread. The World Values Survey confirms that the 42.8 per cent of people interviewed believe that men have more rights to keep their work than women when there is a scarcity of jobs[4]. This change in gender norms due to the crisis might bring back the *male breadwinner family model*, thus walking away from gender equality and equal opportunities.

3.3. Today's Situation

In the PS, today's situation depends on the job losses that occurred earlier. The crisis could have increased or decreased occupational segregation, according to the specific national situations. In Italy, as well as in the most advanced countries, the crisis was a 'macho' one, because it hit the sectors with a higher male employment than female (i.e. industry and construction). Thus, in Italy, today's total employment is more feminized than before the crisis (41.5 per cent in the first three quarters of 2013 (Table 11.5) compared to 39.4 per cent in 2008 (Table 11.2)). Yet, when looking at more disaggregated data, men lose jobs in the industrial sectors while women gain jobs in the service ones. Therefore, the final result is a reinforcement of occupational segregation. Despite the fact that men lost more jobs than women and, consequently, unemployment is less feminized, inactivity is a typically female feature of the labour market (Table 11.5). Not only inactivity as a whole, but inactivity due to discouragement (66.2 per cent) and to family responsibilities (91.5 per cent) are very feminized in the first three quarters of 2013. This data can be seen

---

[3] FIOM is the Italian General Confederation of Labour's (CGIL's) trade union for metalworkers.
[4] www.worldvaluessurvey.org.

Table 11.5   Italian labour market ('000), 2013 Q3

	M	F	Total	Feminization rate(F/total)
Employment	13,103	9,321	22,424	41.5 %
Unemployment	1,681	1,384	3,065	45.1 %
Inactivity	5,256	9,244	14,500	63.7 %
– of which: discouragement	594	1,166	1,760	66.2 %
– of which: family responsibilities	210	2,265	2,475	91.5 %

Source: Istat.

as women's increasing difficulties in reconciling paid and unpaid work, especially after the cuts in social expenditure due to the Italian austerity measures.

The situation in the 'public' SRS depends on the kind of fiscal policy implemented. So, in this case, a distinction must be made. On the one hand, there is the US expansionary fiscal policy while, on the other hand, there is the European sovereign debt crisis. An enormous amount of money has been paid out of state funds worldwide for bank bailouts and stimulus packages, thus leading to an increase in the sovereign debts of some European countries. The European debt crisis has already lent apparent plausibility to the notion that countries of the Euro-zone should reduce their indebtedness drastically. Governments have two ways to reach that goal: limiting public expenditure and raising taxes. The governments of the most indebted European countries have decided on a combination of both options. Restrictive fiscal policy has two consequences: a drop in female employment and an increasing potential to jeopardize women's reconciliation of paid and unpaid work. In an open letter, the European Federation of Public Services Unions (EPSU) has asked the European Commission for more gender equality and awareness in the current crisis[5]. The rearrangement of the public sphere and the withdrawal of the state from its responsibility, due to this restrictive policy, will lead to a worsening of women's living conditions, as women are much more dependent on public physical and social infrastructures. In addition, this worsening is also due to the neoliberal agenda, which enforces further privatizations, thus leading to an increasing influence of private capital on ever larger areas of social life, crucial for women's opportunities to enter the labour market. So, in the end, restrictive fiscal

[5] www.epsu.org/a/6713.

policy will have a 'lag effect' on the financial crisis, which will affect women more than men.

In the 'familiar' SRS, the consequences of the crisis becomes a paradox: too little paid work for everybody and too much unpaid work just for women (Antonopoulos 2009). While downsizing, firing and restructuring are all sources of job losses, gender-blind fiscal stimulus packages and the later fiscal austerity increase domestic and care work. Unfortunately, unlike paid work, these costs remain invisible: they cannot be measured and they are not seen as problems to be addressed. So, the 'familiar' SRS, with women at the centre of it, becomes the shock absorber for the austerity measures. A shifting of burdens from the visible economy of state and market to the invisible one of unpaid work occurs. All this will very likely lead to the intolerable situation of women withdrawing from the labour market, due to the increasing difficulty of reconciling work with family commitments. This is exactly what has been happening in Italy in this period.

4.   CONCLUSIONS

The analysis proposed in this chapter is an attempt to bridge a gap: a gender perspective when looking at the impact of the crisis. In fact, the impact is very gendered, but not only the impact, as the policy responses to the crisis are also very gendered. Therefore, in order to see this gendering, the analysis must look at both the production and the social reproduction systems. The analysis must be carried out at the macroeconomic level, by looking to the 'enlarged' capitalist system, where the unpaid work and domestic labour are taken into consideration. Also the fiscal policy – the former fiscal anti-crisis packages and the later austerity measures of some European countries – is a very gendered variable. Expansionary fiscal policy must be assessed as to whether it is designed to protect women as well as men, thus also checking the situations in the public jobs and the distributions of public subsidies for unemployment. Austerity measures must be assessed to see if their cost in terms of cuts in public expenditures is fairly distributed between the two sexes (it is worth remembering that it is not an aim of the chapter to evaluate their ability to solve the European debt crisis, but I do not think they do).

The feminist debate on productive and reproductive work has returned in this time of crisis, emphasizing the gender-segregated labour market, the gender pay gap and the unsolved issues of domestic unpaid work and immigrant domestic labour. Despite years of feminist theory on women's invisible reproductive labour, the dominant economic and political thinking still does not count and value it. Most analyses with a gender perspective propose a reform of the financial architecture with more democratic control (Antonopoulos 2009; Elson 2002); the need for a gender economic view, which includes social reproduction as a basis for anti-crisis policies; sustainable livelihoods, decent work, gender equality and women's rights. Moreover, specific recommendations as far as fiscal policy is concerned include the gender budgeting of the fiscal stimulus packages and of the austerity measures, in order to build an economic system that includes unpaid as well as paid work as a basis for policy-makers.

Unfortunately, although the crisis has shaken the belief in the free market, it has not altered the theoretical, political and ideological foundations of the neoliberal agenda. So far, the only change is that nation states have temporarily reappeared as the vehicle to allocate national tax money to bankrupt firms and banks. Yet, burdening national budgets with these enormous debts will lead to further privatization, and the additional rollback of welfare regimes will result in a worsening of the conditions of women's lives.

The only hope left is that the crisis will be an opportunity for putting the unsolved question of the social reproduction problem at the core of economic analysis.

REFERENCES

Antonopolous, R. (2009), *The Current Economic and Fiscal Financial Crisis: A Gender Perspective*, Working Paper n. 562, Levy Economics Institute of Bard College.
Apicella, C.L. *et al.* (2008), 'Testosterone and financial risk preferences', *Evolution and Human Behavior*, **29** (6), 384–90.
Badgett, M.V.L. and N. Folbre (1999), 'Assigning care: gender norms and economic outcomes', *International Labour Review*, **138** (3), 311–26.
Barba, A. and M. Pivetti (2009), 'Rising household debt: its causes and macroeconomic implications – a long-period analysis', *Cambridge Journal of Economics*, **33** (1), 113–37.
Barber, B.M. and T. Odean (2001), 'Boys will be boys: gender, overconfidence, and common stock investment', *Quarterly Journal of Economics*, **116** (1), 261–92.
Bellofiore, R. (2013), 'Two or three things I know about her: Europe in the global crisis and heterodox economics', *Cambridge Journal of Economics*, **37** (3), 497–512.
Benería, L. (1979), 'Reproduction, production and the sexual division of labour', *Cambridge Journal of Economics*, **3** (3), 203–55.
Benería, L., A.M. May and D. Strassmann (2011, eds), *Feminist Economics*, Cheltenham, UK and Northampton, MA, USA: Edward Elgar Publishing.
Bernanke, B. (2013), *The Federal Reserve and the Financial Crisis*, Princeton: Princeton University Press.

Boeri, T. (2000), *Uno Stato Asociale: Perché è Fallito il Welfare in Italia*, Roma, Bari: Laterza.

Brancaccio, E. and G. Fontana (2011), *The Global Crisis: Contributions to the Critique of Economic Theory and Policy*, Abingdon: Routledge.

Budlender, D. (2007), *A Critical Review of Selected Time Use Surveys*, Geneva: United Nations Research Institute for Social Development.

Charles, M. and D.B. Grusky (2004), *Occupational Ghettos: The Worldwide Segregation of Women and Men*, Stanford: Stanford University Press.

Coulson M., M. Branka and H. Wainwright (1975), 'The housewife and her labour under capitalism – a critique', *New Left Review*, **89** (January–February), 59–71.

Dalla Costa, M.R. and S. James (1972), *The Power of Women and Subversion of the Community*, Bristol: Falling Wall Press.

Del Boca, D. (2009), *Famiglie Sole: Sopravvivere con un Welfare Inefficiente*, Bologna: Il Mulino.

Dütting, G. (2009), 'Feminists in Europe responding to the financial crisis', *Development*, **52** (3), 338–44.

Elson, D. (2002), *International Financial Architecture: A View from the Kitchen*, Mimeo.

Elson, D. (2010), 'Gender and the global economic crisis in developing countries: a framework for analysis', *Gender and Development*, **18** (2), 201–12.

European Commission (2009), *Opinion on the Gender Perspective on the Response to the Economic and Financial Crisis*.

European Commission (2013), *The Gender Gap in Pensions in the EU*.

Farber, M. and J. Nelson (1993, eds), *Beyond Economic Man: Feminist Theory and Economics*, Chicago: University of Chicago Press.

Fitoussi, J-P. and J. Stiglitz (2009), *The Ways Out of the Crisis and the Building of a More Cohesive World*, Documents de travail n. 17, OFCE.

Fleming, R. and A. Spellerberg (1999), *Using Time Use Data. A History of Time Use Surveys and Uses of Time Use Data*, New Zealand Statistics Report.

Hartmann, H., A. English and J. Hayes (2010), *Women's and Men's Employment and Unemployment in the Great Recession*, IWPR Publication C373, Institute for Women's Policy Research.

Himmelweit, S. and S. Mohun (1977), 'Domestic labour and capital', *Cambridge Journal of Economics*, **1** (1), 15–31.

Hooper, J. (2011), 'Italian firm women-only job cull inflames gender controversy', *The Guardian*, 30 June.

ILO (2013), *Equal Pay – An Introductory Guide*.

Istat (2008), *Time Use in Daily Life*.

Kliman, A. (2011), *The Failure of Capitalist Production*, London: Pluto Press.

Luckerath-Rovers, M. (2013), 'Women on board and firm performance', *Journal of Management and Governance*, **17** (2), 491–509.

Magdoff, F. and J.B. Foster (2009), *The Great Financial Crisis: Causes and Consequences*, New York: Monthly Review Press.

McKinsey & Company (2007), *Women Matter: Gender Diversity, a Corporate Performance Driver*.

Molyneux, M. (1979), 'Beyond the domestic labour debate', *New Left Review*, **116** (July–August), 3–27.

OECD (2009), *Fiscal Packages across OECD Countries: Overview and Country Details*.

Otobe, N. (2011), *Global Economic Crisis, Gender and Employment: The Impact of Policy Response*, Employment Working Paper n. 74, ILO.

Pasinetti, L.L. (1998), 'The myth (or folly) of the 3% deficit/GDP Maastricht "parameter"', *Cambridge Journal of Economics*, **22** (1), 103–16.

Peterson, J. (2012), 'The Great Crisis and the significance of gender in the U.S. economy', *Journal of Economic Issues*, **46** (2), 277–90.

Picchio, A. (2003, ed.), *Unpaid Work and the Economy: A Gender Analysis of the Standard of Living*, London and New York: Routledge.

Prügl, E. (2012), '"If Lehman Brothers has been Lehman Sisters. . .": gender and myth in the aftermath of the financial crisis', *International Political Sociology*, **6** (1), 21–35.

Ruggeri, D. (2010), 'Gender perspectives of the financial and economic crisis', *International Journal of Green Economics*, **4** (3), 217–30.

Sapienza, P., L. Zingales and D. Maestripieri (2009), 'Gender differences in financial risk aversion and career choices are affected by testosterone', *Proceedings of the National Academy of Science of the United States of America*, **106** (36), 15268–73.

Scheele, A. (2009), 'Hat die wirtschaftskrise ein geschlecht?', *Blätter für Deutsche und Internationale Politik*, n. 3.

Schiller, R. (2008), *The Subprime Solutions: How Today's Global Financial Crisis Happened, and What to Do about It*, Princeton: Princeton University Press.

Scott, J. (1986), 'Gender: a useful category of historical analysis', *American Historical Review*, **91** (5), 1053–75.

Standing, G. (1999), 'Global feminization through flexible labor: a theme revisited', *World Development*, **27** (3), 583–602.

Taylor, J.B. (2009), *The Financial Crisis and the Policy Response: An Empirical Analysis of What Went Wrong*, NBER Working Paper n. 14631.

UN (2009), *Emerging Issues: The Gender Perspectives of the Financial Crisis*, Commission of the Status of Women, 53rd session.

Walby, S. (2009), *Gender and the Financial Crisis*, paper presented for the UNESCO Project on Gender and the Financial Crisis.

Williamson, J. (2004–05), 'The strange history of the Washington consensus', *Journal of Post Keynesian Economics*, **27** (2), 195–206.

Wray, R. (2009), *Money Manager Capitalism and the Global Financial Crisis*, Working Paper n. 578, Levy Institute.

12. Financial and nuclear meltdowns: the fragility of chain-reaction critical processes

Alessandro Vercelli

1. INTRODUCTION*

The financial 'tsunami' that hit the USA and Europe in 2008 and culminated in the bankruptcy of Lehman Brothers in September 2008, triggered a 'meltdown' of the financial system that was somehow thwarted only by an unprecedented public bail-out of many big financial institutions. In March 2011, while the effects of the financial crisis were not yet fully re-absorbed, a real tsunami hit the Tohoku region in North-East Japan and triggered the partial meltdown of the nuclear reactors 1, 2 and 3 of the Fukushima1 plant. In my opinion, the analogies between these two episodes go much beyond terminology. Although the common features of nuclear and financial chain reactions have been almost completely neglected in the scientific literature, I claim that we may draw from them pregnant insights. In what follows I focus on their foundations and hint at some of their implications.

I want to show in particular that, in order to understand and prevent catastrophic events in finance and nuclear energy generation, we have to focus on the critical chain reactions characterizing accident-prone systems. This sort of structural instability has to do both with the complex links between the parts of the system (as emphasized, among others, by Haldane and May 2011, Johnson 2011 and Lux 2011) and with the complex dynamics of the system as a whole. A thorough analysis of critical dynamics should combine both aspects, but a full-fledged implementation of this promising research strategy needs more time than we have at our disposal to avoid further catastrophes in the near future (Sornette and von der Becke 2011). In this chapter I claim that the analysis of the

* The research leading to these results has received funding from the European Union Seventh Framework Programme (FP7/2007–2013) under grant agreement no. 266800.

dynamic properties of critical chain reactions in fragile systems may give important insights on their dynamics and controllability. This may be shown through elementary models that avoid any confusion between complex and complicated dynamics. These models show that the critical processes characterizing nuclear reactors and finance dynamics are critical or structurally unstable, in the sense that an infinitesimal shock perturbing a critical process is sufficient to change radically the dynamic behaviour of the system (a critical survey of different notions of instability and their implications may be found in Vercelli 1991). The stabilization strategy of these processes has proved so far unable to prevent a multitude of minor crises and the emergence of rarer deep crises leading in both cases to a 'meltdown'. This calls for a much more effective preventive strategy.

2. THE CHAIN REACTION OF A NUCLEAR REACTOR

A nuclear meltdown is an informal term for a severe accident bringing about a, generally partial, melting of the nuclear reactor's core seriously jeopardizing the process of energy generation and its safety. The term is not officially defined by the Nuclear Agencies, such as the International Atomic Energy Agency (IAEA) or the US Nuclear Regulatory Commission, but is commonly used by journalists and experts. In order to understand under which circumstances a nuclear meltdown may develop, I have to focus on the process of nuclear fission that occurs in the core of a nuclear reactor.

Both nuclear energy generation and nuclear weapons exploit the properties of nuclear fission. The nuclear fission is rooted in the high 'fragility' of the nuclides (or isotopes) of heavy elements such as Uranium (^{235}U) and Plutonium (^{239}Pu). When a heavy nuclide is hit by a neutron, it is likely to undergo a process of 'fission' that breaks the nucleus into two or more fragments, emits free neutrons and releases at the same time a great quantity of energy in the form of radiation (gamma rays and neutrinos) and heat. The most important fission reaction for nuclear energy generation is that of uranium-235, when hit by a slow-moving (thermal) neutron:

$$^{235}U + \text{neutron} \rightarrow \text{fission fragments} + 2.4 \text{ neutrons} + 192.9 \text{ MeV}$$

This reaction releases a huge amount of energy (hundreds of millions of eV, i.e. electronvolts, while chemical reactions release an amount of energy not exceeding a few eVs). In addition, if the ejected neutrons hit nearby heavy nuclides, they produce with a high degree of probability one or more further nuclear fissions. This may trigger a chain reaction that under given conditions may be self-sustained. A nuclear chain reaction is thus a formidable source of energy that may be used for civil purposes. The trouble is that it also releases a great amount of radiation, as the fission fragments are subject to radioactive decay while much of the energy released has the form of radiation (gamma rays and neutrinos). The difficult challenge of nuclear engineering is that of producing a great amount of energy in a continuous way without releasing radiation outside the nuclear plants. This is by no means an easy task, since the physics of nuclear plants shows how intrinsically unstable is the dynamic process of nuclear energy generation.

The crucial part of a nuclear reactor is its core consisting of an assembly of fuel rods. The core is usually surrounded by a neutron moderator (regular water, heavy water, graphite, and so on) that reduces the kinetic energy of newly produced neutrons in consequence of fission events, since slower neutrons are more likely to induce further fissions. In addition, a nuclear reactor is typically characterized by an exogenous source of neutrons: a primary source that speeds up the start of a critical chain reaction or a secondary source that improves the convergence towards the critical state and its sustainability through time.

In order to study the chain reaction of a nuclear reactor the analysis has to focus on the population of free neutrons N. The dynamic behaviour of a nuclear reactor may be described in the simplest possible way by the following differential equation (Lewis 2008):

$$dN/dt = \alpha N/\tau + N' \tag{1}$$

where N is the number of free endogenous neutrons in a reactor core, N' is the number of neutrons injected in the core by an external source, τ stands for the average lifetime of each neutron before it escapes from the core of the reactor or is absorbed by a nucleus, while the parameter α is a constant of proportionality. In order to allow a more intuitive understanding of the complex dynamics of a nuclear reactor we translate this differential equation in a difference equation assuming that the length of the period is τ (so that $\tau = 1$). We get:

$$Nt = kNt - 1 + N' \tag{2}$$

where the parameters N' and k are assumed to be constant. In nuclear engineering the parameter k is called the 'effective multiplication factor' and expresses the average number of neutrons released by one fission that bring about another fission. This number is crucial to study the dynamic properties of the core. When $k < 1$, the system is subcritical and cannot sustain a chain reaction. In this case the system is stable, but the energy released rapidly fades away. The number F of fission events triggered by an exogenous neutron is given by $F = N'/(1 - k)$, where $1/(1 - k)$ may be defined as the 'multiplier' of exogenous neutrons that determines the equilibrium population of neutrons within the reactor. When $k > 1$ the system is *supercritical* and triggers a chain reaction that increases exponentially the number of fissions and, thus, also the population of neutrons progressively amplifying the energy released and undermining its control. The chain reaction may be exploited for a sustainable production of energy only in the borderline case, when $k = 1$. In this case the system is *critical* and the mean number of free neutrons remains constant bringing about, *ceteris paribus*, a stationary process of fission events and energy release. The only useful state of the core of a nuclear reactor is thus a bifurcation point that nuclear engineering tries hard to stabilize.

The dynamic behaviour of the reactor's core under the three different hypotheses mentioned above may be represented in a simplified way as in Figure 12.1.

On the ordinates axis it is measured N_{t+1} and on the abscissa axis N_t. The equation (2) has a slope that depends on k, while the locus of possible equilibrium values (stationary since it is assumed that the exogenous neutron generation rate N' is constant) is represented by the bisecting line where $N_{t+1} = N_t$. The subcritical case represented in Figure 12.1a is characterized by a stable equilibrium N^* that is a function of the rate of exogenous generation of neutrons:

$$N^* = N'/(1 - k) \tag{3}$$

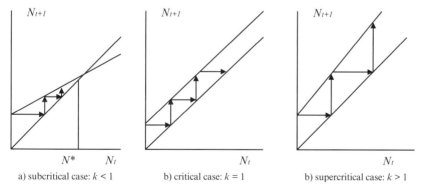

a) subcritical case: $k < 1$ b) critical case: $k = 1$ b) supercritical case: $k > 1$

Figure 12.1   Dynamic regimes of a nuclear reactor

The supercritical case represented in Figure 12.1c has no realizable equilibrium while the population of free neutrons and the number of fission events grows exponentially. In the critical case represented in Figure 12.1b equilibrium is inexistent when $N' > 0$ or indeterminate when $N' = 0$. The critical case is a borderline singularity that is structurally unstable as an infinitesimal perturbation to k may transform the system into supercritical or subcritical (Vercelli 1991).

The fine tuning of k is very difficult, since the physical processes underlying the aggregate value of k are probabilistic and are subject to complex dynamics. The parameter k depends on the following main factors (Lewis 2008):

$$k = P_i P_f \eta - P_a - P_e \tag{4}$$

where P_i is the probability that a particular neutron strikes a fuel nucleus, P_f is the probability that the struck nucleus undergoes a fission, η is the average number of neutrons ejected from a fission event (it is between 2 and 3 for the typical fuel utilized in nuclear plants: ^{235}U and ^{239}Pu); P_a is the probability of absorption by a nucleus of the reactor not belonging to the fuel, and P_e is the probability of escape from the reactor's core. In other words, the product of the first three variables measures the strength of the fission chain reaction, while the probability of absorption and escape measure the average leakage from the system. In consequence of the probabilistic nature of its underlying process, k necessarily fluctuates off its critical value. When $k < 1$ the efficiency in energy generation declines, when k > 1 the safety of the reactor is undermined. A nuclear reactor thus requires reliable mechanisms of regulation that keep the average of the fluctuations of k at its critical value while constraining as much as possible their amplitude.

3.   THE PROPAGATION PROCESS IN A MONETARY ECONOMY

A financial 'meltdown' is an informal term used in finance to designate a severe crisis that undermines the capability of the financial system to support the real economy, triggering a serious recession. This term is not rigorously defined in academic economics, but it is in common usage among practitioners, experts and journalists. This terminology has been probably imported from nuclear physics to emphasize a situation, similar to that of a nuclear meltdown, in which the financial system becomes unable to play its crucial role of support to the real economy, while the decision makers lose control of its dynamics. In this case, however, the metaphor should not be taken literally, since a financial meltdown is typically characterized by a credit crunch and a sudden loss of liquidity: it is a freeze rather than a meltdown. In order to understand under which conditions a financial meltdown may happen, the focus must be on the circuit of economic and financial transactions.

The economic activity is characterized by a mechanism of propagation of impulses that has several analogies with the nuclear chain reaction discussed above. While in a nuclear reactor the process of propagation of an impulse is based on the alternation between fission events of nuclides hit by free neutrons and the consequent ejections of free neutrons originating new fission events, in economics the process of propagation of an impulse is based on the alternation of income flows y received by economic units and their expenditure flows e financed by the previous income flows. Focusing on the real side of the economy, the cumulative effects of this alternation triggered by an impulse e' representing the exogenous expenditure (autonomous investment plus public expenditure) converge towards a finite measure y^* when the marginal propensity to consume $c < 1$:

$$y^* = e'/(1 - c), \, with \, 0 < c < 1$$

where $1/(1 - c)$ is the so called multiplier introduced by Kahn (1931) and Keynes (1936) to study the effects of public expenditure and to determine aggregate income. Here c expresses the propensity of economic units to translate the inflows of income in outflows of expenditure and plays the same dynamic role of the effective multiplication factor k in the equations 2 and 3, describing the dynamic behaviour of a nuclear reactor. In this simple version of the multiplier model, the stability of the real system is assured by a positive marginal saving rate, implying a net leakage from the system. The analogy with the subcritical case of a nuclear chain reaction is striking, as in both cases the propagation process has a similar dynamic structure (Figure 12.2).

A positive aggregate saving rate is the normal case observed in the past most of the time in most countries. However, in the last decades the saving rate greatly diminished in developed countries, progressively pushing the real economic system towards a critical regime, so reducing its stability. In a few countries, and most notably in the USA, the saving rate became slightly negative, or almost so (Guidolin and La Jeunesse 2007), just before the outbreak of the subprime crisis in 2007 contributing to the subsequent economic and financial instability. In addition it must be emphasized that the stabilizing role played by a positive saving rate

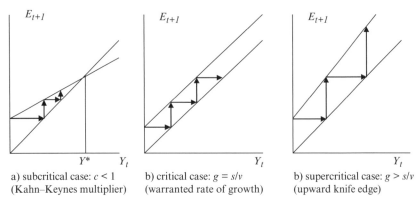

a) subcritical case: $c < 1$ b) critical case: $g = s/v$ b) supercritical case: $g > s/v$
(Kahn–Keynes multiplier)   (warranted rate of growth)   (upward knife edge)

Figure 12.2   Dynamic regimes of a monetary economy

crucially depends on the simplifying assumption underlying the standard Kahn–Keynes multiplier model that all the investment is exogenous. This assumption restricts the validity of the model to the short period as the effects of income variation on the capital stock are neglected. The latter relation is usually expressed by 'the acceleration principle' or 'accelerator'. Its simplest version is the following:

$$I_t = v\,(Y_t - Y_{t-1})$$

where I_t stands for the induced investment and v is the capital/output ratio. As soon as the impact of endogenous investment on the income–expenditure chain reaction is considered, the potential instability of the process becomes evident, as has been first pointed out by Harrod (1939). When $I_t = S_t$ the aggregate endogenous expenditure E_t is equal to the aggregate income in the previous period Y_{t-1} and the system operates under a critical regime:

$$v\,(Y_t - Y_{t-1}) = s\,Y_t$$

from which we derive immediately:

$$(Y_t - Y_{t-1})/Y_t = g = s/v.$$

where $g = s/v$ is what Harrod called 'warranted', that is sustainable, rate of growth (Figure 12.2b). Unfortunately this steady state is a 'razor's edge': an increase of expenditure over income, however small, would render the system supercritical, determining an unsustainable rate of growth (Figure 12.2c), while any reduction of expenditure would transform the system into subcritical (Figure 12.2a). I do not pursue further this line of investigation from the point of view of the real economy, because the instability of the economy crucially depends on the financial side of the income–expenditure process. In a modern monetary economy, an excess of endogenous investment over saving in a given period is made possible by the credit system. In logical terms an excess of expenditure over income could be financed by dishoarding reserves accumulated in the past. However, hoarding and dishoarding had a crucial role in the ancient world, while accumulation and depletion of reserves have only a secondary role in modern capitalism. A persisting excess of investment over saving or, more generally, of expenditure over income has to be financed through borrowing. To understand the intrinsic criticality of contemporary financialized economies, the focus has to be on the monetary and financial side of transactions and economic decisions (Minsky 1982, 1986; Kindleberger 1989; Vercelli 2011).

The first monetary chain reaction that has been systematically explored in the economics literature is rooted in the alternation between credit and bank deposits. Additional credit translates into additional bank deposits that allow the concession of further credit and so on. According to the monetarists, this process explains the money supply M as exogenously determined by the monetary base B, assumed to be under the strict control of monetary authorities. The alternation mentioned above is characterized by a crucial leakage imposed by the legal reserve ratio α of banks while another two significant leakages are the excess reserve ratio β and the currency drain ratio γ. The credit multiplier may be thus expressed in the following way (Krugman and Wells 2009):

$$M = B(1 + \gamma)/(\alpha + \beta + \gamma)$$

The system is subcritical, since there is a leakage in the system represented by $(\alpha + \beta + \gamma)$ and the multiplication factor $1 - (\alpha + \beta + \gamma)$ < 1; however, the lower the desired reserves $\alpha + \beta$ the more the system approaches a critical state. This is what happened in the recent years as financial innovation helped the financial institutions to elude the legal requirements, while the excess reserves ratio tended to vanish and the currency drain ratio became increasingly irrelevant. In the USA and other countries this tendency contributed towards increasing the instability of the system. The nexus between the credit multiplier and financial crises has been hinted at since long ago but never seriously analysed. For example, Friedman and Schwartz observed that a liquidity crisis in a unit fractional reserve banking system is precisely the kind of event that triggers – and often has triggered – a chain reaction. And economic collapse often has the character of a cumulative process. Let it go beyond a certain point, and it will tend for a time to gain strength from its own development as its effects spread and return to intensify the process of collapse (Friedman and Schwartz 1963, p. 419).

In a fractional-reserve banking system, in the event of a bank run, the demand depositors and note holders would attempt to withdraw more money than the bank has in reserves, causing the bank to suffer a liquidity crisis and, ultimately, to perhaps default.

The monetarist belief in the exogeneity of the monetary base fell into disrepute since the early 1980s. This assumption requires demanding conditions such as constant velocity of money circulation or at least its independence of the business cycle, while the empirical evidence suggests that it is quite volatile and strongly pro-cyclical. For example, Goodhart (1984, p. 188) wrote that the base money multiplier model is 'such an incomplete way of describing the process of the determination of the stock of money that it amounts to misinstruction'. The credit multiplier has been rejected in particular by the advocates of an endogenous money theory advanced since long ago and subscribed among others by Schumpeter and many post-Keynesians (for a recent assessment see Lavoie 2003). Endogenous money theory states that the supply of money is credit-driven and determined endogenously by the demand for bank loans, rather than exogenously by monetary authorities. In this case, the analogy with a nuclear reactor's instability is even stronger. The trouble with criticality is that, even in the absence of significant external shocks, a small change from within the system may be sufficient to trigger an unstable chain reaction. That is why criticality characterizes many catastrophe-generating systems (Sornette 2004).

In a given period t, each economic unit is characterized by a financial inflow y_t and a financial outflow e_t. The ratio e_t/y_t is a significant index of its current financial condition as it affects both its liquidity and solvency (Vercelli 2011). It is also an index of the financial multiplication factor. Its value may easily be higher than unity and may persist in such a state for a relatively long time. In this case, the dynamics of the financial system is supercritical, a 'bubble' in the economic jargon that typically occurs during a boom. This is made possible by credit that creates inflows *ex nihilo* in the expectation that the consequent increase in outflows will generate higher inflows in the future that will permit the repayment of debt with an interest. The increase in the extant credit of the private sector typically happens in the period of vigorous economic expansion, when the euphoria of the agents leads them to seek a higher leverage. As soon as the ensuing financial bubble(s) burst(s) the system becomes subcritical to reduce the excessive leverage. Also in this case, as in a nuclear reactor, the critical state is the only one sustainable in the long run, while a deviation from it tends to increase. In order to understand the sudden switch from supercritical dynamics to subcritical dynamics and vice versa, a second source of criticality that interacts with the first one must be introduced. The current values of the liquidity ratio affects its expected values, the sum of which determines the solvency of the economic unit. Whenever the solvency ratio k^* that measures the ratio of discounted expected outflows and inflows is < 1, the unit has a positive net worth and is solvent; $k^* = 1$ is the critical value beyond which the unit becomes virtually insolvent since its net worth is negative. To avoid bankruptcy, the economic units have a desired value of the insolvency ratio sufficiently far from the critical value to withstand unexpected contingencies. The interaction between k and k^* determines the cyclical behaviour of financial conditions (Vercelli 2011). This dynamic mechanism produces semi-periodic minor financial crises during business cycle downturns and a few, much rarer, major financial crises that degenerate into recession or depression in consequence of contagion. To understand why, we have to add to the first chain reaction induced by the expectations, a second chain reaction that depends on the financial linkages between units (Haldane and May 2011; Lux 2011). In minor crises the contagion is limited in extent, time and space, while in the major crises its effects are pervasive and quite difficult to stop.

4. NUCLEAR AND ECONOMIC CHAIN REACTIONS: ANALOGIES AND IMPLICATIONS

The chain-reaction criticality characterizing the dynamics of both a nuclear reactor and a monetary economy raises similar issues of regulation and risk management. Criticality implies that predictability and controllability is severely limited and active regulation is arduous and unreliable. In nuclear reactors the principal instrument of regulation is given by control rods that may be inserted to variable degree in the core of the reactor to slow down the chain reaction as soon as it becomes supercritical or to accelerate it as soon as it becomes subcritical. In the economy the chain reaction may be slowed down and moderated by reducing the leverage of economic units and improving their solvency indexes. However, while successful regulation is manageable in both cases under routine circumstances, it may become prohibitive under unexpected scenarios. The regular working of the reactor is constantly monitored by highly trained technicians. They may, for example, insert control rods to reduce or increase k. Unfortunately, these active interventions of regulation are subject to errors that can trigger an uncontrollable process, leading to the partial meltdown of fuel. Serious mistakes have been made quite often even by the best trained technicians being unable to forecast the complex dynamics of a nuclear reactor, following an unexpected event (that does not need to be a large shock). That is why the training of nuclear plants technicians includes an extensive programme of simulations to refine their ability to cope with unforeseen circumstances. It is impossible, however, to simulate all the possible scenarios and the risk of inadequate behaviour remains extremely high. The Chernobyl accident, for example, had been triggered by an incautious stoppage of the reactor 2 to perform a test meant, ironically, to improve its safety. Analogously, the subprime crisis has been triggered by systematic and reiterated misbehaviour of many subjects, including the over-exposure of financial institutions and households, the illusion that structured securities could spread risk in a more efficient way and the lax supervision of monetary authorities reluctant to interfere with private decisions. The intrinsic weakness of active regulation in these two fields has led the experts to focus on mechanisms of passive regulation that are automatically switched on in case of necessity.

In nuclear reactors the principal mechanism of passive regulation is provided by the neutron moderator (often regular water) surrounding the fuel bars. The controllability and safety of nuclear energy generation depends crucially on the amount and nature of the neutron moderator. There is an optimal amount of a given kind of moderator, as less moderation reduces the probability of fission while more increases the probability of escape. In addition most moderators become less effective with increasing temperature, so that if the reactor overheats the chain reaction tends to slow down. For example, regular water, which is used as moderator in most reactors, starts to boil and reduces the effective multiplication factor. However, there may be an unexpected leakage of water or steam as well as a failure of the systems to pump new water into the reactor's core as in the case of Fukushima1 after the flooding of the emergency pumps. In the economic system passive regulation is delegated to the invisible hand of the market. However, only in the case of an ideal model of a perfect-competition market may we rely on its virtues of self-regulation (Arrow and Hahn 1971). Unfortunately, real markets do not comply with the long list of demanding assumptions that define a perfect-competition market so that the 'invisible hand' is often weak, trembling and coerced by big companies or public agencies. In real markets, as in existing reactors, the failure of self-regulation may originate a cascade of further failures that may bring about their 'meltdown'. In both cases, the likelihood of local failures that may have much wider, even global, consequences calls for a global regulator that imposes strict standards to local units and has the power to enforce them. This is not the case either in the nuclear energy field or in economics and finance. In both cases the authorities are national and the efficiency of their interventions is jeopardized by local interests and regulatory capture.

5.   CONCLUDING REMARKS

In this chapter I have focused on the far-reaching analogy between a nuclear and financial chain reaction, criticality claiming that reflections on this analogy and its implications may be suggestive from different points of view. In particular, it may provide a more concrete intuitive perception of the causes and consequences of both nuclear accidents and financial crises. In the case of nuclear energy generation, most people believe that the understanding of its risks is restricted to nuclear physicists. The analogy with finance, of which anyone has some direct experience, may help the layman to understand, if not its details, at least the nature of the risks involved in nuclear energy generation. In finance, on the other hand, the causal links are mediated by long chains of effects transmitted through layers of derivatives and networks of units; they depend, in addition, on expectations quite vulnerable to cognitive and emotional shocks. The analogy with nuclear reactor dynamics may help us to grasp the concrete implications of complex dynamics in financial processes. In particular, the consequences of a nuclear accident, at least their short-term effects, are much more tangible as the explosions and leakages of radioactive vapour are immediately visible while the leakages of radiation can be easily measured in an objective way, and their effects on human health (in particular cancer) are vividly perceived by everyone.

I believe that the analysis started in this chapter may be significant to assess the risks involved with the operation of fragile accident-prone dynamic systems such as nuclear reactors or financial systems. The risks involved with nuclear energy generation are not just a matter of faulty design of existing nuclear reactors, but they are intrinsic in the complex dynamics of its underlying process even when active and passive regulation seems to be carefully designed. The risks involved with sophisticated financial systems spring not only from the fraudulent or myopic behaviour of 'rotten apples', but from the in-built criticality of financial processes. We have to understand that the frequent occurrence of nuclear accidents and financial crises are both deeply rooted in the structural instability of their underlying processes, and that a correct management of the hard risks involved by their complex dynamics requires the adoption of precautionary policies much stricter than the current ones (Chichilnisky *et al.* 1998).

REFERENCES

Arrow, K.J. and F.H. Hahn (1971), *General Competitive Analysis*, Amsterdam: North-Holland.
Chichilnisky, G., G. Heal and A. Vercelli (eds) (1998), *Sustainability: Dynamics and Uncertainty*, Dordrecht, the Netherlands: Martin Kluwer.
Friedman, M. and A.J. Schwartz (1963), *A Monetary History of the United States: 1867–1960*, Princeton: Princeton University Press.
Goodhart, C. (1984), *Monetary Policy in Theory and Practice*, London: Macmillan.
Guidolin, M. and E.A. La Jeunesse (2007), 'The decline in the U.S. personal saving rate: is it real and is it a puzzle?', *Federal Reserve Bank of St. Louis Review*, **89** (6), 491–514.
Haldane, A.G. and R.M. May (2011), 'Systemic risk in banking ecosystems', *Nature*, **469** (7330), 351–5.
Harrod, R.F. (1939), 'An essay in dynamic theory', *Economic Journal*, **49** (193), 14–33.
Johnson, N. (2011), 'Proposing policy by analogy is risky', *Nature*, **469** (7330), 302.
Kahn, R.F. (1931), 'The relation of home investment to unemployment', *Economic Journal*, **41** (162), 173–98.
Keynes, J.M. (1936), *The General Theory of Employment, Interest, and Money*, London: Macmillan.
Kindleberger, C. (1989, revised edition), *Manias, Panics and Crashes: A History of Financial Crises*, New York: Basic Books.
Krugman, P. and R. Wells (2009), *Macroeconomics*, New York: Worth Publishers.
Lavoie, M. (2003), 'A primer on endogenous credit-money', in L-P. Rochon and S. Rossi (eds), *Modern Theories of Money in Capitalist Economies*, Cheltenham, UK and Northampton, MA, USA: Edward Elgar Publishing, pp. 506–43.
Lewis, E.E. (2008), *Fundamentals of Nuclear Reactor Physics*, San Diego: Academic Press by Elsevier.
Lux, T. (2011), 'Network theory is sorely required', *Nature*, **469** (7330), 303.
Minsky, H.P. (1982), *Can 'It' Happen Again? Essays on Instability and Finance*, Armonk, NY: M.E. Sharp.
Minsky, H.P. (1986), *Stabilizing an Unstable Economy*, New Haven and London: Yale University Press.
Sornette, D. (2004, 2nd edition), *Critical Phenomena in Natural Sciences: Chaos, Fractals, Self-Organization and Disorder: Concepts and Tools*, Heidelberg: Springer.
Sornette, D. and S. von der Becke (2011), 'Complexity clouds finance-risk models', *Nature*, **471** (7337), 166.
Vercelli, A. (1991), *Methodological Foundations of Macroeconomics: Keynes and Lucas*, Cambridge: Cambridge University Press.
Vercelli, A. (2011), 'A perspective on Minsky moments: revisiting the core of the financial instability hypothesis', *Review of Political Economy*, **23** (1), 49–67.

Index